# Selling Transracial Adoption

Elizabeth Raleigh

# Selling Transracial Adoption

*Families, Markets, and the Color Line*

TEMPLE UNIVERSITY PRESS
*Philadelphia* • *Rome* • *Tokyo*

TEMPLE UNIVERSITY PRESS
Philadelphia, Pennsylvania 19122
*www.temple.edu/tempress*

Library of Congress Cataloging-in-Publication Data

Names: Raleigh, Elizabeth Yoon Hwa, 1977– author.
Title: Selling transracial adoption : families, markets, and the color line /
    Elizabeth Yoon Hwa Raleigh.
Description: Philadelphia : Temple University Press, 2017. |
    Includes bibliographical references and index.
Identifiers: LCCN 2017021821| ISBN 9781439914779 (hardback) |
    ISBN 9781439914786 (paper) | ISBN 9781439914793 (e-book)
Subjects: LCSH: Interracial adoption. | Social service. | Families. |
    BISAC: SOCIAL SCIENCE / Social Work. | SOCIAL SCIENCE / Ethnic
    Studies / General. | FAMILY & RELATIONSHIPS / Adoption & Fostering.
Classification: LCC HV875 .R25 2017 | DDC 362.734—dc23 LC record
    available at https://lccn.loc.gov/2017021821

Printed in the United States of America

9  8  7  6  5  4  3  2  1

*To my mother, Laura Mackie (1946–2013)*

# Contents

Acknowledgments                                                          ix

Introduction                                                             1

1   Staying Afloat in a Perfect Storm                                    36

2   Uneasy Consumers: The Emotion Work of Marketing Adoption             64

3   Transracial Adoption as a Market Calculation                        94

4   "And You Get to Black": Racial Hierarchies and the
    Black–Non-Black Divide                                              128

5   Selling Transracial Adoption: Social Workers' Ideals and
    Market Concessions                                                  163

    Conclusion: The Consequences of Selling Transracial Adoption
    and the Implications for Adoptive Families                          190

Notes                                                                   203

References                                                              215

Index                                                                   229

# Acknowledgments

First, I thank the adoption social workers, lawyers, and counselors who participated in this study. While I may be at times critical of adoption practice, after every interview I was always heartened by my participants' thoughtfulness and dedication to child welfare. I am grateful to them for their work and for generously sharing their time and candid insights on race, family, and private adoption.

This book would not have come to fruition without the support of several people and institutions. I thank Sara Cohen and the team at Temple University Press for their skillful guidance. Sara Dorow, a pioneer in adoption research, and an anonymous reviewer both offered valuable feedback and advice. My colleagues and students at Carleton College welcomed me into their community and continue to invigorate and challenge me as a teacher and scholar. A special thank-you goes to the students in my sociology of assisted reproductive technology and adoption class, who help me see the material in new ways. In particular, I thank Emily Scotto for her feedback on the manuscript. The Andrew W. Mellon Foundation's Career Enhancement Fellowship provided a lifeline of financial support that allotted me the time to finish the project.

Several mentors generously gave of themselves to guide me through the research process. Thanks go to my former advisors Grace Kao, Charles Bosk, Barbara Katz Rothman, and Kristen Harknett for believing in the project even before it was a dissertation. Richard Lee was kind enough to step in and serve as an official mentor and brave four days of Florida heat and humidity in late August. Over the years, Scott Wong has offered sage advice and key introductions. And Lynn Davidman introduced me to sociology and offered me my first academic job as a research assistant my sophomore year of college.

Without the intellectual engagement of fellow adoptee scholars, my work would not be as good and not nearly as meaningful. I thank Joyce Maguire Pavao, Kim Park Nelson, and Amanda Baden for being trailblazers and Kimberly McKee, JaeRan Kim, Shannon Gibney, Sara Docan-Morgan, and Jennifer Kwon Dobbs for their commitment to adoption studies.

I count myself lucky to have good friends who are engaged and thoughtful adoptive parents. All have enriched my life and my work. I have known Rachel Gilbert since we were mistaken for each other in grade school, and she and her husband, Geoff, are like family to me. Matt and Joni Karl are cherished friends, and they have my utmost respect and gratitude. Martha Crawford read an early draft of the book, and she assured me I was on a good track. And Frank Ligtvoet and the rest of the inaugural All Together Now adoption group were open-minded listeners and advocates.

Long gone are the days of college, but I am fortunate that my friendships with Aubrey Ludwig Ellman, Jenny Kane, Adele Campbell-Nelson, and Karla Sigler have persisted despite my flaky and intermittent communication. And to friends in Northfield—especially the "moms gone mild" and "the group"—I offer thanks for being sounding boards and for enveloping me in a community of supportive friends.

As I get older, I know how privileged I am to have my family and how fleeting time can be. My mother, Laura Mackie, was gone too soon, but I know that she would have unwaveringly supported this project, just as she was proud of all my endeavors. I am thankful for her love. I wish my dear father-in-law, Patrick Raleigh, had lived to see this publication, but I am grateful that my wonderful mother-in-law, Marilynn Raleigh, is here to read it. Having her move to Northfield has been such a gift.

My dad, David Mackie, has always been an anchor for me, and I love him from the bottom of my heart. My sister, Amy Raccagni, is among the most giving people I have ever met. I thank her for her love and friendship. And I thank my brother, Darren Mackie, for being a loving brother and a devoted uncle.

And last, my enduring love goes to my husband, Nikos, and my daughter, Paige. I thank Paige for her generous heart and the joy that she brings me. Being a mother taught me a lot about adoption, and I understand why people are willing to sacrifice so much to have the experience of raising a child. Paige is the personification of love, and I don't know how I got so lucky to be her mom. And I thank Nikos for believing in me and for his ever-present love and support. He is the 100 percent perfect person for me.

# Selling Transracial Adoption

# Introduction

bigail Johnson sits in the conference room of Clerestory Adoptions, a private adoption agency offering a multitude of international and domestic adoption programs.[1] The room looks like any generic conference room, with a large oval table and several matching chairs around it. The office is by no means luxurious, but the room is tidy and professional. This could be any corporate office, but instead of forecasts of annual sales and profit margins, the charts on the wall detail a roster of adoption programs offered by Clerestory Adoptions and the number of parents currently enrolled. As this book shows, the numbers do not look good.

I am at the agency to interview Abigail, a relatively young social worker who got her start working in adoption right out of college. She is an earnest person, and her brown eyes are thoughtful when she pauses to answer my questions. As someone whose job it is to run information sessions describing the range of adoption programs her agency offers, Abigail is used to fielding inquiries from anxious prospective clients. But the questions I want to broach differ from those of would-be adoptive parents.

Whereas most people seeking out Clerestory Adoptions are looking for a way to expand their families, and therefore want to know pertinent information like how long the adoption will take and how much it will cost, I am here to interview her about her thoughts and insights about whether and how private adoption operates as a marketplace and her role in it. Although the formal adoption of any child by American parents usually involves the irrevocable transfer of parental rights and responsibilities, private adoptions

via domestic and international placements distinctly differ from public foster care adoptions in that they operate on a fee-for-service model. This fiscal
reality puts these adoption workers in the awkward position of having to
generate sufficient revenue to cover their operating costs while still focusing
on serving children and families.

Because adoption operates in a bureaucratized system overseen by a matrix of laws regulating the exchange, to locate and legally transfer a child
from one family to another, prospective adoptive parents must rely on third-
party facilitators. These adoption attorneys, counselors, and social workers
are charged with administering the adoption process. In this sense, private
adoption workers operate under a model of client services in which the revenue that they take in from paying customers forms the foundation of their
organization's long-term solvency. Thus, adoption professionals take on the
role as the de facto adoption sellers, who must promote their services to
discerning customers. However, these social workers also have to live up to
their roles as child welfare professionals, charged with advocating for the
best interests of children. This dual mandate can pose a potential conflict of
interest, since workers must simultaneously serve both adoptive parents and
children, suggesting that workers sometimes have to compromise one priority to meet the other.

Although most adoption social workers espouse the view that the child
should be the central client, this book shows that when adoption is pitched,
the needs of the paying customer (i.e., the prospective adoptive parent) get
elevated. If the parents are the clients, this means that the child, at least tem-
porarily, becomes the object of exchange. Recall the old adage that adopted
children are "chosen children."[2] Under this purview, the child gets positioned as something to be selected, or in other words, he or she embodies a
dual role as subject and object.[3] As subjects, they are the recipients of vital
social services geared toward placing them in permanent families. But these
children also take on an objectified role because to be chosen, it inevitably
means that another child gets passed over. This selection process is counter
to the idea that children are supposed to be universally priceless, but as I
detail, some children embody a greater market value than others.[4] Thus, the
process of choosing and being chosen is one of consumption. Prospective
parents can choose their children, but some parents have more limited
choices in terms of what is available to them.

Knowing full well that some prospective parents face curtailed market
options and that some children are in greater demand than others, adoption
workers face the task of making families while also keeping the interests of
the agency at the forefront. Describing this quandary, Abigail details how
these logistical considerations shape which children get served and why. She
says, "I think that some programs are easier than others. Not only because
there is a need, but it is not the scariest place to go work. We just started up

our Chad program.[5] You have to look at which places you are able to work in. There are tons of kids in need of homes in places where social workers don't want to go work in or where it is going to be too expensive because you have to pay off too many people." In other words, helping needy children becomes somewhat of a numbers game, and if a region is too "scary" or involves paying off "too many people," the program is abandoned in favor of an easier place to set up shop.

International adoption is not the only segment of the adoption marketplace touched by these issues. In private domestic adoption—that is, the adoption of an American child who has never been in the foster care system—the influence of the market is palpable. Like international providers, domestic adoption agencies have to recruit sufficient numbers of customers whose fees keep the agency afloat. But there is a key difference, because in private domestic adoption, they must also enroll sufficient numbers of pregnant women wanting to make adoption plans. Keeping up a "supply" can be difficult, considering that there are more people hoping to adopt babies than there are expectant women wanting to relinquish them. So adoption agencies often struggle to refill the pipeline. Given this market imbalance, many providers have to devote a considerable proportion of their revenue to advertising and outreach. For example, the annual report from one adoption agency discloses that it spent almost 20 percent of its $3.78 million budget on advertising. This figure brings into stark relief the paradox of private adoption: it is a profession devoted to child welfare but sustained by advertising for children and customers.

As Abigail attests, her agency has to balance competing priorities, and they are often pulled between fiscal and family considerations. First and foremost, their mission is to serve kids in need of a home. However, other factors about a country must be considered, such as the perceived safety of the country and the economic sustainability of running an adoption program there. They do not need to make a profit from a program, but they have to make enough money to pay the bills. Abigail reveals how the bottom line affects the decision-making process, stating, "We are opening and closing programs to see which ones we can afford. It is an industry at the end of the day, I suppose." Once the words were out of her mouth, Abigail stops abruptly, realizing that she may have crossed a line. Next she ruefully utters, "I am totally going to get fired for this conversation."

Her blunt assessment that adoption "is an industry" further underscores the paradox of private adoption. It is a practice devoted to child welfare, but to serve children, adoption workers have to take into account market factors such as supply and demand to determine which programs stay open. I begin with Abigail's quote because it illustrates that despite the reluctance to talk about money and markets in adoption, they matter—*a lot.* She worries that by calling adoption an industry she has somehow crossed a line, illustrating the hesitancy some workers feel when talking about child welfare in such crass terms.

During the course of my research, I learned that many dedicated adoption workers, like Abigail, were drawn to adoption because they possessed a deep commitment to child welfare. They were less interested in the financial considerations involved in sustaining a small business. This quixotic approach to private adoption was all right when business was booming, because these workers did not have to worry about paying the rent or making payroll. Perhaps secure in their solvency, it was easier to focus solely on the child welfare aspects of their profession. However, over the course of the last decade, there has been a shift in the adoption industry as workers have been faced with new regulations and a decreasing supply of young and healthy children. These babies and toddlers were once the mainstay of private adoption, but the number of children available—especially overseas—trickled to a halt. Hence the market changed, and the business aspects of adoption began to take precedence as providers struggled to adjust to these new conditions. One social worker I spoke with summarizes this new era, stating, "This is a business, and we have to make business decisions."

The goal of this book is to provide a closer analysis of these business decisions by analyzing the uncomfortable spaces where love and markets intermingle. In doing so, I argue that private adoption offers a window into the social construction of racial boundaries and the meaning of family. In the broadest terms, I aim to answer two questions: What does privatized adoption teach us about kinship, and what does it teach us about race? To answer these questions, I focus on adoption providers and the markets in which they operate. I illustrate how these workers are sellers of kinship, tasked with pitching the idea of transracial adoption to their mostly White clientele.

Once establishing the utility of the market framework, I push forth two arguments. The first is that most prospective parents come to private adoption hoping to replicate as many aspects of biological reproduction as possible. Put another way, applicants who are willing to pay the higher costs associated with private adoption are often hoping to locate the youngest and healthiest child possible. Indeed this was the rationale that helped catapult intercountry adoption to its heightened popularity. Even though there are still plenty of parents who are willing to endure the long waits and high fees associated with private adoption, the supply of young and healthy children is diminishing. Thus, prospective adoptive parents have fewer options. Cognizant of these constraints, adoption providers have had to adjust their sales pitch when promoting their services. With fewer desirable children to go around, many social workers advise their clients to take on a consumer mentality and rank their priorities. By detailing how adoption providers frame these decisions, I show that adoption providers promote and sell transracial adoption as a means to maximize other market variables. Whereas transracial adoption often gets idealistically depicted as a family form where "love sees no color," the goal of this book is to complicate this assessment: it is not that color does not matter; rather, color indeed does matter, but how it matters depends on how race commingles with other market variables.

This brings me to my second argument: that transracial adoption serves as a powerful indicator of racial boundaries. When White parents choose the race of the child they are willing to adopt, they are literally marking their own version of the color line, delineating who they could accept as a son or daughter, and conversely who they could not. Thus, my goal is to mount the argument that the racialized practices in private adoption serve as a powerful reflection of race in America. I aim to illustrate that not only do adoption agencies' practices mirror the racial divide, but these policies are complicit in redefining the racial boundary, essentially reconfiguring a delineation that positions monoracial native-born African Americans on one side and other minority children on the opposite side.

One contribution of the book is that my research captures how adoption providers respond to the downturn in international adoption. Adoption demographer Peter Selman calls this period "the 'beginning of the end' of wide-scale intercountry adoption."[6] During this era, private adoption underwent a massive transformation since there were fewer Asian and Hispanic babies available for adoption. This shortage meant that adoption providers had to rethink how they sold transracial adoption, putting more emphasis on the placement of foreign-born African children and U.S.-born biracial (i.e., part White) Black children. I am able to show how the market shift helped reformulate the racial boundary, effectively expanding it to include these children. Adoption workers played up these distinctions by differentially pricing, labeling, and allocating biracial Black children. Likewise, adoption agencies also perpetuated the idea that the placement of foreign-born Black children would be different from adopting a native-born Black child, permitting White parents to characterize their African children as "not Black." Taken together, these racialized policies and practices actively bolstered the delineation between children who are full African American and those who are not.

Having built the argument that it is vital to take into account the shrinking marketplace to explain the increase in transracial adoption, this book moves to its final goal: to identify the implications of this practice. I am particularly interested in how this customer-centric approach can potentially undermine adoption workers' authority to prepare adoptive parents for the responsibilities and complexities of adopting across race. If adoption providers are concerned about maintaining market share and do not want to lose potential customers to competitors who offer an easier and less invasive process, it becomes more challenging to maintain the standards that adoption social work was built on.

Although there has been a growing consensus among adoption scholars that the market framework provides a fruitful tool for analysis,[7] this approach is often decried by adoptive parents. Such pushback against the market metaphor makes sense given the stigma that still surrounds adoption.[8] These parents and their children are vulnerable to intrusive questions such as "How much did he cost?" The unacceptableness of bringing up money in adoption is so high that there are several posts on popular adoption blogs advising adoptive parents how to respond to this inquiry and other "stupid things people say about adoption."[9] As one blogger writes, "What an awful question to ask someone. We are talking about a child. She cost nothing. Do I ask you how much your biological child cost, with her hospital fees, doctor visits, shots? Yes, we had adoption fees and travel costs, but 'she' did not cost anything. She is a child, just like my biological child."[10]

Notice how the author adamantly argues against the market framework and redirects the narrative by equivocating the costs incurred via adoption as similar to the financial outlay biological parents pay for prenatal care and delivery. This rhetorical strategy reinforces the predominance of what Judith Modell calls the "as if begotten" model in adoption.[11] Under this practice, once legally adopted, the son or daughter becomes de facto biological kin such that "the adopted child is granted an entirely new birth certificate, with the names of his or her adoptive parents on the document and the name of the birth parent nowhere in sight."[12] By rewriting the *birth* certificate, adoptive kinship is likened to biological kinship and the adopted child is seen as "just like my biological child."

The message equating adoption to biological kinship emerges early in the adoption process. For example, at preadoption conferences geared toward audiences of prospective adoptive parents, it is common to see vendors selling T-shirts with catchphrases like "adoption is the new pregnant" or "pregnant on paper."[13] Although it is understandable why a prospective adoptive parent would want to celebrate the formation of her family through a visible declaration of impending maternity, the reliance on a pregnancy discourse has troubling implications. The blogger who insists that adoption fees are like delivery fees implicitly puts forth the argument that a child's existence begins at adoption, instead of at birth. The adoption fee does not bring the baby to fruition; the birth mother (sometimes called first mother) already devoted the time, energy, and labor to bring about this occurrence.

Perhaps one reason for the overreliance on the adoption-as-birth metaphor is that the alternative—the market metaphor—is untenable. Even though private adoption routinely requires the transfer of thousands of dollars from one party to another, any allusion to private adoption as baby buying threatens what sociologist Viviana Zelizer calls "the exaltation of children's sentimental worth."[14] However, as Zelizer shows in her landmark study tracing the desirability of babies put up for adoption throughout the twentieth century, private adoption has always been a marketplace where some children were in greater demand than others. Whereas in the 1900s, would-be adoptive parents sought out older children who could contribute to the upkeep of the household, in contemporary adoption it is the babies who are the most valuable. Zelizer argues that this change catalyzed a new demand for babies and "stimulated a new kind of baby market."[15]

Of course, in the legal adoption marketplace children are not purchased outright. Instead, it is useful to conceptualize the adoption marketplace as a socially constructed arena that is necessary to facilitate the exchange of a child. Within this arena, adoption becomes both child welfare and child commodification. As Margaret Radin and Madhavi Sunder write, "Market relations reflect, create, and reinforce social relations. But they are not the whole of those relations."[16] In this regard private adoption is a peculiar marketplace, where parents are not reducible to pure consumers and children are not merely objects. But the paradox is that to transfer children from one family to another, supposedly priceless children are inevitably marketed and priced. One could argue that there has to be a price associated with adoption because how else could one pay for the costs associated with this circulation? This explanation rings true, but it is only part of the story. If it were the case that all children were equally priceless, then the total cost for an adoption would be the same regardless of the child. But that is rarely the case, and as this book details, in private domestic adoption children are differentially priced according to their market value.

Several scholars have noted that race plays a key role in determining a child's market value, with Black babies garnering a lower fee than White babies.[17] This practice has been well known among adoption practitioners, but it was rarely, if ever, discussed among the general public. This changed in 2013 when National Public Radio launched the Race Card Project, asking listeners to weigh in on race and cultural identity in six words or less. An uproar occurred after a woman submitted the phrase "Black babies cost less to adopt," effectively outing this fairly common custom.[18] The reporter covering the issue spoke with adoption workers about the rationale behind this two-tiered pricing structure. The brief news story details how many social workers viewed the fee differential as a child welfare tactic that increased the likelihood of placing Black children in permanent families. Despite being founded on good intentions, many workers were clearly distressed with the scrutiny it garnered. No adoption worker would go on record about the practice, leading the reporter to conclude, "No one is comfortable about this."[19]

As debates surrounding transracial adoption and the marketplace swirl, the voices of adoption workers have been largely absent from the discourse. There is a plethora of blogs written by members of the adoption triad with adoptive parents, adopted persons, and birth mothers (and to a lesser extent fathers) weighing in on their experiences.[20] Yet there are few, if any, blogs written by adoption social workers. Granted, many probably do not actively publish via this medium since they have to uphold the confidentiality of their clients. But the lack of input from adoption providers is also mirrored in the research literature. Despite the fact that adoption workers could presumably be afforded a layer of protection as confidential informants, there are few studies leveraging their expertise.

This book is unique because it is one of the only studies to explicitly focus on adoption providers. Instead of their voices being a side note, I argue that hearing from these workers provides a rich opportunity to plumb sociological questions about the intersections between markets, kinship, and race. By highlighting the perspectives of adoption workers, I am able to uncover the ambivalence many feel about their seemingly contradictory roles as child welfare advocates and client services personnel. These workers view private adoption as an integral component of social service work. Yet many of these women also feel conflicted, citing concerns about the ethics of treating child adoption as an "industry." Although members of this profession may be reluctant to risk their jobs by going publicly on record, once guaranteed a confidential space where their names and identifying information would not be revealed, these workers had a lot to say.

After Abigail voiced her concern that her comments would ultimately get her fired, I offered to omit that portion from the transcript. But she demurred, saying, "No, no. I think that it is very important to discuss. It is important for the fact that when these kids are like fifteen, sixteen, seventeen years old, you know that it is going through their minds. Or when they are thinking about building their own families. We can frame it in all of the positive language in the world, but kids are smart."

As Abigail alludes to, in contemporary practice there has been what the sociologist Pamela Anne Quiroz calls "a shift in the discursive practices of adoption to broaden the acceptance of adoptive families. Old terminology (e.g., blue-ribbon babies, natural parents, illegitimate, unadoptable, feeble-minded) has given way to a set of kinder, more inclusive terms."[21] With this softer language, the adoption narrative gets reformulated such that a first mother gets recast as a birth mother, not the "real" or "natural" mother. These expectant women are said to make an adoption plan, not "give up their child" for adoption. And subsequently, the children brokered in adoption get referred to as in need of care, not "available" for adoption.

But despite these efforts to reframe private adoption as an empowered and altruistic decision made by an autonomous birth mother, the market aspects are still unavoidable. Although Abigail is adamant that "you're not buying a child; it is not like that," private adoption is a form of social service where the parent paying the bills becomes the de facto client. Some critics of adoption refer to this business model as finding children for families, rather than the child welfare model of finding families for children.[22]

The former positions the child as the object, while the latter frames the child as the client.

This distinction resonates with Michele, another social worker I interviewed. Unlike Abigail, who is relatively new to the field, Michele has been working in adoption for more than twenty years at a large full-service agency that offers a plethora of international programs as well as private domestic adoptions. Michele sees her adoption agency as one of the good ones, separating her practices from that of other agencies that "are not operating aboveboard." Michele surmises, "There are agencies that basically find children for parents. Our agency finds parents for children."

Although the differences between these two phrases are subtle, the stakes are high, especially since children are seen as priceless, and thus attaching price tags to them is discomforting, to say the least. According to Zelizer, the allusion to child markets is so fraught because, as critics argue, "Some goods and services should never be sold, and . . . some market arrangements are inherently pernicious."[23] Maintaining the distinction between a commercial enterprise and an altruistic one is essential, since these approaches occupy what Zelizer calls "hostile spheres."[24] Any overlap between the two is risky because it threatens the sacredness of children. Thus, any baby market is seen as a dangerous "black market" rather than a socially sanctioned arena of exchange.

For adoption stakeholders, the very idea of combining the terms "market" and "baby" is rife with controversy because the idea of commodifying children threatens the underlying foundation of the adoptive family. As Debora Spar notes, "The debates in this field are passionate, with adoptive families and adoption agencies pitted against those who condemn the process."[25] She identifies one side of the debate as "those who see adoption as a purely social interaction: it is about building families and rescuing children and assuaging the pain of missing people." In contrast, critics of adoption argue that "adoption is not only a market but indeed a market of the worst possible sort" that commodifies innocent children by putting a price on their heads.[26]

Of course, it is folly to create a forced choice either extolling private adoption as an altruistic child welfare practice or condemning it as baby selling. As Joan Williams and Viviana Zelizer argue, the questions of whether the commodification of children exists and whether commodification is good or bad are oversimplified. They contend, "Economic sociology shows that we need to steer away from the question of 'to commodify or not to commodify,' and appreciate instead that people strive to define the moral life in a wide variety of social contexts that involve *both* economic *and* socioemotional relationships."[27]

Notably, adoption is not the only transaction where markets and altruism intersect in a bureaucratized system. In his research on organ donation, sociologist Kieran Healy emphasizes the value of acknowledging the eco-nomic and social aspects of the exchange. He probes how organ donation agencies create what he calls the "cultural account of donation," or in other words, "sets of ideas and stories, meant for public consumption, about the nature and meaning of what they are doing."[28] Since the message of organ donation grows out of an altruistic framework (e.g., providing the gift of life), workers are especially wary of sullying the narrative with allusions to the business of donation. But Healy reminds us that there can be no organ dona-tion without a "procurement organization" that oversees the logistics of the transfer. These operational aspects tend to be ignored, since the few extant studies tend to focus on organ donors and the recipients.[29] Likewise, adop-tion research tends to focus on adopted children and parents and not on the organizations that bring these parties together. These workers serve as mid-dlemen (and women) charged with facilitating the placement.

Like Healy's work, this book is built on the idea that an industry can be both altruistic and transactional. Thus, in the adoption marketplace, child commodification and child welfare can both occur. With these caveats in mind, my aim is to push forward the conversation by examining how a so-ciologically informed market lens help us further understand where adop-tion, race, and kinship intersect. Williams and Zelizer remind us that the market framework is particularly useful for this type of inquiry, since "mar-kets often work *too well*: among the many things they deliver efficiently are race, gender, and class privilege."[30]

These privileges are especially apparent when considering the circum-stances that lead children to be placed in the adoption pipeline in the first place. In countries where there is a wider social safety net and greater access to contraception and abortion, very few women voluntarily relinquish chil-dren for adoption. For example, domestic adoptions in Sweden are quite rare: according to the last available data, only *forty-one* couples were able to adopt domestically in 2016.[31] Barbara Katz Rothman writes of this improb-ably small count, reflecting that few "Swedish women found themselves in a situation where placing their babies out for adoption was their best option. When you take away most of the social forces operating upstream that put women in that awful position, you are left largely with personal idiosyncrasy, personal reasons."[32]

Unlike in Sweden, where a minute proportion of newborns are placed for adoption,[33] the social issues operating upstream in countries such as Guate-mala and China create a much larger supply of children. For example, de-mographers estimate that at the height of Guatemala's adoption trade, a staggering one out of one hundred live births resulted in a newborn sent to the United States for adoption. In China, the percentage is not as high, but the magnitude of the effect is significant, such that at its peak almost 14,500 babies a year were sent abroad to a handful of "receiving" countries—more than thirty-nine a day.[34] Under these conditions, the factors leading tens of thousands of birth mothers to relinquish their children are not about choice; more accurately, they suggest a profound lack of choices for these disenfranchised women.

The popular adoption narrative focusing on the benefits bestowed to adoptive parents and children ignores those whom Rickie Solinger calls the "beggars" in adoption—that is, the women who relinquish children.[35] Solinger powerfully states that socioeconomic inequities are often obscured and replaced by the euphemistic narrative of choice, stating, "The argument that simple 'choice' actually underlies the very popular (though much denied) idea that motherhood should be a class privilege in the United States—a privilege only appropriate for women who can afford it."[36]

Writing from the perspective of a sociologist and adoptive mother, Rothman expounds on this idea:

> Those of us who adopt, and the culture of adoption that supports us, like to think that birth mothers act out of choice, that—especially in contemporary, more open adoptions—we are the "chosen people" of those birth mothers. It begs the whole question of what "choice" means, where individual agency comes into play. It's hard to imagine a woman who "chose" to place her child for adoption in the same way I "chose" to adopt: out of no need but her own desire to do so. True enough, once pregnant, once well on the way to a motherhood that she does not want, adoption may be only one of a woman's options, and any given adoptive family only one of her choices. But even under these most ideal of circumstances (not faced with a strong desire for sons in a country with a one-child-only policy, not faced with war and famine and heartbreak of all kinds), it's hard to imagine a woman choosing to become a birth mother without the circumstances pushing hard in that direction.[37]

Like Rothman, historian Laura Briggs recognizes that choice is often a misnomer in adoption and argues for "a history of adoption that pays as much attention to the position of those who *lose* children in adoption as to those who receive them."[38] Her work offers a context to help us understand the political backdrop that pushes women into adoption. Briggs advocates, "We need to widen our lens beyond the largely White and middle-class women who are the subject of that primary narrative and pay attention to how Black and Native women in the United States, and those outside the United States, came to give their children up for adoption, or lose them involuntarily."[39]

One goal of this book is to pick up where other scholars left off by drawing attention to other voices that are usually sidelined in adoption. By

focusing on adoption workers—that is, those who work in the marketplace—
I am able to paint a more thorough picture of how the market operates. I am
particularly interested in the boundary of race and how the color line plays
into what races prospective parents are willing to adopt. There is an old saying advising prospective parents that if they would not marry someone of a
certain race, then they should not adopt a child of that race either. Nora,
another social worker I interviewed,[40] brings up this point: "The rule of
adoption is you don't adopt a child of another race unless you like the grown-
ups. Your kids are going to grow up and be one of those grown-ups. Do you
eat in those restaurants? Do you mingle in those neighborhoods? Do you
shop in those stores? If you don't like the grown-ups, don't adopt one of their
children." Likewise, Gretchen states, "There is that old joke about, if you
wouldn't marry one, don't adopt one." She admits, "Of course, that is a very
crass comment, but I think it really holds true in a lot of ways."

The maxim comparing transracial adoption to interracial marriage
makes sense considering that for years sociologists have looked to intermarriage as a gauge of softening racial and ethnic boundaries. First, intermarriage signals that the social distance between the White and non-White
spouse has eroded enough for the couple to be able to marry.[41] Second, intermarriage serves as a catalyst for generational assimilation for the children of
intermarried couples.[42] For subsequent generations, ethnic differences become less salient in everyday life, and as the assimilation process occurs,
ethnicity becomes less a master status and more a symbolic identity.[43]

This model is often referred to as "classic assimilation" as it was developed to characterize the experiences of White ethnic immigrants in the early
1900s.[44] One oft-cited example of this phenomenon is the test case about how
the Irish became White.[45] Whereas Irish immigrants once were "an interme-
diate race located socially between black and white" and were routinely dis-
criminated against in terms of employment and housing,[46] after subsequent
generations the "No Irish Need Apply" signs disappeared as these immigrants and their descendants assimilated into the American mainstream.[47]

Following this model, some contemporary racial scholars argue that a
similar process is occurring for new waves of immigrants who came to the
United States following the landmark Immigration Act of 1965.[48] This legislation was monumental since it opened the doors for Asian immigrants who
had been largely banned since the Chinese Exclusion Act and greatly increased the pathway for immigration from Latin America.[49] Since its passage, the foreign-born population has steadily risen such that more than one
in ten Americans is foreign-born.[50]

Yet there is a huge distinction between the cohorts of Italian, Irish, and
Polish immigrants that composed the former wave of U.S. immigration and
the cohorts of Asian and Hispanic immigrants who largely make up the latter. Namely, most of these post-1965 immigrants are not White. Based on

this crucial racial difference, many argue that these newcomers and their children cannot possibly follow the same path as the White immigrant families did before them.[51] With this in mind, there is a fierce debate among immigration scholars regarding post-1965 immigrants' trajectories of assimilation and whether they will follow the classic path of upward assimilation or whether the prospects for the second and third generations will be segmented or even downward.[52]

Since not enough time has elapsed for successive generations of post-1965 immigrants to make their way through the assimilation process, it is impossible to know exactly what the assimilation process will look like for these relative newcomers.[53] Part of the debate about assimilation rests on whether there is a changing conception of race in the United States. While the color line used to be roughly based on a White–non-White divide, many argue that this boundary is evolving toward a Black–non-Black one.[54] If this is the case, this new demarcation will greatly shape the assimilation prospects for Hispanic and Asian immigrants and their children.

The nuances of the assimilation debate go beyond the scope of this brief overview, but for our purposes it is important to pay attention to the underlying argument that there is greater latitude for Asians and Hispanics to assimilate than there is for Blacks. Drawing on evidence from surveys on racial attitudes and demographic data on housing patterns and interracial marriage, Eduardo Bonilla-Silva argues that East and South Asians, as well as light-skinned Hispanics, are becoming "honorary whites."[55] In other words, even though these racial minorities are not White, they occupy a more privileged position compared with dark-skinned Hispanic and Black Americans. Along the same line, George Yancey argues that even as Hispanics and Asians become largely incorporated into the American mainstream, Blacks are further left behind: "Because nonblack racial groups can avoid the label of being 'black,' they can eventually be given a 'white' racial identity."[56] Unlike these non-Black racial minorities, "African Americans are in a quasi-caste system by which they occupy the lowest level of social prestige in the United States and it is in the social interest of all nonblack racial groups to keep them at the bottom."[57] Herbert Gans describes how this segregation is the foundation of what he labels African American exceptionalism. "Although a significant number of African Americans have become middle class since the civil rights legislation of the 1960s," Gans argues, "they still suffer from far harsher and more pervasive discrimination and segregation than nonwhite immigrants of equivalent class position. This not only keeps whites and blacks apart but prevents blacks from moving toward equality with whites."[58] Whereas the color line seems to be expanding to make room for most Asians and some Hispanics, African Americans remain the consistent exception to the assimilation narrative.[59] In fact, the proportion of White intermarriages with Asians outnumbers the proportion of

White-Black intermarriages despite the fact that the Black population in the United States is more than double that of Asians.[60]

Evidence of this new racial division is especially apparent in rates of intermarriage. On the basis of an analysis of 1990 census data, Qian and Lichter find that Blacks are among the least likely to marry Whites compared to Asians or Hispanics. Characterizing this trend, they conclude that "fair skinned minorities are more likely to marry Whites than darker skinned minorities."[61] Furthermore, in a study of 2005 American Community Survey data, Jeffrey Passel, Wendy Wang, and Paul Taylor find that among the newly married, Whites who intermarry tend to choose Hispanic and Asian partners, and are the least likely to intermarry with Blacks.[62]

Although intermarriage among Whites has stood as the gold standard for evaluating racial boundaries, in some respects adoption may be a far more racially deliberative process. Certainly, research on assortative marriage shows how variables like race and class shape who marries whom.[63] But these patterns do not take into account the subjective elements of love and romance based on shared values and mutual attraction that also fuel romantic pairings. These factors may soften the effect of racial difference. For example, in her qualitative study on White-Black interracially married spouses, Heather Dalmage finds that some couples did not actively set out to form an interracial union, but they "fell in love and that was it."[64]

Moreover, forming an engagement to marry requires the consent of both participants and therefore is more likely to reflect changing racial attitudes of the White and non-White person forming the union. On the other hand, transracial adoption is more one-sided. Unless the non-White child is old enough to consent to the adoption—a rarity in private adoption since the children tend to be quite young—the decision to adopt across race is initiated by the White parent(s) and not the child.

The difference between intermarriage and transracial adoption is even more pronounced considering that romantic partnerships are largely based on mutual attraction and compatibility among couples. In contrast, in private adoption prospective parents will often commit to a child—especially a young healthy child—without having met him or her first. Thus in private adoption, prospective parents usually are not choosing a child based on his or her personality. Extending the marriage market metaphor, if anything transracial adoption could be seen as an arranged marriage where one party is the chooser (the prospective parent) and the other is the proverbial chosen child. Based on this model, adoption workers act as matchmakers of sorts, helping their clients weigh variables of race, age, and health to identify the profile of the son or daughter they hope to adopt. Thus, when White parents adopt across race, they literally mark their delineation of the color line.

Recently scholars have examined how adoption serves as a window into the racial hierarchy and how Black children are relegated to the bottom of the spectrum. Kazuyo Kubo summarizes a review of the literature, arguing, "The common discourse that is engendered from their stories is that the racial division between white and black is too wide to cross, in contrast to the differences between whites and Asians."[65] Similarly, Rothman concludes that cohorts of Chinese and Korean children may become "successfully moved into whiteness."[66] But in contrast, the color line does not yield as readily for African American children. She continues, "Children of African descent cannot cross racial lines. As long as the idea of race continues in America, black children will grow up to be black adults, no matter who raises them or where."[67] Along the same line, Sara Dorow's work contextualizes the surging interest in adoptions from China. She finds that White parents adopting transnationally from China highlights the importance of racial boundaries in the decision-making process, finding that "blackness serves as a mediating backdrop" in White parents' decisions.[68]

We see this grim hierarchy also play out at the national level. For example, in Hiromi Ishizawa and colleagues' research on intercountry adoption using census data, they find that the majority of White parents adopted an Asian child, suggesting that this phenomenon is "rooted in the choice to adopt black versus nonblack where white parents feel Asian children are more assimilable to mainstream white culture than black children."[69] Similarly, White transracial adoptive parents are three times more likely to adopt Asian and Hispanic children than Black children.[70]

These studies illustrate a remarkably consistent racial hierarchy that positions Whites at the top, Asians and Hispanics in the middle, and Black children at the bottom. With this in mind, Pamela Quiroz argues that private adoption practices serve as a type of racial project that reproduces the color hierarchy.[71] She attests, "Racial projects have found their way into the adoption arena affecting children of color" such that "private adoption practices provide a window into the shifting dynamics of race in the United States demonstrating that rather than moving towards a color-blind democracy, we instead live in a context where race continues to matter substantially."[72] This leads Quiroz to argue, "Nowhere is America's schism with race more evident than in private domestic adoption."[73]

## Frontstage and Backstage Perspectives: Focusing on Adoption Workers

This schism with race became readily apparent when, several years ago, I interviewed Hannah, an adult Korean adoptee, about her experiences growing up with White parents. During the conversation I asked Hannah if her parents ever mentioned why they decided to adopt from Korea. Her response was quite candid as she disclosed that her parents told her they chose to adopt from Korea over Vietnam, another country where healthy infants were available, because "Vietnamese children looked Mexican."[74] Not wanting a child who could be mistaken for Latina, Hannah's parents pursed adopting from Korea. Although Hannah's parents were surprisingly forthcoming about their racial preferences, prior research indicates that few adoptive parents are willing to frame their decisions in such stark terms.

This reluctance makes sense, considering that in her study of White transracial adoptive parents Kathryn Sweeney finds, "Parents may be race conscious, yet struggle with explaining their choices within the confines of language that is considered non-racist and non-colorist."[75] Prior studies indicate that rather than reduce their adoption journey to a series of rational calculations about skin shade and racial profiling, adoptive parents tend to draw on narratives of fate to explain how "the universe conspired" to bring them their son or daughter.[76] Given the palpable hesitancy to explicitly own how racial hierarchies factor into the decision-making process, adoptive parents may not make the best informants regarding this line of inquiry. For example, Patricia Jennings argues that most of the transracial adoptive mothers approach parenthood from a color-blind perspective, lamenting, "Only a small number of women in this study had a critical grasp of race relations."[77]

With this in mind, my research follows a different path of data collection, focusing on adoption workers. Specifically, this book analyzes what sociologist Erving Goffman might call the frontstage and backstage of private adoption. He argues that on the frontstage a public performance is enacted which is "molded and modified to fit the understanding and expectation of the society in which it is presented."[78] In the case of private adoption, the presentation of the adoption information session serves as a type of performance where adoption professionals are tasked with marketing adoption to prospective customers. Yet, given the moral prohibition against the commodification of children, the actors must sell adoption while adhering to a more socially palatable script. This is easier said than done since the information meeting is the time when private adoption veers to the commercial because adoption workers are tasked with selling adoption—describing the array of programs they offer, detailing the characteristics of the children placed, and discussing the associated fees.

Nora bluntly acknowledges the fine line that exists between an information meeting and an infomercial, stating, "It is like a marketplace, absolutely. But there is no way around that. Or else the adoptive parents wouldn't come." She continues, "Even one could argue that the photo listings are shopping, like a Sears and Roebuck catalog. It has to start like that. There is no other way to give people the information that they need." Interestingly, Nora raises the question of what type of information is considered the most pertinent to convey during the initial meeting. Is the goal to educate prospective parents about the complexities surrounding becoming an adoptive family, or is the goal to inform prospective clients about their consumer options? Should social workers warn prospective parents of the challenges and responsibilities inherent when parenting across race, or should they table the discussion lest they scare away potential customers? These questions are important, especially since prospective adoptive parents often look to adoption workers to set the tone of the discourse.[79]

In her research on Korean adoption, Kristi Brian examines these issues through her analysis of adoption information sessions.[80] She identifies how adoption facilitators tend to discuss adoption in terms of applicants' consumer options, writing, "I expected to find international adoption, in general, promoted in a manner that appealed to prospective parents' sense of altruism or international relief efforts. Much to my surprise, I found instead that adoption facilitators focused primarily on appeasing adoptive parents' expectations in the area of customer service."[81] While her work is valuable in identifying the inherent tensions which portray international adoption as an altruistic but consumer-friendly process, since Brian analyzes only three adoption agencies specific to Korea, it is unclear whether and how the consumer approach applies to other segments of the adoption marketplace.

In Dorow's comprehensive ethnographic study of transnational adoptions from China, she includes a subset of interviews with adoption workers, examining the behind-the-scenes labor involved. She writes, "The work of facilitators begins in the pre-adoption phase of preparing and shepherding parents through the many steps of the process, in anticipation of crossing borders."[82] A crucial element of this work includes the "cultural training" geared to "prepare parents for transnational and transracial kinship."[83] As Dorow notes, these trainings often coalesce around the idea that adopted children should have some knowledge of their heritage, and White parents should be introduced to the idea that their Chinese children will experience racism. However, many of her respondents were wary of treading too deeply into the discourse of racial difference with their clients, since "none of them wanted to scare parents off with a lot of intervention." She describes how "even those who were committed to thorough pre-adoptive training admitted they were wary of doing 'too much' around race and culture issues."[84]

Dorow's informants frame their reticence to introduce tough conversations about race and adoption as a pedagogical strategy, rationalizing that it is usually after placement that parents are more "ready to hear it."[85] But the hesitancy to introduce uncomfortable topics also likely stems from a desire to placate the parent-customer who may already be reeling from the seemingly unending bureaucratic steps that an overseas adoption mandates. Since agencies compete to recruit applicants who can likely choose among several organizations offering adoptions from China, few agencies would want to impose additional hoops, especially if they believe that "the other stuff is almost more immediate."[86] Dorow highlights a conversation with Carrie, an adoption social worker, who frankly discusses this conundrum: "My salary, and Norma's salary, is paid by a secondary client, whose goodwill we must maintain."[87]

Dorow's findings raise fascinating questions about the role of adoption facilitators as the arbiters of transracial adoption. Fueled by a belief and perhaps a business strategy that pushes difficult discussions about race down the road, Dorow argues that there is "the professionalized emphasis on finding the 'right' level of Chinese culture."[88] Notably, her informants espouse the idea that some White parents can do "too much," whether that be move to a more Chinese neighborhood or enroll their family in Mandarin classes. For example, Carrie declares, "I have concerns about the families who become totally Asian. . . . [D]on't they have any self respect about their own background?"[89] The idea that parents should do something with Chinese culture but not too much reinforces what Dorow calls the "tacit normalcy" of Whiteness that often operates in the background of discussions on racial socialization among social workers facilitating Chinese adoptions.[90]

Notably, Dorow conducted her research during a time when transnational adoptions from China were booming. The pace of business was so fast that one social worker she interviewed ruefully referred to her agency as "China-R-Us."[91] This book serves to juxtapose how the slowdown magnifies this consumer mentality, raising new questions as to whether a discussion of race at the preadopt stage will go even further underground as social workers have greater incentive to cater to the needs of the paying clients and not scare off potential customers before they are "ready to hear." Thus, this book contributes to the existing literature by describing how adoption workers promote transracial adoption during a market downturn as opposed to during the boom years.

Beyond Brian and Dorow's work, Quiroz's study of adoption agency websites is one of the few other systematic studies of private adoption institutions addressing issues of race and the color line.[92] Based on a sample of private adoption agencies' websites, she positions these texts as racial projects and analyzes how Black children are segregated into lower-tier programs. Describing this separation, Quiroz writes, "Regardless of the functional, benign, or even altruistic motives claimed by adoption agencies, racial distinctions are perpetuated and the color line protected when African American and biracial children are separated from virtually everyone else in adoption programs."[93] Although Quiroz's research was instrumental in establishing how racial hierarchies infiltrate adoption, her research is also limited since it is based on content analyses of polished and vetted text.

Only a handful of studies explicitly focus on adoption social workers' attitudes, usually investigating best practices in the wake of new policy initiatives such as the Multiethnic Placement Act (MEPA) and the Interethnic Placement Act (IEP). These two pieces of legislation prohibited adoption providers from taking race into account when making adoption placements for taxpayer-funded adoptions, such as through foster care.[94] In response to these new regulations, Jan Carter-Black interviews ten African American social workers working in foster care and finds "overall, a concern for the potential harm of MEPA-IEP."[95] However, the sample only includes social workers who facilitate foster care adoptions, since private adoption tends fall outside MEPA's purview.

Similarly, in response to the ratification of the Hague Convention on Intercountry Adoption, a treaty that set uniform ethical standards for cross-national placements, Jo Bailey interviewed thirteen international adoption workers asking how the new requirements would impact the industry.[96] The new rules stipulated that, to receive Hague accreditation, agencies must have a governing board, possess two months cash reserves, and carry a minimum threshold of liability insurance commensurate with the size of the agency.[97] The workers Bailey interviewed presciently predicted that smaller agencies will be adversely affected by these regulations and may say, "We're done, we're finished, or we're gearing down to close our doors."[98] But since Bailey conducted her interviews in 2007, well before the downturn in international adoption hit a crisis point, for some agencies it would be several more years until the threat of bankruptcy really set in.

In addition to interviewing adoption social workers about their views on specific policies, other studies have sampled social workers about their opinions on transracial adoption. Derek Kirton examines British social work students' opinions on transracial adoption, finding that support for cross-race adoption is generally strong but even stronger among White students.[99] A more recent study of U.S. social work students echoed a similar trend, suggesting that support for transracial adoption is a shared philosophy, especially among White social workers.[100] While these two studies identify consistent support for transracial adoptive placements among White social work students, it is unclear how many sampled students actually go on to administer transracial adoptions.

Missing from the analysis is a multifaceted analysis of the frontstage and backstage of private transracial adoption. The aim of this book is to bridge this gap in the literature by illustrating the reach of the market. I show how the business of adoption permeates the way that adoption professionals talk about their work when backstage and how it shapes their actions when they are pitching their services to potential clients frontstage.

To study the frontstage, I acted as a participant observer at information sessions and preadoption conferences geared toward audiences of prospective adoptive parents. Over the course of two years, I attended forty of these presentations, sitting in the audience among prospective adoptive parents who, like me, were frantically taking notes and trying to discern how adoption works. Considering that the average age of parents using private adoption is forty years old,[101] as a graduate student in my early thirties, I was only a few years younger than many of the audience members, who were just starting their potentially multiple-year journey toward adoptive parenthood. Since adoption is a largely female-driven process, I did not look out of place as a lone woman. But given that more than four out of five private adoptive parents are White,[102] I may have stood out as one of the few women of color in the audience. Had I disclosed my social location as a mother of a child born to me, I likely would have stood out all the more, since the vast majority of applicants pursue private adoption only after facing significant barriers to biological reproduction.

Another aspect of my social location that is important for readers to know is that I am a Korean adoptee. Born in Korea but raised by White parents in the United States, I am one of the two hundred thousand children sent abroad to the United States and Western European countries in the post-Korean Conflict period.[103] Long before "rainbow families" were in vogue, I grew up in a transracial family with a White mother and father, a White sister who is my parents' biological child, and a brother adopted from India. Thus, I come to this project with somewhat of an insider status, since my social location as a Korean adoptee shapes how I think about race and adoption.[104] But I am also an outsider, since I am not a social worker and have never worked in adoption. Although my position as an insider-outsider may be of interest to readers, I want to stress that I write from the perspective of a race and family sociologist as much as, and probably more than, from the perspective of an adult adoptee.

As Paul Hodkinson writes, "Holding a degree of insider status clearly can have implications for the achievement of successful and productive interactions with participants."[105] One aspect I noticed throughout my fieldwork was that my status as a transracial Korean adoptee likely gave me additional "backstage" access to respondents who may have been otherwise reticent to discuss their work. Goffman characterizes the backstage as a space where one can let one's guard down. He gives the example of the corporate executive whose office provides a space to "take his jacket off, loosen his tie."[106] Moreover, the backstage is a space where performers can go "off script" and deviate from the dominant narrative. Even though I identified myself as a sociologist and researcher, because of my social location as a Korean adoptee, I had the sense that adoption professionals saw me as one of them. In other words, I was a potential colleague who had a deep understanding of the adoption process. As someone who grew up in an adoptive family, I did not have to be convinced that adoptive families were just as legitimate as biologically related families. I could attest that love was thicker than blood.

The data from backstage derives from interviews with twenty-five adoption providers from seventeen different adoption organizations. I use the umbrella term "adoption providers" because their jobs span a breadth of responsibilities including writing home studies so clients can be approved to adopt by family court, answering phone calls from people initially reaching out to the agency, and coordinating domestic adoption programs. I was also able to speak to adoption professionals who occupy a management role, including executive directors of adoption agencies and independent attorneys who built their practice around guiding parents through the independent domestic adoption process. Whereas most of my in-person interviews took place on the East Coast, I was able to supplement my data collection through phone interviews with adoption workers in the Midwest, the South, and the West Coast. Like social service in general, women make up the vast majority of the adoption work force, a trend that is reflected in my all-female sample. Additionally, all but two of the women I interviewed were White. While it would be interesting to note when women of color voiced different opinions regarding their work, since there are so few minority women working in adoption I do not make any further distinctions in order to not jeopardize their anonymity. For all of my respondents, all identifying information has been changed.

It is important to underscore that I take a somewhat liberal interpretation of the term "backstage." Through my interviews, I am able to access adoption workers' thoughts and insights that they normally would not publicize during a frontstage information meeting. Yet my research methods did not enable me to go fully backstage and observe adoption workers in conversation with each other, carrying out their everyday responsibilities. Despite this limitation, this work is the only monograph that analyzes both international and domestic adoptions from the perspective of adoption practitioners. It captures a unique point in adoption history when workers are struggling to adapt to a shrinking market and tightening restrictions.

In 2009–2010, when I was conducting my research, it had been five years since the number of international adoptions hit their peak. At this time, in the United States there were still 150 Hague-accredited adoption agencies in operation. But it became apparent in my research that international adoption workers knew the tide was turning. There were tightened restrictions across several major sending countries as popular programs either limited the number of healthy infants sent abroad or closed down entirely. For example, China—a program known for sending more than five thousand infant and toddler girls to the United States a year—curtailed the number of these placements, and Guatemala and Vietnam closed their adoption programs entirely. Ethiopia was one of the few remaining countries sending infants. But by 2010, even Ethiopia was slowing down. At its peak, the country sent 2,511 children to the United States, with 61 percent of the children younger than two years at the time of placement. In other words, one of the last countries supplying infants and toddlers was drying up.

One question that logically emerges is whether readers can be confident that I actually got backstage access and was not just given a reiteration of the frontstage party line? Here it is useful to go back to Abigail, the social worker featured in the opening quote. The first time I met Abigail was not during our interview but at an adoption information session where I sat in the audience as an observer. During this two-hour presentation, she and her colleague delivered a comprehensive overview of their many programs. Not once throughout the information session did she discuss with the audience how Clerestory Adoptions was struggling to find an economically viable international adoption program that did not require paying off too many people or liken the practice to an industry. Instead, she stuck to the script detailing their long history of serving adoptive families and their commitment to child welfare. Yet during the backstage interview, she let down her guard to the extent that she worries, "I'm totally going to get fired for this conversation."

Other women I interviewed expressed similar sentiments and shared their ambivalence about their work and their roles in perpetuating an industry. Even though my focus is on the market aspects of adoption, my hope is that my interviewees will see that the intent is not to vilify their choices or private adoption in general. If anything, I left each interview with a deep respect for my respondents, many of whom were grappling with similar questions. These women took time out of their busy schedules to talk to me and they were forthcoming even when the questions might have made them uncomfortable. I recall the end of my interview with another respondent, Amanda. We had already touched on controversial subjects such as charging less for Black babies, supply and demand in adoption, and whether she thought it was acceptable to allow White parents to specify that they would be willing to adopt a biracial Black child but not a monoracial Black child. She gamely answered my inquiries, even though she was clearly curious about my intent, commenting, "I'd be curious to see where this [project] goes." My research led me to some conclusions that adoption workers may not necessarily agree with, especially in regard to social workers' ability to adequately prepare White parents adopting across race. Even though some may disagree with my findings, I want it to be clear that I remain incredibly grateful to these professionals for their honest appraisals of their joys and frustrations working in this field.

For example, I spent an hour and a half talking with Erin, a bright and dedicated social worker who came to adoption work because she wanted to work in child welfare in developing countries. Although her livelihood depends on making adoptive placements, Erin strongly advocates that the best child welfare model would be to keep kids in their biological families. She states:

And my frustration with adoption agencies—not so specifically this agency to this degree—[has to do with] really balancing our adoption work with our responsibility to do humanitarian aid work or any kinds of programs that can help keep kids in families. At the other agency I worked for, we did do more, and I felt better about that in a lot of ways, just because that is a better longer-term solution. Obviously, I wouldn't be working in adoption if I didn't support it, but there are definitely times when I think there are some gray areas where I am not comfortable.

Notice how Erin's words echo Zelizer's theory of the hostile spheres of commerce and love, where on one side of the equation adoption exists as humanitarian child welfare, and on the other side it is a commodified marketplace for children. In private adoption, Erin's job mandates working in the liminal space between these spheres. It is in those "gray areas" that we can learn the most about race and family.

## Previous Research on Kinship Marketplaces

Sociologists have accumulated a substantial body of research illustrating how market aspects permeate everyday life and, in turn, how those marketplaces are socially constructed and reproduced. William Julius Wilson's work on marriage markets is particularly instructive, as he was one of the first to contextualize family formation in economic terms. He posits that the low rates of marriage among African American women are partially due to the high rate of underemployment and incarceration among African American men, which led to a shortage of suitable marriage partners.[107] Since Wilson, sociologists of the family have routinely applied market principles in their analyses of dating, mating, and childbirth.[108]

Landes and Posner applied this market framework to adoption, arguing that the practice should operate as a free market exchange.[109] In their infamous paper, they propose setting differential prices for adoptable children, citing the immense waiting times to adopt a healthy White infant contrasted with the "glut" of children in foster care. They compare the large number of children in foster care awaiting adoption as "comparable to unsold inventory in a warehouse."[110] Since the demand for these children was so low, they argue, their price should be too. Unsurprisingly, casting adoption as the sale of children in such stark rational terms provoked numerous outraged responses.[111]

Much in terms of family building has changed since the publication of Landes and Posner's work. Most significant is the explosion of assisted-reproduction technologies (ART) that have altered the market options for

adoptive parents. At the national level, researchers have identified a significant overlap between ART users and adoptive parents. Using data from the
1988 National Survey of Family Growth (NSFG), researchers once characterized adoption seeking as "primarily a function of the desire to have children
coupled with inability or difficulty in having them."[112] A follow-up study
from the 2002 NSFG reiterates the strong association between infertility and
adoption, showing that women who have used infertility services are ten
times more likely to have adopted than women who have not.[113]

Because of the inexorable link between infertility and adoption, Rene
Almeling's work on the market for human gametes is particularly relevant
as it lays the groundwork for a sociologically informed discussion of pricing
babies.[114] She uncovers how the market value of eggs and sperm is based on
the supply of each as well as the status of the donor. Since sperm is easier to
obtain, it effectively drives down the price, and the male donors are treated
as replaceable workers. On the other hand, egg retrieval requires a surgical
procedure so the supply is harder to harvest, enabling women to command
a higher price for their donation.

Another important insight from Almeling's research is that markets are
shaped by social constructs such as gender. She argues that the discourse
surrounding egg donation is deeply feminized, such that egg donors are
characterized as altruistic women more interested in helping people become
parents than rational laborers selling their eggs for thousands of dollars. The
moral policing against donating solely for profit is so strong that fertility
workers are quick to scorn "girls who just want to lay their eggs for some
quick cash."[115]

If the moral stakes are tenuous in assisted reproductive technologies
where workers only trade in human gametes, they are even higher in surrogacy where a woman is paid to gestate and give birth to someone else's
baby. Take, for example, the case of Baby M, an infant born to a paid
surrogate who refused to relinquish custody. The resulting custody battle
was the first to test whether a surrogate was a mother or a contract worker.
Although the paid surrogate eventually won partial custody of her daughter,
her case is unusual because she was both the biological and gestating
mother.[116]

Nowadays fertility specialists seek to limit a surrogate's claim on a baby
by separating the egg donor and the gestational surrogate such that one
woman provides the genetic material and the other the womb.[117] In this new
frontier of assisted reproductive technology, it is possible that there are four
or five parents—the sperm donor, the egg donor, the gestational surrogate,
and the intended parent(s) who procure and pay for the services creating
their son or daughter.[118]

Although much has been written on the ethics surrounding surrogacy,
especially transnational surrogacy, in which intended parents outsource the

gestation and labor to poorer women in developing countries,[119] for our purposes the most applicable research is on the experience of the surrogates themselves. Amrita Pande's work interviewing gestational surrogates in India shows how workers validate their labor, conceptualizing themselves as respectable workers despite the public shame they endure for taking part in something seen as akin to sex work.[120] Even though these women at times see themselves as workers, many view their labor as an altruistic journey that provides the gift of life for parents longing for a baby.[121] Some anticipate and perhaps naively hope for an extended relationship with the intended parents after the birth.[122] Yet as Zsuzsa Berend depicts in her analysis of American surrogate chat rooms, the relationship with the intended parents quickly fades after the birth of the baby.[123] Likening it to a "romance," she shows how surrogates are often showered with attention while pregnant, but once the surrogate completes her contract and the transactional payment occurs, the relationship dissipates and disappoints.

Whereas human gamete donors and gestational surrogates can claim identities as workers who are engaged in creating a baby for another party, birth mothers do not have that option. Unlike surrogates or egg donors, the law prohibits birth mothers from making money from the placement of the baby. The approbation against the appearance of baby buying is so strong that many states have regulations specifically detailing how much money can be spent to support the pregnancy of a woman making an adoption plan.[124]

In contrast to the recent explosion of studies on gestational surrogates, there is a notable absence of literature on the experience of birth mothers. One reason is likely that the shame and stigma that surrounded the decision to place makes birth mothers a difficult population to identify and study.[125] The few studies that exist find that the grief and loss is palpable but may fade over time, especially given the trend in the United States toward open adoptions where there is some expectation of ongoing contact and the exchange of photos and letters between the birth and adoptive families.[126]

Perhaps because there are so few studies highlighting the voices of birth mothers, the prevailing narrative surrounding adoption tends to focus on the gift exchange rather than on loss or commodification. As Appurdai writes, "Gifts, and the spirit of reciprocity, sociability, and spontaneity in which they are typically exchanged, usually are starkly opposed to the profit-oriented, self-centered, and calculated spirit that fires the circulation of commodities."[127] The altruistic message embedded in the gift exchange does the emotional work of smoothing over the birth mothers' losses as well as the commodified nature of the transaction by anchoring it in more comfortable territory. Barbara Yngvesson describes this phenomenon, arguing, "In spite of efforts to reconceptualize the physical movement of a child between persons or nations as placement rather than gift, the gift child remains a powerful and persistent image in adoption discourse."[128] Additionally, Dorow's work on transnational adoption from China provides further insight into why the gift narrative prevails. She argues, "The gift further serves to offset the discourse of the client, that is the 'placement' practices of the adoption profession and, more important, the commodified nature of the contractual market."[129]

But at closer analysis the gift metaphor falls short when describing these transactions. In Marcel Mauss's model, a gift is exchanged between two parties and there is an anticipation of reciprocity where the gift giver will later receive something of equal or greater value in return.[130] Donors of eggs and sperm sell their gametes; they do not give them away hoping that the recipient will later return the gesture. Surrogates trade their literal labor for wages; they do not give the baby away hoping to receive one down the road. In contrast, adoption is an unequal exchange, the transaction or placement of a child from a disenfranchised parent without the resources to care for the child to a more privileged parent who can not only afford to raise a child but also pay thousands of dollars to procure one.

The market aspect of adoption is even more apparent when considering the costs associated with different types of adoption. According to results from the National Survey of Adoptive Parents, more than nine out of ten parents utilizing international adoption report that the total cost exceeded $10,000 (Vandivere, Malm, and Radel 2009). However, the true cost of adopting internationally was likely much higher. According to the latest report issued by the U.S. Department of State, the median cost of an international adoption was $31,120[131]—which is more than half the median household income.[132]

Data for private domestic adoptions are harder to come by, but the total cash outlay tends to vary widely. Results from the National Survey of Adoptive Parents show that only one-third of parents report that their domestic adoptions cost more than $10,000.[133] Notably, adopting from foster care required the smallest expenditure with more than half (56 percent) of foster care adoptive parents responding that the adoption occurred with no net cash outlay.[134]

Despite the significant differences in costs between foster care, private domestic, and international adoptions, it is clear that the fee may not be the most significant variable since prospective parents could pay very little (if any) money to adopt from foster care. Considering that parents pursuing private adoption are willing to wait years for a baby, while 23,000 children "age out" of the U.S. foster care system every year without being adopted, it is clear that foster care is not seen by many as a desirable market alternative.[135] According to Fiona, another social worker I interviewed, clients pursuing private adoption have emphatically ruled out foster care. She describes their rationale, stating that she has heard many clients say, "It is harder for me to adopt from the U.S. because those kids come with so much baggage; that's why they are in foster care."

While there may not be a lot of crossover between private and publicly funded adoptions, it is important to recognize that parents *do* adopt from foster care. In fact, about one-third (37 percent) of adoptive parents choose to adopt via foster care, approximately equal to the percentage of parents utilizing private domestic adoptions. However, foster care adoptive parents fit a very different demographic profile than those who pursue private domestic and international adoptions. Analyzing data from the National Survey of Adoptive Parents, Ishizawa and Kubo find that these foster care adoptive parents are more likely to be lower-income and have families blending biological and adopted children.[136] The latter suggests that infertility may not be a driving factor, and indeed, foster adoptive parents are the least likely to say that infertility was a motivation for adoption.[137]

Early in my data collection, I made a conscious decision to focus on private international and domestic adoption. My reasoning was threefold. First, there is a far more established canon of research on foster care than private adoption. Because the U.S. Department of Health and Human Services mandates data reporting, there is a long history of social and behavioral research on foster care adoptions.[138] However, there is less extant research on private adoption, especially domestic transracial adoption. Second, the market paradigm is completely different in foster care adoptions that occur at little to no cost. In fact, 93 percent of foster care adoptive parents continue to receive monthly adoption subsidies even after the adoption is finalized.[139] These payments lower the net cost for foster parents who would have had to forgo the monthly payments associated with child expenses if they adopted the child in their care.[140] Third, there tends to be little institutional overlap between private and public adoption agencies. Whereas it is common for private agencies to offer an array of domestic and international programs, few offered choices across foster care, domestic, and international programs, starkly illustrating how adoption operates as a segmented marketplace.[141] For example, the presenter at Forever Family crisply informs her audience, "We do not deal with foster care."

Having decided to purposely restrict my sampling frame to private adoption, I did not seek out any foster care adoption workers. Nora, a social worker featured earlier in the chapter, was one of the rare adoption providers simultaneously working across the three market segments. She describes her frustration with foster care's diminished reputation: "There is a bias in our society against adoption. There is a quadruple bias against foster care. . . . Foster parents are seen as the low end, and foster kids are seen as children of the lower class." Penelope, another private adoption social worker, voices similar concerns about the characterization of children available via foster care, lamenting, "Then there's that whole thing with kids in the foster kid system: they are free, and they are so cheap and how that aligns with them being damaged, and damaged goods on sale."

These assessments closely echo prior findings that children eligible for adoption from foster care are more likely to be seen as having "problems" compared with children available via international adoption. Sociologists Yuanting Zhang and Gary Lee argue that the "characteristics of minority children available for adoption in the United States are phrased in terms of social problems such as possible parental drug addiction and adverse neighborhood influences on child development."[142] According to Nora, it is not just the parents who hold these views; private adoption agencies also impart this message. She attests, "There is an incredible social bias [against foster care]—way, way more than adoption. And the agencies perpetuate it."

The message that foster care adoptions are subpar did at times emerge during the information sessions I visited. Even though most of the providers facilitated only private adoption, the specter of foster care enshrouded these conversations. The option of foster care was often brought up and then quickly dismissed as an unviable alternative. For example, at a conference designed for prospective adoptive parents, the executive director of one of the sponsoring agencies welcomes her audience during the opening remarks. She explains the origins of her agency and how she came to specialize in private adoption. She describes how "the foster care system was failing" and how her clients "could not find the types of children they were hoping to adopt."[143] The message is clear: foster care offers lower-tier children that audience members probably are not looking for. She offers private adoption as a salvo, depicting her agency as an entity that can help parents "adopt the child that you want."

One reason for this mismatch between the supply of foster care children and the demands of adoptive parents may be the age and race of children available through foster care. Parents hoping to adopt a baby would have a difficult time finding an infant via foster care adoption, as the median age of children adopted via foster care is five years old. Black children are also overrepresented among the foster care waiting child population. Twenty-four percent of the one hundred thousand children waiting to be adopted are Black, whereas only 15 percent of the population of children in the United States are Black. In stark contrast, the number of Asian children waiting to be adopted from foster care is so minuscule that they make up less than one percent of the population of children waiting to be adopted.[144] Once in foster care, Black children—even relatively young infants—are less likely to be adopted into permanent families than older White children.[145]

The fact that foster care children did not fit the description of the child "that you want" became even more apparent during my interview with Lindsay, a veteran adoption social worker. I asked her how many of her clients were considering foster care. She responds that she had "very few from foster care," adding that this breakdown was "for a number of reasons, and a number of valid reasons." Lindsay explains, "If you are single, you are not going to get a child who is under five, or six, or seven." Meeting an older child's needs is difficult, especially "if you are a single working parent." Lindsay is honest about the commitment it entails, elaborating, "To take on an older child with special needs is not something that I would really encourage unless you are really wealthy and have all of the social supports." Dismissing foster care as a viable option, she bluntly states, "I don't think it is that realistic."

As Lindsay deftly points out, parents have valid reasons for choosing the pathway of private adoption. This assessment rings true considering that most prospective adoptive parents do not deliberately set out to make a statement about the nature of kinship and the hierarchy of race and the color line. Rather, they are trying to become parents—usually after facing significant barriers to this goal. Private adoptive parents want to become parents so badly that they are willing to undergo a tremendous invasion of privacy, pay thousands of dollars, and endure uncertain and excruciating waits. My intent is not to judge their choices. It is worth repeating that as a mother to a child born to me, I had the privilege of sidestepping these thorny issues and did not have to negotiate tenuous questions about kinship and racial boundaries as I was forming my family. For others who do not have this privilege, I imagine that this book could feel like a personal attack.

As adoptive father and adoption advocate Adam Pertman argues, "I don't believe we should second guess how people choose to adopt any more than it's our business to tell someone to parent a child from foster care rather than have another fertility treatment."[146] And at the individual level, of course, this is true. The point of this book is not to second-guess people's choices, especially families who are conspicuous and at times vulnerable. I am not interested in critiquing an individual's journey to adoption. Nor am I interested in judging how White parents go about raising their non-White children. I have witnessed firsthand, not only from my own upbringing but now from dear friends who are transracial adoptive parents, that the majority of White transracial adoptive parents deeply and unconditionally love their children. I hope that these readers can see that my intent is not to judge their actions or their families.

However, I strongly believe that it *is* fruitful to go up a unit of analysis to understand how the idea of transracial adoption is promoted and sold to prospective parents. To do so, we need to hear directly from adoption professionals—that is, those tasked with putting the adoptive family together. From these providers, we can learn how markets, race, and family intersect. But to adequately talk about markets, it is vital that we are able to talk about adoption in terms of supply and demand—a framework that, admittedly, does not always sound right.

## Supply and Demand: "It Doesn't Sound Right"

Alyssa Hollis is the director of True Heart Adoptions, a domestic adoption agency whose organization is a branch of a larger social service agency. She has been working in adoption for thirteen years. Before the start of her adoption career, she served as a counselor for teen parents who were struggling to get by. "I became so struck that over the years women were not considering the option of adoption," Alyssa recounts. "It was quite apparent [that] they were all living in crisis mode: Do I have enough to eat? Do I have enough to feed my kid? But they were all parenting. So I would eventually ask them, 'So why did you choose to parent?' and all of them had an answer that had something to do with abortion. Either I was too late for an abortion or I didn't know where to get one or I didn't want one. And then they were all parenting by default. And then I just started to think, 'Well what happened to adoption?' and learned more about it on my own and got really into it and have been doing it exclusively."

Her agency is small by design, keeping a waiting list of only about twenty families. Because Alyssa can fall back on the umbrella organization for additional financial support, she does not have to rely solely on application and placement fees from adoptive parents to meet her expenses. With this safety net, Alyssa indicates that her organization has the "luxury" of keeping only a small pool of waiting families so that she and her colleagues can focus on the needs of women and children, rather than waiting parents. "Since we are supported by a larger agency," she states, "we have the luxury [that] if we can't pay our bills this month, it is okay. And the other places that have sixty families, they don't have that luxury." Alyssa continues, "We don't want to be placement-oriented. We want to be about the baby and helping a woman make the best choice for her baby and for herself. And if it is adoption, great. But if not, okay. So we don't want the pressure of sixty families waiting to be parents."

Despite the fact that Alyssa's parent organization provides a fiscal safety net, she still recognizes that her agency has to manage its revenue. She relents, "You know, it is a business. We provide a fabulous service, but at the end of the day, we are a business. Which I would never want you to quote, since it doesn't sound right." This raises the question: Why does it not sound right to call adoption a business? How does framing the placement of children in terms of supply and demand, or inventory and revenue, violate the moral boundary between child commodification and child welfare? If this type of language is supposed to be off-limits, what strategies do adoption workers use when maneuvering across this morally ambiguous terrain?

I spoke with Heather about this issue. She is a social worker in her mid-thirties who has predominantly worked in private international adoption. She got her start at the agency right out of college and then stayed on in a variety of different roles. "Adoption work kind of grabs hold of you," she says, explaining how she has worked at her agency for twelve years. Professionally speaking, Heather states, "I kind of grew up here," relating how she started working here right out of college and then got an MSW along the way.

Near the end of the interview, I asked her what she thought of using market vocabulary to describe adoption trends. Heather responds that she is reluctant to characterize adoption this way, stating, "My gut reaction to all that is very negative, the supply and demand. I don't hear a lot about the marketplace kind of approach, but you definitely hear the supply and demand language—usually in the periphery—and it is very uncomfortable." Following up, I asked what made her uncomfortable about the market metaphor and she responded, "I find it disturbing that people are being reduced to commodities, and it disregards the issues in adoption. But I think that my initial gut reaction is these are humans, and we don't talk that way about humans."

Despite her hesitancy to use this terminology, she relates how some of her clients have referred to adoption in this way. Heather continues, "But I also can see how it gets reduced to that, and it would come up some time in China. A family would inquire why the wait was getting so long, and I would say that there was a backlog of families who were waiting for young children, and they would say, 'Oh, so you say that the demand exceeds the supply.'" The notion of referring to adoption in market terms is so fraught that Heather calls this approach a form of ignorance, stating, "I think that people aren't sensitive to these issues. If you are a businessman, that is how your mind works. So part of what we have to do is educate people not to say things like that. I have heard that from ignorant people, let's say."

Heather's quote brings up a key issue about how to talk about private adoption. Notice that she is not taking umbrage with the fact that the waiting times skyrocketed for China's "traditional" program that routinely placed healthy infant girls. Rather her issue is that framing this trend in terms of supply and demand violates an unspoken rule of referring to adoption as a market. This transgression threatens the foundational premise that transnational and transracial adoption is purely about child welfare.

But what words *should* people use to describe this phenomenon in a more palatable way? Here it is helpful to return to Abigail's thoughts. Recall how she called adoption an industry and then worried that she had crossed a line by referring to it this way. Even though she admits, "It is an industry at the end of the day," she still makes an effort to eschew market language, especially when talking with clients. "In terms of client demands," she states, "we frame everything as there is more of a need in this country. I am trying really hard to get away from the words 'available for adoption.' I know a lot of people say that. We try to keep it as kids who are in need of homes, parents who want to be parents to a child internationally."

Although Abigail describes strategies of moral and linguistic maneuverings to cast adoption in a positive light, Joanna, another interviewee, concedes that the market language can be useful shorthand, but only with the stipulation that it is in the service of helping children. "We view it as child welfare," she explains, "and it is about children in need, and going from there. But, honestly, if we are in a group of like-minded peers, we do use terms like that, as long as it is a group of like-minded peers and there isn't that risk of misinterpretation. But the business terminology is helpful, even if you are talking about it very differently. But it is helpful."

Although the mission is child welfare, Joanna goes on to discuss how it is becoming harder for them to do their work, since countries are limiting the supply of young children released for adoption. She details, "There is a supply and demand issue in many ways that families—although there has been a shift in flexibility, there are still more families who want a young child as healthy as possible, than there are children necessarily available who need placement. So we do use those terms, but again always making sure that it is within a group of colleagues who know that it is within the short form. Obviously, our goal at the end of the day is to change the population of families to meet the needs of the kids."

As Joanna suggests, her organization was at a crossroads. Families were still interested in adoption, and there was still a demand for a young child as healthy as possible. Yet there was a downturn in the supply as country programs closed or significantly curtailed the number of healthy infants they were willing to place. Joanna attests that the child welfare goal is to recruit prospective parents who can meet the needs of older children facing medical issues. And there are parents out there who eagerly sign up to parent children with these challenges. Yet these parents may be more likely to pursue foster care adoptions because the fees are lower, leaving more money to devote to acquiring services for the child. Although this trend toward foster care adoption is a good thing for U.S. foster care children waiting for permanent placements, it does not necessarily bode well for private adoption agencies specializing in transnational adoption. As the next chapter shows, the downturn in international adoption brought many agencies to a crisis point, making it all the more difficult to stay afloat.

## Overview of the Book

To summarize, the main goals of this book are to identify and analyze what private transracial adoption can teach us about family and the demarcation of the color line. To unpack these questions, I identify and address several interrelated lines of inquiry. First, how does the downturn in the private marketplace affect child welfare practice? Second, in light of this downturn, how does the market framework inform how adoption providers sell transracial adoption to prospective parents? Third, how does the tightening privatized adoption marketplace complicate the idea of transracial adoption, especially for Black children?

My aim is to answer these questions by building a successive argument that unfolds over five chapters. Chapter 1 establishes the basis for my argument as to why private adoption can be viewed as a marketplace. In this chapter, I introduce readers to how adoption providers both embrace and reject the market framework. I put the voices of adoption workers front and center, detailing their struggle to keep their focus on the child welfare mission of finding families for children. Centering my analysis on international adoptions, I examine how the declining supply of babies threatens the livelihood of transnational adoption agencies, leading workers to make trade-offs to "keep their doors open." I pay particular attention to the exponential growth of adoptions from Ethiopia, describing how this emerging market was gold to struggling agencies that otherwise would have declared bankruptcy. Then I explore how adoption workers feel about the commodification of children and the use of market vocabulary to describe their business, detailing how some feel some ambivalence about their work.

After describing how the marketplace operates via the backstage, in Chapter 2 I turn my attention to the frontstage of adoption. Broadly, I ask how adoption providers sell adoption to prospective clients. I begin by providing an in-depth description of the typical adoption information session, emphasizing how adoption professionals face the ironic and complex task of assuring prospective parents that adoption is not a marketplace for children while marketing adoption. To navigate through this potential minefield, I argue that adoption practitioners rely on a form of emotion work that eases parents into a consumer mind-set without blatantly overstepping the line between child welfare and child commodification. By examining attorney-led and agency domestic adoptions, as well as international placements, I show how adoption facilitators try to navigate between these so-called hostile spheres of social service and customer service.

In Chapter 3, I leverage workers' expertise to describe how most pursuers of private adoption only "come to adoption" after facing some sort of barrier to biological reproduction. At this tender juncture, adoption workers must tread carefully as they ask potential clients to articulate the type of child they want to adopt. I show how adoption workers often cast this decision in market terms, often urging clients to make the "age-race-health comparison." However, since many international programs have strict eligibility requirements, adoption workers must also convey the difficult information that not all prospective parents will have equal access to all children in the pool.

In Chapter 4, I extend my market analysis of transracial adoption. In the first section, I detail how adoption workers categorically de-emphasize race when talking about the transracial placement of Hispanic and Asian children such that they are seen as "less of a transracial adoption." Whereas much of the literature on transracial adoption frames the decision in terms of White parents adopting Black children,[147] in this chapter I also tease out how the adoption industry differentiates among Black children available for adoption. I show how the practice of charging lower fees for Black children compared to non-Black children reinforces the demarcation of the Black–non-Black divide. However, there are also important exceptions to this delineation. I examine two case studies complicating our understanding of the Black side of this divide. First, I examine the racialization of Black biracial children, detailing how part-White Black children occupy a higher status than monoracial African American children. I then investigate the rising popularity of African intercountry adoptions. If Black children supposedly embody the lowest stratum on the color line, how do we explain the exponential growth of adoptions from Africa, particularly Ethiopia? Based on these data, I argue that the tightening adoption marketplace is helping reconfigure the color line, drawing it between those who are monoracial native-born African American and those who are not.

In Chapter 5, I delve deeper into how adoption providers sell transracial adoption to prospective clients. I show how market concerns lead adoption social workers to downplay the significance of race, often conflating discussions of racial power and privilege with more palatable discussions of multiculturalism. I describe how many White social workers, who are the arbiters of transracial adoptive placements, are reluctant to engage in discussions about race. When adoption social workers *do* bring up race, I detail how they tend to minimize the commitment that transracial adoption entails, often positioning it as one step above travel and budget considerations. There is one important exception to this general disapproval of talking about race. In contrast to this race-evasive dialogue, adoption workers invoke racially explicit descriptions of children, often warning prospective parents that "some children are darker than you would expect." This approach has troubling implications because adoption social workers fail to take advantage of valuable teachable moments to help prepare their clients for the challenges and responsibilities of adopting across race.

In the Conclusion, I reiterate the scope of the book and briefly summarize my research questions and findings. I end the book by tackling the question *so what?* Why does it matter that private adoption operates as a marketplace where parents are turned into clients and children into objects? I emphasize that analyzing adoption through a market framework provides an important piece of the sociological puzzle because it helps us understand why some children are in greater demand than others. What makes some children available for adoption more likely to be "chosen," and how do these decisions help us understand norms about racial boundaries and kinship? I end with a discussion of the implications of the market approach, especially in terms of the best interests of children. I argue that since the goal of adoption information sessions is to recruit potential clients, not scare them away, social workers often gloss over the complexities and responsibilities of becoming transracial adoptive families. Because prospective adoptive parents look to social workers to set the tone of the discourse on transracial adoption, these are missed opportunities to better prepare White parents to adopt across race.

# 1

## Staying Afloat in a Perfect Storm

Danielle got her start in social work right out of college in an entry-level position for Child Protective Services. Her caseload consisted of some pretty troubled families, and she quickly became immersed in issues surrounding child abuse and neglect, foster care, and the termination of parental rights. "It was some of the most intense social work I've ever done," she reflects. Although the work was draining, she loved it and a few years later pursued a master of social work (MSW) degree. "Really it was an epiphany for me that I was supposed to be a social worker," she recalls. Although Danielle knew her calling was in social work, she explains wryly, "I didn't know I was . . . going to work in adoption."

She goes on to describe how she left Child Protective Services when her partner relocated out of state for a different job. Danielle learned about an open position at an agency conducting home studies for parents going through the private adoption process. Many of the agency's clients were White parents applying to adopt transracially, and given that Danielle grew up with a transracially adopted cousin, the job seemed like a good fit. Over the years, she has stayed with the same organization, and her role has evolved from conducting home studies and trainings for adoptive parents to more a supervisory position. Most recently, she has taken on the responsibility of working with parents seeking to adopt through her agency's programs in Africa. All told, Danielle has been at the agency for fifteen years. Counting her previous work in Child Protective Services, she summarizes, "It turns out that adoption has been my career for twenty years."

Near the end of the interview, Danielle gets quiet, reflecting about her career choices. She confides, "I have some ambivalence about this being my life's work. Taking kids from poor countries and giving them to richer countries. Taking kids of color and placing them largely [in White families]." She goes on, stating that while not all the parents she works with are White, the majority are: "In [the] Africa [program], a portion of our parents are African American, but it is still small."

Even though Danielle has helped facilitate hundreds of adoptions, she still worries about the larger implications of her actions, admitting, "It is not necessarily how I think the world should operate. I think that all kids should have a home, but I don't think that poorer people in poor countries should have to give their children to people in richer countries. That is not corrective in any way." Her misgivings are so strong that she repeats, "I think I have some ambivalence about this being my life's work."

Danielle was not alone in her ambivalence about the implications of adoption. Like Danielle, Abigail raised similar questions about adoption. I asked her what she would like to see different in adoption, and from her response, it was clear that she had given the question some thought:

> You are probably not talking to the right person, because I have strong feelings. But all of the money that people are spending on adopting, [I wish] that they would just donate it to the country so that the children could stay there in foster homes, and then [the donors] would adopt domestically through foster care. The idea of international adoption is wonderful, and I support it. These kids need families, but it is putting a Band-Aid on a giant problem, which is poverty; lack of women's rights; lack of access to health care, which is causing premature death; AIDS. These kids are in orphanages, and then they are being adopted by wealthy people from other countries. International adoption is not a sustainable solution.

Her response is telling for several reasons. First, even though Abigail is directly involved in facilitating the transfer of children from poor families to wealthy families, she is able to vocalize her misgivings about the macro-level implications of the practice. Second, she draws an important distinction between private international adoption and public foster care adoptions, elevating the latter as a more virtuous pathway to parenthood. Third, she brings up the issue of money, raising the question of whether the high fees associated with international adoption might be better spent in implementing programs to keep children in their countries of birth. Such a disclosure is noteworthy because if hopeful parents were no longer paying fees to private adoption agencies, Abigail would be out of a job.

Having concluded her appraisal, she immediately concedes the futility of these lofty goals, stating, "That's not going to happen, obviously; there is no way." Brought back down to Earth, she acknowledges that most of her clients do not want to adopt from foster care, and indeed they seek out private adoption to avoid using the publicly funded market segment. "These parents want to be parents, and they want to be parents in a way that feels comfortable to them," Abigail states. "And these kids don't have homes, and they are getting way less than adequate care. It makes sense for the two to meet and for us to put the supports in place so they can have a fabulous life together. International adoption is obviously filling a need."

Abigail's characterization of her work reminds us that the adoption marketplace is not a singular entity. Rather, the arena can be more aptly described as an umbrella term for three distinct segments of child placement—private domestic, transnational, and foster care. As described in the Introduction, this book is primarily focused on private domestic and intercountry adoptions. I exclude the publicly funded foster care system because, as one social worker describes it, foster care is "a whole 'nother ballgame." Although private domestic and private international adoption use vastly different processes to connect parents and children, what they have in common is that prospective adoptive parents are willing to pay thousands of dollars to procure a child who "feels comfortable to them." The role of the social worker is to "put the supports in place," with the hope that these families will "have a fabulous life together."

Despite their instrumental role, before this book there was very little research regarding how adoption professionals approach their work. Danielle's and Abigail's disclosures that they are ambivalent about their careers raises some tantalizing threads to be further pursued. These questions include: How do adoption professionals react to the use of the market metaphor? Do they see it as a justifiable framework? Understanding the range of responses is important, considering that as these interviews were being conducted, many workers were reeling from the market downturn that put their livelihoods in jeopardy. This raised new questions as adoption professionals reappraised their professional standards while struggling to keep their employers afloat.

## Historical Research on Adoption Practitioners

Since there is relatively little current sociological research examining adoption practitioners, studies that elucidate the historical foundations of the adoption market provide much-needed contextualization for understanding these contemporary conundrums. From prior research, it is evident that concerns about the overlapping spheres of child welfare and child commodification have deeply shaped adoption from the start. In her historical analysis of adoption in the United States between 1851 and 1950, Julie Berebitsky details how adoption was not initially part of the canon of social workers' expertise, arguing, "Social workers came slowly to adoption."[1] Part of this reticence could be attributed to the fact that up until the 1930s, the prevailing wisdom was that unwed mothers should keep their infants. But as the demand for adoption grew, social workers endeavored to pull adoption away from the purview of well-to-do philanthropic women and bring it under their jurisdiction.[2] As adoption workers began to professionalize, this raised questions as to whether and how much to charge for their services.[3]

Even then, social workers feared that the exchange of cash would sully adoption, turning it into a transaction that veered too much toward commodification. Thus, some workers argued for the separation of the opposing spheres of child welfare and markets. Wanting to avoid any hint of being tainted by the market, adoption agencies initially only accepted gratitude donations from clients.[4] Yet this practice evolved as social workers increasingly exerted their roles as experts in the field. Berebitsky states that many social workers argued that "they were providing a professional service like any other; lawyers charged fees (even when they lost the case), so why shouldn't trained social workers?"[5]

With the exchange of money becoming standard practice, adoption workers justified their salaries by emphasizing the competencies they brought to child placement, matching families "so seamlessly that adoptive families did not appear to be designed at all."[6] Fundamental to these placements was the reliance on the idea that the best adoptive families did not reveal their adoptive status, since the "notion that resemblance expedited love and difference spelled trouble was accepted by adopters and social workers alike."[7] Ellen Herman calls this ultracurated approach "kinship by design," detailing how adoption professionals pushed forward the idea that "adoption could be governed and safeguarded through documentation, investigation, and oversight by trained professionals."[8]

Standardization of these policies became known as sound adoption practice as social workers endeavored to thoroughly vet all members of the adoption triad before signing off on the match. This entailed an investigation into the potential genetic and moral deficiencies of the birth parents and a forensic probe of prospective adoptive parents' medical and financial histories. To maximize the likelihood of a well-designed placement, children were also scrutinized. Writing a history of the transnational adoption of infants between the United States and Canada, Karen Balcom details how "newborn children were also investigated before they were judged 'adoptable' and placed with new families. These children were carefully observed, given thorough medical exams, and tested against 'normal' physical and mental development in hope of identifying obvious physiological or neurological defects."[9] This practice could routinely take months to complete, meaning that despite the demand for newborns, it was rare for children to be placed before four months of age, since that threshold was seen "as the minimum age below which it was impossible to determine whether or not the child showed signs of normal mental development."[10]

Yet the development and enactment of sound adoption practice had to be tempered by the market realities and the increased demand for even younger infants. Adoption social workers not only had to contend with matching children and parents but also had to determine whom to deny. Berebitsky writes, "Throughout the 1920s, 1930s, and 1940s, the demand for children greatly exceeded the supply of adoptable infants. And, without a doubt, social workers felt immense pressure to meet the desires of desperate, young childless couples."[11] These gatekeepers enacted policies that gave preference to those they believed were the most deserving parents—married, heterosexual couples suffering from infertility. In aggregate such practices "privileged the model of the as if begotten nuclear family" by excluding older couples and those with biological children.[12]

These historical studies are most notable for demonstrating that adoption as consumption and the professionalization of adoption practice were highly intertwined. From the 1940s onward, there was concern among adoption practitioners as to how to balance the needs of paying clients and the needs of children. As Berebitsky presciently details, "A couple paying a fee acquired the power of the consumer, which enabled them to demand better service from the agency."[13] In other words, although adoption social workers may have embraced the quixotic idea of adoption uncontaminated by market realities, this utopia never existed. Herman argues, "Practices associated with the commercial, consumption-oriented culture of a modern market society suggested that adopters had the right to shop for exactly the sort of children they most desired."[14] Moreover, there was competition between brokers and agencies, and between agencies themselves, and professionals realized that to "compete effectively, agencies had to deliver more of what adopters wanted—healthy white infants."[15]

As this market summary indicates, not all children were considered adoptable. Racial minority children and those who did not pass these rigid inspections because of mental and developmental delays were often turned away. This was standard practice, writes Herman, detailing, "Until the 1950s these children were more likely to be institutionalized than treated as candidates for family placement." But things changed with what Herman calls "the special-needs revolution," which "expanded the terms of adoptability and posited belonging as a vital resource for all children in need of parents, including children of color."[16] However, these early placements were still founded on the edict of curated kinship and race matching.

Social workers' initial forays into placing Black, and mixed-race Black and White children followed the edict of the as-if-begotten model, meaning

that these children were usually placed in Black families. However, Berebitsky contends that the shortage of White babies, coupled with the difficulty of recruiting Black families, paved the way for domestic transracial
adoption: "Efforts in the 1950s and 1960s to recruit African Americans as
adoptive parents had some success but still fell short of meeting the needs of
black children. As the shortage of white babies continued, agencies began to
place black children with white families."[17]

The implications of these transracial placements and how they help reconfigure the color line are further discussed later in this book. But for now, the
main takeaways include three ideas that inform the book's discussion. First,
a historical examination of adoption underscores the instrumental role social
workers play. As the purveyors of adoption, these workers professionalized the
standards of what was considered sound practice, determining the eligibility
criteria that made parents and children suitable. Second, the private adoption
of infants was never divorced from child commodification and always occupied a liminal space between social service and customer service. Although
social workers embraced the mandate to work toward a child-centered approach to adoption, there was always concern about losing market share, especially to the lawyers facilitating private placements.[18] And third, race
remains an integral variable in private adoption. Whereas transracial adoption was an almost unheard-of violation of the dictates of kinship by design,
as times changed and the market evolved, these placements gained traction.

While there is more latitude to explore the circulation of children from
a historical standpoint, framing contemporary adoption as a market practice
engenders great discomfort because any critical analyses of the effects of the
marketplace can be interpreted as an assault on the adoptive family. The
stakes are even higher in transracial adoption, in which the family's adoptive
status is rendered visible by racial difference, making these families easily
identifiable and at times targeted. Thus, the dominant narrative tends to veer
toward celebrating adoption and emphasizing the stories of adoptive parents
who welcome children into their homes.[19] While this story is important to
communicate, it tends to ignore the inequities embedded in adoption in
favor of framing it as a mutually beneficial policy that leads to happy endings
for parents and children. On the basis of these messages, Kim Park Nelson
argues that there is a widely held belief "that adoption is a 'win-win-win'
situation in which adoptive parents get the children they want, unwanted
children find families, and birth families are relieved of the burden of unwanted children."[20]

## Adapting to a Down Market

Throughout my interviews, it was clear that respondents were questioning
whether adoption was truly a "win-win." Danielle's disclosure about her

ambivalence working in adoption cuts to the heart of the deficiencies of the win-win paradigm. She acknowledges that adoption—especially transnational and transracial adoption—is often portrayed as the panacea for child welfare ills and a beautiful exemplification of how familial bonds can defy boundaries of blood, race, and nation. Yet she takes issue with this oversimplified characterization, passionately stating, "It is not a way to change the world, international adoption. In fact, it is a testament to how terrible the world is in some ways."

She goes on to discuss how in Ethiopia most of the women relinquishing children face the terrible decision of sending them away or letting them starve. She considers facing this dire predicament, imagining "that I was in Ethiopia and had my children, and I was not able to feed them and had to give them to somebody else. That your choice is keeping your child and not being able to feed them or give them to somebody else. And that is a horrible choice." From her perspective as a social worker, Danielle wants her clients to understand these broader contexts to recognize that international adoption involves losses as well as gains. "I try to be really clear about that with people," Danielle asserts. "This is not just a beautiful, wonderful thing. This is a difficult thing, and I think that adoptive parents and adoption professionals should struggle with that."

While Danielle hopes that her fellow adoption professionals will grapple with these issues and work to engage prospective adoptive parents in these macro-level discussions, in reality there is little allowance for these conversations. Instead, day-to-day issues take precedence, especially as it gets harder to keep a business going. Heather describes this trade-off between wanting to live up to her ideal of what an adoption social worker should do and just keeping up their operations: "Most licensed agencies are operating in ways that are aboveboard. . . . There is another reality where international adoption agencies are having a really hard time right now, and having a hard time staying in business." Realizing that she has just crossed a moral line by likening adoption to a business venture, Heather quickly qualifies her statement, rushing to add, "And we don't like to think of this as a business. And it is not a business, and we are certainly not for profit, any of these organizations. But lots of agencies have had to close their doors. So it is possible that people are resorting to tactics that they maybe wouldn't have five to seven years ago. But it is different now."

As Heather succinctly states, the downturn in the adoption marketplace catalyzed a paradigm shift in which workers had to "resort" to new tactics. To learn how international adoption providers were adjusting to the crisis, I had the opportunity to sit in on a webinar called "Updates on International Adoption" hosted by a large adoption agency offering professional development credits for adoption social workers throughout the country. This was a unique experience because it provided a rare window into how adoption social workers talked with each other. The tone of the presentation was informative but foreboding, as the speaker characterized the state of the industry as filled with "bad news." She began by providing a brief historical overview of trends in international adoption, describing how "when we moved into the eighties, we saw younger kids become eligible for international adoption—infants." She went on to describe how they hit their zenith with record numbers of placements and since then how the market has slowly declined: "It basically grew. . . . We were peaking [with] large numbers of families adopting primarily infant-age children." The speaker went on to say that recently there has been a decline, since "guidelines are more restrictive, [there are] fewer opportunities for singles, and the Hague process can be cumbersome." The slowdown has forced workers to do more with less. She summarized by saying, "As agencies, we are providing services for a longer period of time. What used to take a year and a half as far as processing is taking two, three, or in the case of China, years and years to process. We have also seen countries that have closed—lots of bad news, I know."

Tellingly, as the supply of infants made available through international adoption diminished, interest in domestic adoption seemed to expand. Intercountry providers got further squeezed as the market shifted toward domestic adoption and fewer applicants signed on to work with them. Many of these hopeful parents may have voted with their feet and made the switch to domestic adoption. During one information session hosted by Babytalk, Nina, a new adoptive mother, spoke of this calculus. She described how she and her husband had been "leaning toward international adoption" and had "looked into it for about eight months" before settling on domestic adoption. Although one or two defectors might not have made a difference, in aggregate the lack of new customers, coupled with a declining supply of eligible infants, made it harder for overseas adoption agencies to stay in business. Lindsay, a domestic adoption social worker I interviewed, reflects on this change, stating, "I think that it is inevitable that more people will do domestic as international becomes more complicated."

As the number of prospective adoptive parents considering private domestic adoption grew, there is anecdotal evidence that the supply of children grew alongside it. Although there is not a central clearinghouse reporting the annual number of domestic adoptions, I heard several stories from domestic adoption providers about the uptick in interest among women considering making adoption plans. Many adoption workers attributed their increased caseload to the aftermath of the Great Recession, reporting that impoverished mothers struggling to feed their children were attempting to place their toddlers for private adoption, rather than have the state take them away and put them in foster care for neglect. Although these placements were still a minority of their caseload, many social workers mentioned the rising number of toddler placements. At a preadoption conference, one attorney discussed this trend: "They [birth mothers] can't afford to have foster care come in and take custody of their children. So they want to make a plan for their children, because they think it is a better plan than to have them in foster care. So it is happening more. I had done one such placement in eight years. I have done four this year." Similarly, at an adoption information meeting, a social worker also reports an acceleration in these placements: "I have had three cases this year. . . . One of my families was placing siblings—while she was placing a one-year-old, she was also placing a two-year-old son. It is happening more now because of the bad economy."

As the international market retracted, some adoption providers were prescient enough to develop their domestic programs and were thus able to keep their agencies competitive. For example, I attended an information session sponsored by a domestic adoption agency. Early in her presentation, the social worker, Tracy, offered some history of her agency, describing how they "used to focus on international adoption, but the new director came in with a focus on domestic adoption." She characterized this decision as a strategic business move, disclosing that they "needed something to keep the adoption program up and going."

Cognizant of how these market swings can affect one's livelihood, Tracy described how her agency was one of the lucky ones that ended up on the right side of the business equation. She recounted, "When we first started the agency, the focus was domestic. When the swing of adoption went international, we obviously went with that swing." Although her agency did offer some international programs, it became harder for them to operate after the ratification of the Hague Convention on Intercountry Adoption, which mandated that agencies go through additional steps to be Hague-accredited. These regulations led them to give up their international programs and offer only domestic adoptions. "So we just decided, let's see where we go with just domestic and see where it takes us," Tracy recalled. This business strategy paid off: "So far we have been really successful at it. If the trend starts to go back international, I am sure we will follow it, but right now we are just domestic." While it may have seemed risky to specialize in only one adoption segment, their timing was right as they stopped offering international programs ahead of the slowdown. "Those that closed, they were purely international and didn't do domestic at all," Tracy commented wryly. "And they've now closed and shut their doors."

Whereas not going bankrupt was a persistent theme that emerged from my interviews with transnational adoption professionals, none of the domestic adoption employees or attorneys worried about losing their jobs or their agencies going under. Although Alyssa, the executive director of a domestic adoption agency profiled in the Introduction, worries about paying her utility bills, there was not nearly the same sense of foreboding as was captured in the interviews with those primarily doing international adoptions. Because there was a significant contrast in the tone of the interviews between domestic and international adoption workers, the bulk of the rest of this chapter focuses on how intercountry adoption social workers balanced the needs of children with the needs of their agencies.

## A Perfect Storm

Christian World Adoptions (CWA), a long-standing international adoption agency founded in 1991, shut down operations in 2013. On the front page of its website, it announced the closure, attributing its insolvency to a perfect storm of events:

> Today international adoption—adoption agencies in general and CWA in particular—face a "perfect storm" of circumstances that has made it difficult and in some cases impossible to continue. Many adoption agencies have closed their doors in recent years. Russia's recent ban on adoptions to Americans, the U.S. State Department's decision not to open adoptions from Cambodia, vastly longer adoption wait times in China, and longer adoption times and fewer referrals in Ethiopia have all had an adverse effect on CWA. UNICEF has waged an unrelenting campaign against international adoption for many years. Ongoing mandatory child care costs in Ethiopia despite slower adoptions has been a major drain on our finances. Children living in our partner orphanages have to be cared for, fed and kept healthy every day, even when adoption cases are not moving and the fees we collect do not entirely cover the cost of their care. Costs have been increasing all across the board, including the cost of accreditation and licensing to remain in compliance with U.S. and foreign legal requirements, as well as the number of staff hours devoted to that compliance.[21]

Although CWA does not describe their collapse in explicit market terms, their missive essentially blames their downfall on the shrinking supply of children available for adoption. They list the negative effects of Russia's ban on American adoptions, the slowdown in China, the U.S. government's decision not to allow adoptions from Cambodia, and the decline of placements in Ethiopia. While one of these setbacks may have been manageable on its own, taken together the resulting plummeting supply of children made it impossible to continue operations.

According to CWA, it was not just the decreased availability of young healthy children—the mainstay of international adoptions—that impeded business. In addition, adoptions were taking longer to process as legal requirements increased. They obliquely attribute some of these challenges to the ratification of the Hague Convention on Intercountry Adoption, an international treaty that mandated a set of common practices for countries partaking in international adoptions.[22] Because the paperwork often took longer, agencies had more costs associated with taking care of the children in their adoption pipeline. Since the bulk of agencies' revenue comes from placement fees, and fewer adoptions were being processed, operating expenses kept going up without money coming in.

It is not surprising that CWA, among others, closed. If anything, it is notable that so many agencies hung on for so long considering that by 2015 there were only 5,674 children sent to the United States to be adopted.[23] This sum pales in comparison to a decade before when, at its peak, almost 23,000 children were adopted by American families.[24] Currently, not only are there fewer placements, but the profile of children vastly differs, since the majority of available children tend to be older. Whereas in 2004, 83 percent of children placed via intercountry adoption were younger than two at the time of placement, by 2015 this percentage had decreased to only 28 percent.

Irene, an adoption attorney who provides consultations for prospective clients deciding between domestic and international adoption, describes this era of plentiful adoptions as the good old days. She states, "God, it used to be so easy in the old days. The old days were before China changed, before Guatemala changed. When singles could adopt. The age requirements were always there, but now there are more restrictions in terms of finances, body weight mass, this other crazy stuff."

Irene goes on to explain that during that time, overseas adoptions were seen as more predictable compared with the uncertainties of attorney-led domestic adoptions, where adoption situations often fell through and the timeline and costs could wildly vary. "If they needed to know how much it would cost, with certainty," says Irene, "I would tell them, though it could be more international, you would have more of a budget. The time frame—there used to be certainty on the time frame. . . . Some people just needed that type of certainty. So I might advise them that international would be a better choice for them."

Countries like China and Guatemala were particularly attractive choices because these countries were known for placing relatively healthy non-Black infants and toddlers. In fact, 90 percent of the thousands of children placed from these countries were under two years old at the time of adoption.[25] The timeline was relatively quick in that most placements occurred within a year. But as Irene mentions, things began to change when Guatemala suspended its adoption program and China significantly cut the number of referrals of healthy baby girls they sent abroad. During this time, Korea passed new legislation promoting domestic adoption within Korea.[26] As these policies changed, agencies quickly felt the pinch. Adoption providers began to migrate to other countries such as Ethiopia and Ukraine to open up new programs.[27] However, the number of children (especially young, healthy children) sent from these programs would never approach the same magnitude.

I spoke with Amanda, a social worker who has been working in adoption for more than a decade. She describes how her organization tried to adjust to the change, stating, "A few years, maybe even as recently as two years ago, it really felt we were facing a dilemma. And I am sure other agencies would share the same story." Amanda discusses how the downturn in infant placements affected business, saying, "We were dealing with a high volume of families coming to us, but for an adoption process that existed five years ago . . . back in the time when there were several programs that placed a very high percentage of infants." During this time, business was booming. "There were thousands of infants coming into this country through international adoption each year. China, Guatemala, Russia, Korea, all of these programs were thriving and placing many kids."

But since 2004, the number of internationally adopted children has declined each year. It often fell to Jennifer, an adoption social worker who answered the intake phone lines, to relay these new realities to prospective clients. She describes how given the tremendous waiting times, stringent health and body mass index requirements, and new policies prohibiting single applicants, callers had to readjust their expectations. Jennifer states, "We are really kind of back to where we were when I first started back in the early eighties, and the age range and needs range of the children look a lot like we do now. The demographic of the child is extremely similar and the tight health requirements that prospective adopters need to meet."

Absent blockbuster programs like China and Guatemala, Amanda describes this new era of intercountry adoption, predicting that there will be "fewer families in general. The trend is going to be a decreasing population of children available for international adoption, so [there will be] fewer families." She continues that, on the bright side, the population of parents is becoming "a more diverse, more educated, more prepared, more flexible number of families," but overall numbers are going down. Summarizing this trend, the speaker at the professional development webinar informed her colleagues, "As we look into the future, we are going to see smaller programs where we as an agency place ten to fifteen children a year. . . . The future— rather than a program placing several thousand kids, there are going to be a lot of those small programs."

I had a long conversation with Nicole about the effects of this downturn. As a social worker in her early thirties, Nicole had already been working in adoption for several years. Unlike some of the more veteran social workers with a familial connection to adoption, Nicole was a member of a new generation of social workers who viewed international adoption work as intimately tied to public health and economic development. She describes how a television story sparked her interest in the subject, detailing, "I was a psychology major as an undergrad. I had heard about an adoption story on Oprah or something, and I remember thinking, 'That is so fascinating.' There were so many different angles to the story.... It was a really complex case, and I remember thinking it would be fascinating to work with these complex cases."

Through some serendipitous connections, Nicole was put in touch with the director of an adoption agency and secured a position with them. "There was never a dull moment," she recalls. "I liked working with the families and learning about different cultures and the political issues." Continuing her work in this area, she transferred to a larger adoption agency known as a placement agency. These placement agencies had direct ties with orphanages in sending countries and used their established networks to work with smaller adoption agencies to place foreign-born children across the United States. While these regional affiliates were in charge of recruiting, certifying, and training prospective parents, the placement agency acted as the supplier of children, earning revenue from this service. Nicole's role was to act as a liaison between her placement agency and the parents scattered throughout the country adopting through them.

As the official intermediary, Nicole started doing a lot of traveling for her organization to get the word out about the services they offered. Looking back, she states, "it was sort of like marketing, now that I think about it." I followed up, asking to whom she was marketing, and Nicole clarifies: "Prospective adoptive parents mostly, and sometimes conferences. And [I did] a lot of networking with other agencies that were just other home study programs and didn't have the international programs that we have."

Paradoxically, even though the goal of Nicole's job was to drum up business, she adamantly states that adoption agencies should focus on curtailing the need for adoption. She asserts, "I think that any good adoption agency, their goal is to put themselves out of business because the country doesn't need us and they are closing the program down." Likewise, Danielle is also a proponent of this goal, commenting, "One thing that I would like to see different, is that anyone who is doing international adoption should be pouring resources back into that country to help make international adoption unnecessary." Note that this ideology is not a sustainable business strategy, since closing down programs puts the survival of their agencies—and thus, Nicole and Danielle's jobs—in jeopardy.

Even though these social workers theoretically support the idea that going out of business would be a positive sign that adoption was no longer necessary, in practice the market downturn generated a crisis. Nicole describes the conundrum that her agency faced when countries stopped releasing babies, and subsequently money stopped coming in. Although prospective adoptive parents pay some fees up front during the initial application and the home study process, the bulk of the payment is transferred when parents accept the referral of a child who will eventually become their son or daughter. "We had all of these waiting families, so we were really busy with the waiting families," she remembers. But even though they had full caseloads, Nicole continues, "We weren't making referrals. And basically we have cash coming in when we make referrals because that is when we charge for all of our program services. So it is not like we weren't busy; we just didn't have any children to refer. So it was like, we need babies so we can make money, which is a horrible way to look at it, but that's the reality of how you keep your doors open in adoption."

Nicole was willing to be blunt about the realities of cash flow in adoption, but others were quite uncomfortable talking about the financial aspects of the transaction, especially to prospective clients. I spoke with Erin, a social worker who still considered herself fairly new to adoption, having only worked for six years in the field. She says, "I always have a lot of discomfort talking about fees and feeling the need to really explain what they are used for. And maybe it is my own sensitivity and anxiety about that part of the work, or the commercial aspect of it."

Of my interviewees, Erin was especially conflicted, and it seemed that the day-to-day job responsibilities did not live up to her aspirations working in international child adoption. She describes how adoption "was not a deliberate career choice for me," but with her background in international relations, she had wanted "to take the international relations work in the nonprofit world" and "adoption [as a career choice] just kind of happened in that way." Throughout her tenure as an adoption professional, she has worked at multiple agencies in different capacities, since "adoption programs kind of change, and they slow down, and they close, so I got shifted around."

Erin goes on to recount how she started working with the program in Ethiopia, which was formative because she was "able to work more directly with the families and really get to know some of the kids." She explains how these experiences "ultimately spurred my decision to become a social worker," and after graduate school she "kind of ended up in adoption again."

After earning her MSW, Erin took a job at a placement agency working with the China program. Her new job was challenging, since the country's program had trickled to a halt, and children were no longer being referred for adoption. Had there been referrals, Erin would have been helping families arrange travel, answering questions about what to pack, and relaying happy news and cute photos. Instead, her job was to be the messenger of bad news—or more specifically, no news—to exasperated prospective parents. "That's been probably the biggest challenge coming in as a newish staff person here and inheriting a pretty large caseload of families who are just waiting," Erin discloses. She explains, "A lot of them [parents] initially applied to the agency at a time when the program in China was moving a lot quicker, and it has been really hard for them to adjust their expectations around that. It has gone from eight months, [from beginning the process] to a referral of a child, to . . . four years."

Erin grows visibly upset when she discusses how stressful the work can be at times, stating, "It is sometimes hard when you are getting that initial reaction to bad news. And it is hard because there is not always a lot of information. I have a lot of families, and sometimes there is nothing to update them on. They'll call and say, 'What's happening?' and there is nothing to tell them. Nothing is happening, or I don't have any updates. I think it is hard because I want to be able to give them something, and there is nothing to say."

Later in the interview, I asked Erin whether she often got together with other adoption professionals to blow off steam or share best practices, and she responded that few had time for such luxuries. "I don't know," she says. "Just because international adoption agencies are struggling so much because there are fewer placements, it is harder for smaller agencies to keep afloat. So the struggle of trying to keep good practices while trying to keep the agency sustainable is probably the biggest challenge. And how much that is talked about between agencies I don't know, but it is hard to keep things going without maybe having the luxury of discussing bigger issues."

Another reason why Erin is reluctant to talk to colleagues may be that she was feeling somewhat pessimistic about her career. She relates, "A lot of times when I end up talking about my job, I feel like I end up sounding so negative." Whereas laypersons tend to have overwhelming positive associations with adoption,[28] it was evident that Erin felt more cynical about the practice. She elaborates, "People are like, 'That's wonderful,' and I am like, 'It can be.' But every time I engage in a serious conversation about it, I feel like my concerns definitely come up. I have a hard time stifling them, and there are things about adoption that I am definitely not comfortable with, and I have a hard time with them as a professional."

## Emerging Markets

As the formerly stalwart programs like Guatemala and China sent fewer children or shut down entirely, some agencies looked to emerging markets to try to stem their losses and generate more revenue. For example, the presenter at Cornerstone told her audience, "We explore new countries all of the time." But few sending countries offered the right mix of healthy young children that could be adopted with minimal travel. The presenter went on to say that they "considered Kenya, but they have a six-month residency requirement," making the country an unrealistic option.

When Nepal opened up, many hoped that this country could sustain the market. During a presentation offered by Harmony Services, the social worker described how Vietnam has recently closed, but she glibly noted that prospective clients "will go to Nepal, and they will be fine." However, this turned out not to be the case, since Nepal was allowing adoption only as a pilot program.[29] At an information session hosted by Kid Connection, the presenter informed her audience that Nepal was not a realistic option, since the country was "only accepting a few families per agency." The speaker at Coastal Adoptions reiterated this bad news, describing how the country was "full and not accepting new applications," because it was "absolutely flooded with agencies wanting to work with [it]." However, she told her audience that they just opened up a program in Bulgaria. Realizing that parents may not be familiar with the country, she described it as "a small, picturesque country approximately the size of Tennessee" and encouraged prospective applicants by telling them that "it looks like a promising program."

Likewise, other emerging markets did not seem to be panning out as potential substitutes. The social worker at Harmony went on to describe how they were opening up a new program in Nicaragua, but "the children are not as young as [we had] hoped they would be." India was a similar disappoint-ment because the pace of referrals was "going slowly," since the country "pre-fers working with overseas Indian nationals." Moreover, she lamented that the children did not fit the desired profile, since "most are older and waiting kids. No healthy children between zero and four."

Despite the fact that agencies needed new programs with healthy infants, since "you need babies to make money," many social workers were reluctant to think about their profession in such crass terms. For example, Heather responds, "My gut reaction to all that is very negative, the supply and de-mand." She continues, "I don't know a lot about the marketplace kind of approach, but you definitely hear the supply and demand language, usually in the periphery, and it is very uncomfortable."

Later in the interview, I asked Heather what had changed in international adoption, and she jokingly answers, "Everything." She then elaborates: "Practically speaking, it is so much more difficult." She goes on to talk about her agency's new program in Bulgaria. Whereas the presenter at Coastal Adoptions had no problem discussing the program in terms of its market promise, Heather was more reluctant to frame its newfound popularity in market terms. She states, "When I first started, we had a program in Bulgaria, and we had no interest in the Bulgaria program because the kids were older—about two, and the wait was longer—about a year, and you had to make two trips, and people were like, this is such an outrageous program."

However, as China slowed down, the Bulgaria program gained favor. Although her agency's decision to invest in the Bulgaria program would surely help its bottom line, Heather is quick to divorce the move to reopen the Bulgaria program from any sort of self-interest on the part of her employer. She explains, "We recently reopened our program," couching the decision as good timing, "because they had things on hold on their end for a while." Heather describes how relative to other options, Bulgaria was back in the running, since, "now people are like, 'Oh I can request a child as young as two; that is great.'"

While expanding into new markets offered a lifeline to agencies that needed to develop other revenue streams, this strategy raised concerns among some social workers. I spoke with Kiera, an adoption social worker who specializes in placing children from Eastern Europe. She shares her apprehension that agency representatives may just cut and run, so to speak, once adoption programs close. She avers, "I feel like agencies who are devoted to helping children in need should stay present in the country helping children in need. Not go to the country where they can have more adoptions in an easier way because that also helps the agency stay afloat." Delineating these trends, she describes how she has "worked in adoption long enough to see that. Ethiopia was all the craze and then Kazakhstan." Despite her reservations about this rapid expansion, Kiera rationalizes that the ends can justify the means: "I can see how we pride ourselves on doing good work. And in order to continue to do good work, we have to stay afloat."

Although intercountry adoption agencies looked to Eastern Europe, Asia, and Latin America to fill the gap, Heather contends that "the biggest recent change has been the shift to Africa," particularly Ethiopia. Around the mid-2000s, the number of children sent from Ethiopia began to skyrocket, increasing exponentially from a low of 42 children in 1999 to a peak of 2,511 in 2010.[30] Although part of the interest in adopting from Ethiopia was fueled by an Evangelical Christian movement drawing attention to the global orphan crisis, Ethiopia gained in popularity because it was one of the few international programs that placed babies and toddlers.[31]

The availability of adoptions from Ethiopia provided new opportunities for prospective adoptive parents, but many of the adoption workers I spoke with raised ethical concerns about the implications of the country's rapid rise. Among my respondents, Beth was the most vocal. She runs her own adoption agency that has a long history of placing Ethiopian children. She was one of the first people working on the ground in Ethiopia during the early 2000s, back when Ethiopia was sending fewer than one hundred children a year to the United States. From our conversation, it was clear that she had a deep knowledge of the country and the needs of the children.

Beth was deliberate in her decision to place mostly older children for whom she believed international adoption would truly be their best option. She passionately discusses the early years of her work, stating, "When I first started in Ethiopia, my heart was in it. I went in knowing the people in the group." Because she had long-standing connections with Ethiopians, she purposely did not set up programs in neighboring countries, and instead she chose to focus her work in a single country. "Does it mean there aren't other kids in other countries in need of help?" she rhetorically asks and then answers, "Of course there are. Could I have branched off to other countries? Yes."

Beth adamantly defends her decision to stay small, arguing that continued expansion does not serve the best interests of children. "I needed to make a conscious decision that was not based on economics, not based on my agency staying afloat. It should not be based on that. I think we are not doing a service to children if we base our adoption programs on the survival of our agency."

While specializing in one country may have been good child welfare practice, it was risky business-wise as other placement agencies started opening up shop and pushing her out. "Families have a need for a certain kind of children," she laments. "It all starts out really well. We have orphans, and they are really in need of families. Their parents have died of AIDS," she relates. Someone on the ground in Ethiopia would then approach Beth, asking, "Could you guys [help us]? We are looking for adoptive families." Beth says, "People are really attracted [to helping], and we start to place those kids." Yet those are not the kids who keep an adoption agency afloat. Beth elaborates: "We also know that economically what makes an agency run and keeps you going is not your older children adoption; it is the babies."

Recall Amanda's statement about how her agency needed babies to make money because the revenue they generated enabled organizations to keep their doors open. When I followed up with her to ask whether and how they managed to find babies to make the money, she told me her agency went through a big round of layoffs. However, once Ethiopia opened, the country provided a lucrative stream of revenue, and they were able to remain open. Amanda recounted, "We laid off staff. I think it was just everywhere slowed down. And then Ethiopia took off, and Ethiopia was keeping us open. The Ethiopia team was gold because they were the ones paying our salaries."

Even though the expansion of international adoption undoubtedly provided homes for children in need, Beth worries that emphasizing solvency can supersede concerns about child welfare. She herself admits to being tempted to start programs in neighboring countries so she can stay in business, but she has resisted. "My biggest incentive was not to keep an agency going. My biggest incentive was to place children." However, she wonders if other agencies have the wrong priorities, alleging, "I think for a lot of us, that has switched. When a country closes or a particular situation makes it impossible for a lot of us to make placements out of that country, then you start to look at other places." With an ever-narrowing supply chain, Beth discloses that she has thought about branching out, stating, "I did not anticipate I would be playing that game. But I've had to look at it." Yet Beth worries that this rationalization prioritizes the needs of the business over the needs of children, musing, "But the thinking probably starts there. And I know that there are agencies that justify their actions based on the fact that they are doing good work."

Reflecting on these trade-offs, Erin describes how the market downturn has added a new dynamic to child welfare by creating "this gross kind of competition between agencies to get the best referrals." The competition for children puts an interesting spin on the ideology that adoption finds families for children instead of children for families. Although many of these workers may have started out with the best intentions, the incentive to find children who fit the desired profile for exasperated waiting parents sometimes took precedence. As the next section details, to alleviate strain and expand the supply of adoptable children, some adoption agencies resorted to new strategies to pitch the adoption of waiting children.

## Waiting Child Adoptions

The term "waiting child" is a euphemism that covers a spectrum of medical needs, from healthy children with minor correctable conditions (such as a missing digit) to those with life-threatening illnesses. Undoubtedly, there are some parents who come forward to adopt children with serious chronic medical issues requiring significant treatment and care. But altruistic intentions alone cannot fully account for the rapid increase of these placements. Rather, promoting waiting child adoption offered an additional emerging market that adoption providers could suggest to would-be parents. Erin describes how some of her clients were amenable to this strategy, recounting that her clients were "visualizing the special needs program [as], 'Well, maybe I can't adopt a healthy infant, but I can adopt a child with a cleft lip and palate, and that seems manageable.'"

As the demand for children with cleft lips and palates rose, adoption agencies worked to try to locate more of these children to meet the needs of prospective parents. Erin contends, "Waiting kids are the only ones moving, and that is sadly how decisions are made within this agency, and I am sure within other agencies." The interest in these children grew to such an extent that she acerbically characterizes the waiting child program as "the cleft lip and palate program because it is the only thing families come in thinking about and feeling comfortable with."

Even in China, a country where there are thousands of waiting children identified in need of international adoption, there were not enough cleft lip and palate children to go around. To maximize their chance of getting these referrals, some agencies tried to leverage the system to find enough children for would-be parents. Whereas these days the China Center for Adoption Affairs (CCAA) informs placement agencies when they will be updating case files en masse, it used to be that waiting children were sporadically added to the list. With the time change between China and the United States, it often

meant that the most desirable children would get claimed by the most motivated providers willing to log on from the United States in the middle of the
night. Cognizant of the advantage to be gained, Erin details how her supervisors approached her about it: "They were kind of proposing that I just look
at any and all hours so I could look at the referrals."

With her commitment to child welfare in mind, Erin scoffed at this sug-
gestion, characterizing it as a ploy that positioned children as objects to be
found and reserved, rather than as clients to be advocated for and served.
She bitterly states, "And I kind of felt that this is absurd. I am not going to
seek out kids. I felt like that the whole premise made it that we are looking
for a kid for this family, whereas our mission is to find families for kids who
need families. It feels kind of counterintuitive to be looking for a specific kid
for a family. So I had a lot of resistance to it."

The demand for the most desirable children was rendered even more
visible when the CCAA changed the system so that "now every agency can
access this at the same time." Under these new procedures, Erin describes
the rush to reserve children as akin to a land grab, testifying that she witnessed "this huge scramble to basically lock in the kids who are 'easy to
place.'" Or in other words, she says, "there is this big scramble for cleft lip
and palate. As soon as those kids are posted [*claps her hands for emphasis*],
you can see those agencies reserving those kids for their families." She laments that in the rush to claim the so-called best children, "there are like
1,500 children—literally 1,500 children—on this website that aren't even
being looked at carefully because everyone is scrambling to place these kids
that are thought to be easier to place."

## Two Clients

Although the adage that adoption finds families for children sits at the nu-
cleus of adoption agencies' reason for being, the challenge of staying afloat
in a down market inevitably bestows additional consumer power on the
prospective adoptive parents, the ones paying all the fees. In her ethnogra-
phy of transnational adoption from China, Sara Dorow explores this tension,
describing how the social workers she profiles are often pulled between
wanting to advocate for the child, who they see as their "primary" client, and
appeasing the prospective parents, whose needs are supposed to be secondary. While this prioritization sounds good on paper, in practice these ideals
are difficult to follow since the child embodies "the ideal phantom client,"
while the needs and demands of the paying client are front and center.
Accordingly, Dorow argues, this puts adoption workers in an untenable position: "The (impossible) trick was to keep the child at the center of professional social work practice even as the parent, the 'secondary client' was the
one directly paying for services."[32]

Because of the industry-wide standard of upholding the narrative of finding families for children, most of the women I spoke with tended to abide by this interpretation. Nora, the foster care social worker featured in the Introduction, was an interesting exception. She conveyed a no-nonsense way about her, bluntly describing herself as "a parent who learned" about adoption "on the job." She got interested in adoption after having adopted once domestically and once internationally. Even though Nora pursued private adoption, her professional mission was to place American children out of the U.S. foster care system.

In addition to placing children from foster care, Nora's agency serves as a local affiliate conducting home studies and post-placement reports for families adopting transnationally. At the time of the interview, there was still a demand for this type of service. Nora had few qualms discussing how the fees from international adoptions helped her cash flow. For example, when I asked her how many adoptions they did a year, she responds, "Maybe five to ten [domestic] babies. Twenty foster kids, and we have at least three hundred international. And that's what pays our rent. We do the home studies and the post-placement reports."

Perhaps one reason why Nora is so amenable to discussing intercountry adoption in market terms is her willingness to differentiate between private adoption as a consumer enterprise and public foster care adoption as a more altruistic endeavor. I asked Nora whether she noticed a difference in the demographics of parents who pursue international adoptions versus foster care adoptions. She emphatically answers, "Yes, I am going to say mean stuff. People with more money tend to go international. People who have money will look for younger, healthier toddlers." Referring to the recent downturn in intercountry adoption, she continues her train of thought, "China is—was—Ethiopia now. People with means, people who are socially mobile, will do that more. People don't go international for several reasons. They don't go because they don't have the money or because they really want to help an American kid."

I highlight Nora's testimony because it offers an interesting counternarrative to the voices of the other women I interviewed. Nora had no pangs about framing international adoption as a source of revenue. Perhaps because her focus was foster care, she was less interested in futilely trying to separate the hostile spheres where children and money overlap. She did not seem to mind giving the customers what they wanted.

For Erin, this rationalization was not as easy. She reports that she sought out social work to protect and advocate for children, and she resents how the demands of the parents can sometimes get in the way. Reflecting on this irony, she relates, "One of the biggest struggles for me as a professional is balancing the two clients, so to speak. Most people get into adoption—at least I got into this field—to focus on the child welfare piece and really focus-

ing on the kids. But you also have these other clients who are the parents."
Alluding to the fact that many of the parents look to private adoption only
after a struggle with infertility, Erin says that she tries to keep "understanding where they are coming from. It's for me easy to lose sight of the fact that
they've had a long, however many years, [wait] that has led up to the fact of
them getting here. And they want things to happen quickly."

Pausing for a moment, Erin collects her thoughts on this issue. But as she
resumes talking, her answer comes rushing out in a burst of pent-up testimony. She shares, "In some ways I feel like adoption takes on, versus other
social service fields, almost a customer service component. These families
who want to adopt, they come here, and they want a baby, and they want
[*trails off*]. And they are paying fees for a variety of services. It almost becomes in a way an exchange, in a way that if you are just doing other kinds
of social work, that doesn't come up as much."

Erin laments that private adoption was more transactional than other
forms of social work. Instead of her hoped-for work as a child welfare
professional, she is tasked with being a customer service representative. The
prospective adoptive parents become consumers with a desire for a baby and
the means to pay a fee to procure one. Contemplating these dilemmas, Erin
continues, "I am sort of rambling, but it is hard because clients have said
things like, 'This is what I am paying you for. And why can't you make this
happen?' And the system is constructed in a way that makes it feel more like
customer service."

Erin was not the only adoption social worker to cite the difficulties in
balancing the needs of the paying client with the child client. Michele also
describes this negotiation, stating, "We live in a very consumer-oriented society, and we have been dealing with the majority of families who are coming
in based on infertility." She conjectures that as fertility patients, prospective
adoptive parents were accustomed to being courted by assisted reproductive
technology providers and saw themselves as the patients and clients, elaborating: "They have [had] a certain type of treatment when they are walking
in the door. With that experience behind them—and they are also facing big
fees ahead. So they have an expectation of the ways they are supposed to be
treated, the services that they'll get." Michele continues, "I think it is a fine
balance between—I feel that I have to focus on the best interest of the child
but also realize that the adoptive parents [are] being customers of a certain
type of service." Reiterating this potential conflict of interests, she repeats,
"It is a fine balance."

To summarize, the goals of this chapter are twofold. The first goal is to
delineate why it is appropriate to use the market metaphor in private adoption. By highlighting the voices of adoption practitioners, my aim is to show
the extent to which business decisions permeate adoption practice. Even
though adoption providers are often attracted to the social work aspects of

adoption, the fiscal realities of running and maintaining a small business in a down market often take precedence. Second, this chapter demonstrates the futility of trying to separate the spheres of child welfare and child commodification. Although some respondents were clearly uncomfortable with (and occasionally disapproving of) the market metaphor, statements like "We need babies to make money" underscore how international adoption providers are simultaneously asked to be child protectors and child providers.

Nicole echoes this sentiment, explaining how even some of the much-touted humanitarian programs agencies sponsor are geared toward developing the adoption pipeline. She laments, "I think that adoptions should be about child welfare, but so often they are about child placement. So many agencies have these large humanitarian aid projects, but having the money tied to adoption, a lot of times it means that they are only doing projects in countries they are placing children from, and that is a way to keep the government in your favor."

Despite her cynicism, it is important to emphasize that she remains a proponent of international adoption. When I asked her what she would like to see different in international adoption, she responds, "I guess just more awareness about adoptive families." She mentions that she is wary of describing her work to critics who are quick to lambast intercountry adoption: "I guess sometimes I hesitate to tell people that I work in international adoption because they want to get on their soapbox and tell me that all international adoptions are corrupt." While Nicole acknowledges, "I think that I am more cynical of international adoptions than most people who work in the field," she defends the practice, continuing, "I don't think that all international adoptions should be banned. And I think that people have a hard time understanding that."

## The Shadow of the Black Market

During my interviews, I purposely avoided bringing up the subject of black market adoptions since the focus of my inquiry was on the intersection between child welfare and child commodification when everything appears to be aboveboard. Although there have been several documented incidents of corrupt practices,[33] I deliberately eschewed questions regarding child trafficking. Broaching the theme of adoption as a legitimate marketplace was controversial enough, and I did not want to turn off potential respondents by delving into the black market.

Again, it is useful to return to the historical literature on adoption to remind us that worries about corruption arose from the beginning of organized adoptions. Balcom traces what she calls "the traffic in babies" between the United States and Canada from the 1930s to the early 1970s, detailing how social workers on both sides of the border used high-profile stories of baby smuggling to assert the need for their expertise in the first transnational placements.[34] As with international adoptions today, Balcom asserts that the act of crossing the border, with two different governments, child welfare organizations, and sometimes cultures and languages, created chaotic conditions under which corruption could bloom. "As babies crossed borders," she argues, "they slipped between legal jurisdictions, and arenas of governmental responsibility."[35] She meticulously details that these were not isolated incidents, but rather, such placements were orchestrated by organized baby rings.

This was the case of the 1950s Montreal baby market serving predominately Jewish American parents who were searching for babies in Canada. These prospective parents looked to Canada since the prevailing wisdom of this era of "designed kinship" was to limit Jewish applicants to Jewish babies—and there were not enough of these U.S. babies to go around. She details how baby-ring organizers were able to take advantage of the Quebecois birth registration system that was solely under the jurisdiction of religious authorities. This aided the process of "laundering" a Catholic Canadian-born child into a Jewish American-born one: "Lawyers helped adoptive parents find rabbis who would register children presented to them as Jewish, or even 'born to' the adoptive parents." By forging the birth certificate, this practice obliterated the existence of the birth mother, paving the way so "new parents could take their Jewish-American born-to-them infant home to the United States and show the false birth registration in the unlikely event they were stopped at the border."[36]

The adoption-social-workers-turned-reformers that Balcom chronicles saw it as advantageous to highlight unregulated and corruptible border crossings because it helped them reinforce their professional authority. In other words, the social workers viewed corruption as a consequence of a broken private market, and they viewed the development of regulated adoption practice as the cure. In contrast, for contemporary social workers, contending with the existence of corruption is more complicated since it would mean acknowledging that even with "sound" practice, the potential for unethical behavior exists.

Perhaps because of these stakes, throughout my interviews few women raised the issue of corruption. Kiera did voice her concern about the high fees her agency (among others) charged for their services, wondering if it fueled unethical behavior. "The one thing that really bothers me is the amount of money exchanged," she testifies. "I know that it is a bureaucratic system, and I know the amount of work that goes into it, but I am afraid on some level, how much of those expenses cover real services, and how much does it feed an industry?"

She then brings up the Hague Convention and how the legislation was supposed to curb unscrupulous behavior, stating, "I think that with the

Hague there are precautions taking place, but you think of small countries like Guatemala and how many kids are being placed." She acknowledges that part of this trend has to do with the lack of social services in Guatemala, but on the other hand, Kiera worries that part of this surge is based on market factors: "True, there is no abortion—but with some countries, it is like demand and supply. It makes me very uncomfortable. I hope that children find families because they really need families and not a way for their birth families to make a living."

Kiera's concern that the demand for babies creates an incentive for poor women to relinquish their children was echoed in Beth's discussion of how some adoption facilitators take advantage of the system to make a profit by locating infants. "People are going out, not the agencies per se," Beth relates, "but people who are realizing this is a lucrative business are going in the villages and offering money to birth mothers so a family can have a baby."

Knowing this behavior is occurring, Beth describes the leap of faith she takes when "I take representatives and have them sign all of the documents that say they won't traffic children or buy and sell. I think that everyone has been educated and whatever. [But] I don't know that person." And even though she is legally protected, she still struggles with knowing that "if they do something wrong, or even the next person they connect to does something unethical, that connects me to them. I am constantly struggling with that."

Beth also worries that the potential for corruption can grow, especially as more agencies move in and begin placements. She cites an ethical quandary where a government official asks for $20, likening these types of payments to a form of bribery. She asserts that this type of behavior often takes place, even by "good agencies with good intentions," but is overlooked as adoption workers justify their actions in the name of child welfare. Beth agonizes over these payments, concerned that they fuel corruption, stating, "The other component is we don't understand the culture on the other side. We think that if we give $20 to this official to get gas for a car that is a government car, that we are not bribing, but we really are."

In the context of the overall fees, $20 may seem like a small amount, but in poor countries like Ethiopia, where the per capita annual income is $590, this is not an insignificant sum.[37] Moreover, Beth asserts that as more agencies set up shop, "the ante keeps going up," and the costs of doing business keep growing. Similarly, Abigail corroborates Beth's concerns, averring that bribes are so commonplace in international adoption that the cost of these payouts factors into whether agencies can afford to open up programs in new sending countries. She divulges, "There is so much corruption, and people get paid off for every other thing when families are adopting abroad."

Whereas these women were quite frank in their acknowledgment of potential corruption, others were more hesitant, dismissing documented cases of child trafficking as isolated incidents that are the inevitable and unfortunate fallout of intercountry adoptions. Heather described her work in the China adoption program, emphasizing its transparent process such that "people feel very confident that things are done aboveboard." While she concedes that "there are always people who can abuse systems," citing "stories where an orphanage director here [in China] took money," Heather downplays such allegations while also confirming them, testifying, "That happens everywhere."

She asserts that the potential for corruption in adoption is not limited to intercountry adoptions. Heather states matter-of-factly, "It happens in the United States," continuing, "Unfortunately adoption is a system that can really bring corruption." Even though she acknowledges the potential for bribery and corruption that can lead to child trafficking, she defends private international adoption, testifying, "I think that anyone would tell you that despite these anomalies, the Chinese really run a very efficient and trustworthy program."

During the information sessions, only occasionally did the topic of corruption come up. When speakers mentioned it, it would usually be to dismiss its relevance to their field, framing it as a sporadic occurrence that had been blown out of proportion. In other words, corruption tended to be perceived as the unfortunate consequence of having a few bad apples that should not spoil the bunch. For example, at one conference I sat in on an update on international adoption sponsored by representatives from an adoption advocacy group. During the presentation, the director provided a rundown of different sending countries, noting that Nepal suspended their pilot program since finding irregularities "with fraud and child buying." Despite these concerns, she hoped, "it will hopefully open again." She detailed how Guatemala also faced "fraud and corruption," but in response the country is trying out new DNA testing procedures. Although she warned us, "They are not trying to speculate about when it might reopen," it is likely that it would never approach the same magnitude, since "if they reopen, they are using international adoption exclusively for children over age five and special needs."

In spite of these documented cases of child trafficking, several presenters were quite vocal that adoption remained a human rights issue that gave children access to permanent families.[38] The director went on concede that there has been "commercialization of the process and corruption" but countered that "the response should not be to shut the whole thing down." She later reemphasized this point, attesting, "We don't pretend that corruption doesn't happen, but we think that the response is inappropriate."

At a different preadoption conference, another woman gave an update on international adoption, decrying Guatemala's decision to shut down their adoption program. She likened closing the Guatemalan program to "throwing the baby out with the bathwater," describing how the sending country ratified the Hague Convention without having systems in place to abide by it. Because the United States is also a signatory to the treaty, the United States had no choice but to halt processing adoption visas, lest it be seen as noncompliant. On the basis of these events, the presenter lamented that "Guatemala was available as an opportunity for children" and that the Hague Convention was "used as a Trojan horse to shut the system down." She went on to underscore that "the vast majority of placements were highly ethical, but in any system that is private and individual, there is potential for activity to not be up to ethical standards." While she admitted, "Some entities took advantage of the situation," and she recognized that "we need to protect the rights of birth mothers and children," she pointed out that closing the program puts children at risk.

The existence of a black market for children is the unfortunate corollary to a legal adoption marketplace. Although all the providers I spoke with insisted that these practices did not apply to their specific agencies, the fact that it exists at all was a source of deep unease for adoption social workers. Many of these women had devoted their lives to the welfare of children and families, choosing to work in careers where their salaries could hardly be the main draw. In spite of their commitment to the field, several had strong reservations about private international adoption, especially once taking into account the big-picture social issues relating to women's rights and global poverty. These are smart and dedicated women who are trying their best to do good social work under conditions that keep getting harder. Given the market downturn, understandably, these workers were also worried about their jobs. By the time I spoke with them, it was clear that the international market was drying up; many had already survived a round of layoffs. As fiscal realities crept up on their aspirations as social workers, they faced new dilemmas as they came to terms with the inextricable mix of social service and customer service expected in private adoption.

## From Backstage to Frontstage

In sum, the goal of this chapter is to establish that the market metaphor is an appropriate lens through which to view private adoption. Although social workers may want to situate child adoption solely within the domain of child welfare, I show that it is unrealistic to expect that the economics of keeping an adoption agency afloat do not matter. This is especially the case for transnational adoption, in which workers have had to contend with massive constrictions of supply, frustrated customers, and industry-wide layoffs.

While these conditions have been fairly widespread across international adoption agencies, it is a rarity to hear adoption workers speak so bluntly about their ambivalence. Given that adoption is solely supposed to be a "win-

win" that finds parents for children, any hint of the reverse can pose as a threat to the public narrative. Through my interviews, I was able to capture more of a backstage perspective where adoption professionals were free to go "off script." Throughout the interviews, adoption workers detailed the drawbacks of working in private adoption where clients' needs can supersede children's needs, making the profession feel "more like customer service" than social service. Although these conversations yield new insights into how adoption professionals characterize their roles, it is important to emphasize that my backstage is limited to adoption workers' self-reports.

Despite this caveat, my methodological approach *does* allow me to compare and contrast how adoption workers act in the frontstage versus how they talk about their profession when not trying to recruit paying customers. As Michele reports, "it is a fine balance" navigating between serving the needs of the child and parent clients. The next chapter further examines this tightrope, focusing on the frontstage of the adoption marketplace—that is, the arena where adoption workers market their services to prospective adoptive parents.

# 2

# Uneasy Consumers

*The Emotion Work of Marketing Adoption*

When the elevator doors open at Kids Connection adoption agency, visitors are greeted by a friendly receptionist and framed professional photographs of smiling adoptive parents and their children. These photos are success stories, meant to reassure anxious prospective parents who have come to this place looking for a way to expand their family. Because the practice of creating a family from social rather than biological bonds remains outside the traditional practice of kinship,[1] these images remind prospective applicants that adoption is a viable path to parenthood. Moving down the hallway past portraits of diverse families in every constellation, the attendees begin to arrive in a room set up with folding chairs and a screen that will later display a presentation describing the myriad of adoption programs Kids Connection offers.

The audience consists of mostly White couples, many of whom look to be in their late thirties and early forties. These demographics make sense since nationally, adoptive parents are more likely to be older and White compared with the population of parents who have children biologically.[2] Several of the couples in attendance hold hands and murmur quietly to each other as they wait for the presentation to begin. Other attendees peck at their smartphones. One gets the sense that this is not the first waiting room they have been in and that prior to attending this meeting, like the majority of people who adopt, these hopeful parents have already sat in the waiting rooms of doctors and fertility specialists trying to conceive.[3] In addition to the married heterogamous[4] couples facing infertility, there are also a few homogamous couples and single prospective adoptive parents who also face hurdles to biological reproduction.[5] For these audience members adoption may be their best—or only—chance to have children.

While waiting for the presentation to begin, some of the attendees leaf through the pamphlets provided by Kids Connection. As Ward Gailey argues, the content of these promotional materials communicates the message that prospective clients have an array of choices available to them. She states, "Web sites, brochures, and other advertising materials from a range of private agencies and independent adoption intermediaries reveal how much these agencies and brokers stress that such prospective parents have the 'right' to 'adopt the baby you want.'"[6]

Indeed, the message that private adoption could fulfill hopeful parents' desires for a suitable child was literally front and center on Kid Connection's brochure. At the top of the glossy pamphlet, above a picture of a White woman holding a racially ambiguous light-skinned infant, was the slogan "We Deliver."[7] Considering the costs associated with professionally printing these materials, the wording cannot be accidental. It may be a less-than-subtle nod to the fact that most clients who pursue private adoption face barriers to biological reproduction and cannot conceive and carry a baby on their own. Read on a different level, the word "deliver" invokes a promise of convenience and customer satisfaction. This double entendre is likely deliberate because, from the outset, adoption providers face the task of reassuring prospective clients that their organization can locate a satisfactory child while providing a high level of service. Notice how these promotional materials position prospective adoptive parents as the main client. Whereas adoption social workers in Chapter 1 discussed their reservations compromising the edict that the child is the central client in adoption, in agencies' marketing materials the message that the parents are the empowered consumer is unwavering.

To sell private adoption to prospective clients, providers rely on a number of strategies to advertise and market their services. The website is often the first touch point as it provides an anonymous opportunity for curious parties to browse through an agency's programs. As Pamela Quiroz argues, "Websites provide public representations of agencies' practices, [and] they offer a window into adoption policy."[8] These sites do not just provide information but are designed in order to maximize the likelihood of attracting potential customers. She continues, "Agencies advertise and compete with each other for a limited population of adoptive clients. Presumably, these factors lead agencies to present themselves in the best possible way."[9]

Adoption conferences are another pathway for adoption providers to market their services. These large regional conferences are similar to other types of commercial expos in that consumers pay a fee to register and spend the day wandering through the exhibition hall and attending sessions to learn more about their options. Although the sessions at these conferences vary, they usually cover topics such as deciding between international and domestic adoptions and whether to use a domestic adoption agency or an attorney. Others included topics such as health concerns in international adoption and affordability concerns.

In the exhibition hall there are tables staffed by representatives from adoption agencies and independent adoption attorneys who are there to share information about their services. Some of these displays are more polished than others. Many of the big name adoption agencies have large-scale displays with professionally designed graphics, and others have a more handmade look. Regardless of the quality of the printing, the exhibitors come to these conferences to pitch their services and recruit potential clients who are considering embarking on a multi-thousand-dollar journey into private adoption. For example, I spoke with one woman who told me she "had an exclusive" on an orphanage in China that had some of the best babies. Another woman passed out business cards proudly proclaiming her status as the stork attorney. In addition, I passed by several tables advertising a cottage industry of adoption services, from those who promised to help create successful parent profiles to woo expectant women considering adoption, to others who specialized in identifying fruitful geographic market segments to place classified advertisements soliciting potential birth mothers.

Having perused adoption providers' websites or attended an adoption conference, prospective clients who want to move forward with adoption will often attend an information session hosted by a specific organization. These information sessions are offered for free and are open to the public. They serve as the first point of sustained professional contact between adoption providers and potential customers.

In *Adoption Nation*, adoption advocate and adoptive father Adam Pertman describes his journey from infertility to adoption. Like many adoptive parents who faced barriers to biological reproduction, Pertman went through the process of "fertility drugs, in-vitro fertilization, donor eggs, the whole shebang."[10] Having sustained invasive treatments and ongoing disappointment,[11] Pertman positions himself as one of the thousands who left the fertility clinic empty-handed and "kept going right into the offices of adoption agencies and lawyers."[12] Although we know that there is a strong association between infertility and adoption,[13] before this study we knew little about what occurs once prospective parents arrive at these purveyors of adoption.

Whereas the goal of Chapter 1 is to leverage the voices of adoption workers to show the futility of segregating the spheres of child welfare and child markets, in this chapter I deepen my analysis to detail how these discourses become enacted during the work of recruiting new applicants. In other words, in Chapter 1 I frame the adoption market as a noun, detailing whether and how adoption professionals see their work as affected by business decisions. Having reported from the backstage, in this chapter I move to the frontstage and subtly pivot my analysis to frame the word "market" as a verb. I examine how adoption providers promote their services, or how they market themselves to potential clients. Specifically, I am interested in how adoption providers draw on and utilize messages about child welfare and child commodification as they make their pitch.

I argue that adoption providers must first remind their customer base— and perhaps themselves—that private adoption is fundamentally about child welfare. This discursive strategy serves the purpose of alleviating the potential guilt that could emerge when shifting gears and discussing adoption as a consumer practice. By establishing the caveat that, at its core, adoption is about child welfare, workers are exonerated and then free to subtly shift their marketing ploy toward a more consumer-friendly stance.

To thread the needle between social service and customer service, I argue that adoption practitioners rely on a form of emotion work that eases parents into a consumer mind-set without blatantly overstepping the line between child welfare and child commodification. Coined by sociologist Arlie Hochschild, the term "emotional labor" broadly encompasses the unwritten and often uncompensated work that is geared toward managing clients' feelings.[14] These jobs tend to disproportionately fall to those in the service sector—including social workers. "Day-care centers, nursing homes, hospitals, airports, stores, call centers, classrooms, social welfare offices, dental offices," writes Hochschild, "in all these workplaces, gladly or reluctantly, brilliantly or poorly, employees do emotional labor."[15]

Key aspects of this work include putting clients at ease, eliciting trust, and gaining business. Hochschild continues, "When an organization seeks to create demand for a service and then deliver it, it uses the smile and the soft questioning voice. Behind this delivery display, the organization's worker is asked to feel sympathy, trust, and good will."[16] Notably, this emotion work can be hard to recognize unless there is a "pinch" between "a real but disapproved feeling on one hand and an idealized one on the other."[17]

For private adoption workers, the emotional labor revolves around managing the dissonance between adoption as consumerism and adoption as care, and the "pinch" can be felt as they try to find the balance between the two. In order to bridge these separate spheres, adoption social workers use what Hochschild calls "feeling rules" to set a script or a "moral stance" for how providers should navigate this terrain. The parameters of these feeling rules can be seen in the language adoption providers utilize during these information sessions. For example, one adoption social worker tells her audience, "We come to work for the children." Certainly, these dedicated child welfare professionals help find homes for thousands of children who need families. With that being said, the presenter is free to pivot her message, as she emphasizes they offer "a tremendous variety of opportunities" for prospective parents.

The need for this type of emotional labor can be especially acute since prospective adoptive parents are often in a vulnerable state when they first attend an information meeting. Many may be reeling from miscarriages and failed infertility treatments, or they may be trying to come to terms with the idea that adoption could be the only viable path to parenthood. Certainly there are applicants who choose adoption as their primary method of becoming mothers and fathers, but we know from prior research that those considering adoption are ten times more likely to have undergone infertility treatments.[18] Some attendees may be feeling resigned to adoption as they psych themselves up to embark on a potentially expensive and lengthy process. At this tender juncture, applicants come through the door of adoption providers and once they arrive they are asked to reconsider their definitions of family.

Prospective adoptive parents are faced with questions such as, "Would you consider having an open adoption that entails contact with birth family members, parenting a child who does not share your racial background, or raising a child who was potentially exposed to alcohol or drugs in utero?" Biological parents usually have the privilege of maintaining control over these issues as they can choose the race of their co-progenitor, and pregnant women have control over what substances to consume during gestation. Moreover, biological parents can claim motherhood and fatherhood from conception and do not have to contend with the rights and feelings of a birth mother and/or birth father. But these issues are common in adoption. Even adoptive parents in closed adoptions where the birth parents' identities are not known still have to make room for these shadowy figures in the child's origin story. These questions can upend ideas of kinship, pushing prospective adoptive parents to reconfigure notions of blood that are typically the bedrock of parenthood.

And finally, prospective adoptive parents are catapulted into a position where they have to articulate what characteristics they want (and conversely do not want) in a son or daughter. Sure, one could virtuously attest that she or he would be willing to parent a child who had a major noncorrectable health concern, was conceived via rape or incest, or has birth parents that regularly drank or consumed drugs. But in adoption, these choices are not theoretical; instead they have concrete implications. Since children fitting these profiles tend to be in greater supply than demand, indicating a willingness to parent a child with this background almost ensures being matched with a child who fits these characteristics. These can be heart-wrenching decisions, especially considering that hopeful parents may have started out wanting what biological parents often get—a healthy newborn that racially resembles both parents. Armed with the knowledge that prospective adoptive parents enter the adoption marketplace from a vulnerable position, adoption providers proceed carefully during these initial meetings.

To understand how adoption workers navigate feeling rules when they sell adoption to prospective parents, I became a participant-observer, attending over forty conference and information sessions.[19] Although I was geographically limited to the East Coast, I was able to personally attend twenty-five sessions scattered throughout the Northeast and Mid-Atlantic. To increase the range of my project, I also sat in on fifteen webinars offered by adoption agencies across the country. These webinars provide a low-stakes way for those considering adoption to learn more about a particular adoption agency. Of note, these webinars are not asynchronous prerecorded videos but live sessions featuring a dynamic interchange between presenters and audience members who can have their questions answered in real time. The sessions usually lasted about an hour and a half in person (although one lasted almost three hours) and were slightly shorter online.

I cultivated a sampling frame of adoption providers using a three-pronged approach. First, I used a master list of adoption agencies accredited by the Hague Convention on the Protection of Children, a multinational agreement designed to protect and streamline the movement of children across countries for the purpose of adoption.[20] Agencies must be accredited to process international adoptions from one of the ninety-five countries that have ratified this treaty.[21] To receive accreditation, agencies must meet minimum standards in terms of reporting adoption services and activities, satisfy educational requirements for supervisory staff, offer at least ten hours of training to adoptive parents, and carry a certain amount of liability insurance.[22] Second, I identified agencies and information meetings from an online resource called *Building Your Family: Infertility and Adoption Guide*, a go-to resource that lists events hosted for prospective adoptive parents.[23] From this source, I was able to identify additional adoption agencies as well as individual private attorneys who solely provide domestic adoption services (and hence do not need Hague Accreditation) or provide international adoptions from countries that had not ratified the Hague Convention. Third, to ensure that I captured the full range of adoption agencies, I identified agencies that had been denied Hague Accreditation and included some of these organizations as well.[24]

It is important to acknowledge that there is a good deal of variation among the adoption agencies I visited in terms of size, religious affiliation, and geographic location. It would be interesting to delve deeper into how this variety shapes institutional practices. But since private adoption is a relatively small world, I chose to not paint detailed descriptions of agencies out of concern that they would become recognizable to those who are familiar with adoption. Along the same line, I purposely do not link the names of the women I interviewed with the agencies they worked for, out of concern that despite their pseudonyms the women could be identified given their institutional context.[25]

During the time I conducted my fieldwork, it was not uncommon to see some of the same audience members as I made the circuit across information sessions offered by local providers. For example, I remember repeatedly seeing an unmarried White woman in her late thirties who was trying to figure out whether adoption as a single applicant was going to be her path to motherhood. She was quite gregarious and would often engage other audience members, so I learned a little bit about her backstory. I first saw her at a conference geared toward prospective adoptive parents. There she attended the same session I did which detailed the differences between domestic and international adoption. Seeing her across multiple venues underscored the fact that potential clients often do "shop around" before committing to a specific adoption agency or country program. She must have decided that international adoption was going to be a better fit because a few weeks later I saw her again at an information meeting specifically discussing transnational adoption. She and I crossed paths at yet another information meeting offered by a competing intercountry adoption agency. By the last session she proudly disclosed to the group that she had settled on adopting from Ethiopia and was going to officially start the paper process.

I still remember her because she seemed so resolved and excited to move forward with adoption. The agency she selected was one of the few that was still accepting applications from single women hoping to adopt an Ethiopian child as young as possible. Years later, I wonder whether she was able to submit her dossier in time to be considered or whether the slowdown in Ethiopia meant that she was not able to adopt. Moreover, I wonder whether she fully understood the commitment she was making when she decided to become a transracial adoptive parent and whether her agency adequately prepared her for the challenges ahead.

Like myself, these prospective adoptive parents eventually reached what sociologists refer to as a "theoretical saturation,"[26] when each additional information session stopped yielding new insights. Since past research indicates that only a fraction of women considering adoption ever follow through,[27] it is likely that some attendees decided not to move forward with the application process. Thus, presenters at these meetings have their work cut out for them in that they are trying to convince audience members to first consider adoption, and second to sign on with their specific services. As adoption ethicist Madelyn Freundlich argues, "The growing number of agency programs in these countries and others has led to increased competition and the need for each agency to position itself as able to provide the most desirable children in the most expeditious manner."[28] This sense of competition among providers clearly resonated with one speaker who told her audience, "This whole presentation has to be about what separates us from other agencies."

Most adoption information sessions assume that audience members have no previous knowledge of adoption, and presenters often begin by describing the differences between domestic and international adoption.[29] Next they go on to detail how in private domestic adoption, the pregnant woman considering an adoption plan usually chooses the adoptive family among several different profiles. Although there are occasional exceptions, most of the children placed via private domestic adoptions are infants, usually newborns. Prospective parents have the choice of using a full-service adoption agency or hiring an attorney who advises clients how to locate an expectant woman looking to place her child.

Presenters then explain that, in contrast, international adoption often entails the placement of a toddler or older child born overseas (recall from the previous chapter that infants are rarely available). If applicants are hoping for a child as young and healthy as possible, prospective parents sign up for one of the few countries placing these children and eventually are given a referral for a child meeting those qualifications. Internationally, adoptive parents who are willing to adopt an older child or one with a significant medical need often apply through a separate and often-expedited less-expensive program for waiting children.

After ironing out these details, the speaker usually describes the general characteristics of the children available for adoption, such as their age, health, gender, and race. Following these descriptions, presenters discuss more of the "nuts and bolts" of the application procedure, explaining how long the application process takes and the many bureaucratic steps involved. Then they briefly touch on the associated fees and payment plans. After finishing this overview, the facilitators open the floor to questions.

Early in the session, most presenters thanked the audience members for coming. They briefly acknowledged the significance of their attendance, especially for audience members who had struggled with infertility. One presenter obliquely spoke of the "long road" many had likely traversed before getting to the session. At another meeting, the presenter cast herself as a sympathetic listener, empathizing that some applicants may feel "battered and bruised with what they've been through already." A third presenter indirectly referred to applicants' infertility struggles by stating, "We know that when families come to us, they have been on a rocky road." Others were more candid about the fact that many audience members had likely already unsuccessfully tried to conceive via assisted reproductive technology (ART), making sure to drive home the point that adoption could deliver a child to them, even if ART had failed.

For example, I sat in the crowded ballroom of a conference center one Saturday morning and listened to the keynote speaker address an audience of mostly White women and men who were considering private adoption. The featured presenter was an adoption consultant who specialized in working with prospective adoptive parents with infertility problems. Her overall message to her rapt audience was that adoption works. She likened ART to being on a roller coaster ride of "hope, anxiety, waiting, and disappointment" over and over again. In contrast, she told her audience that adoption is like "crossing a bridge," and "if you get on the bridge and have the fortitude to stick with adopting, the chance of success is 100 percent." She reminded them, "That is not a statistic you've heard in a really long time."

At another information session, the presenter touted a similar message that adoption successfully creates families when other attempts have yielded only disappointment. The social worker told her audience, "I have been doing this long enough to have seen families go through the process. I have seen families in info sessions bring children home." Cognizant that her goal is to persuade people not only to choose adoption but also to sign on with her agency, she emphasized her organization's success rate, stating, "This process really does work. Ninety-seven percent of those families who register with us bring children home."

Additionally, many presenters identify themselves as having an insider status, usually as adoptive parents but occasionally as adult adoptees. This strategy helps speakers make a personal connection with audience members and offers prospective applicants hope that they too can successfully grow their families. One presenter played up her coworkers' credentials as not just adoption professionals but also as adoptive parents, stating, "We don't just talk the talk, but we walk the walk." Another speaker mentioned that an adoptive parent founded her agency, stating that they "practice what they preach." She continued that many of the staff are transnational adoptive parents, so at holiday parties, "It is like the United Nations." Others mentioned how they also had adult adoptees working for them, with one stating, "Our team—we are all very family orientated. We have adult adoptees and adoptive families with children adopted internationally."

Placing adoptive parents as spokespersons for adoption agencies not only helps reassure prospective parents but also serves as a savvy business strategy. For example, at a conference panel focused on the future of international adoptions, one agency employee drew on her insider status as an international adoptive parent to try to convince prospective adoptive parents that despite the downturn, overseas adoption is still a viable pathway. She offered a cautionary tale about her own "failed" attorney-led adoption before she successfully adopted a child from Russia through her employer. The presenter detailed how she and her husband had contracted with a lawyer who told them that if an adoption did not go through, she would refund the money they had already paid. Yet because the presenter did not get the agreement in writing, by the time the pregnant woman changed her mind about the placement, all the money in escrow had already been billed, and the attorney refused to honor their verbal agreement. With this experience in mind, she advised her audience, "I think that it is safer to use an adoption agency."

Beyond employee testimonials, some providers invite previous clients who adopted through their agency to address audience members' questions. By sharing their journeys, these parents serve as the ultimate endorsement and reminder that the agency produces many satisfied customers. For example, at a meeting of a local adoption support group, the guest speaker was an adoption attorney who brought along one of her happy clients. The new adoptive mother cradled her cooing baby and told the audience, "I was just like you a year ago . . . and without [name of the attorney], I wouldn't be here today." Inviting this mother accomplished a dual purpose as the attorney proved to the audience that first and foremost independent infant adoption does work. Second, by showcasing a White mother with a White baby, the attorney was able to subtly inform clients that despite the relative shortage of White infants, her client prevailed and was able to locate the baby of her dreams.

At a session for Cornerstone, the organizers invited a heterogamous married couple that had recently adopted a toddler from Russia. These parents heartily endorsed working with the agency, revealing that they had devoted two years toward pursuing an attorney-led adoption and "had some heartbreaks" along the way. After these disappointments they wanted to adopt internationally because "we knew [that] could be successful." They then went on to say that they chose Cornerstone because "you never felt like you were doing it alone," and "the agency helps protect you."

Similarly, at Baby Talk's information session, Jessica, a new adoptive mom, gushed about her experience with the agency. She detailed, "We came to Baby Talk after trying fertility and that not working out for us. We didn't know anyone in our family who had ever adopted. . . . I remember being at the general information meeting and thinking how excited I was. And I did have a lot of questions. Everything in our journey toward finally bringing home our son has been a fantastic experience."

These newly minted parents provide a concrete depiction of an adoption success story offering a lifeline for uncertain folks trying to make up their minds about adoption. Even agencies that do not have guest speakers often try to assure prospective parents that they too can be adoptive parents. For example, at Loving Family, a domestic adoption agency, the social worker comforted audience members by conveying the message that they could successfully adopt a baby. She told them that adoptive parents come in all forms, stating, "Adoptive parents are in their late thirties, early forties. Sometimes secondary infertility problems, sometimes no infertility. There are interracial couples, same-sex couples, white collar, blue collar. People who have a desire to expand their family through adoption. *They are like you.*"

With these assurances, the adoption information session enacts a specific type of emotional labor, and providers tread softly over the topic of infertility and the expensive and arduous process ahead. Good presenters assuage parents' fears on multiple levels. Although the type of emotion work varied by whether the audience was predominantly interested in domestic or international adoption, one thing that all sessions had in common was the strategy of assuring parents that adoption was an honorable practice firmly grounded in its mission for child welfare. In order to move the conversation into the commercial domain, presenters had to unquestionably establish that adoption is first and foremost devoted to finding parents for children. In the following section I detail how adoption workers convey this message.

## Children as Clients

Perhaps because of the large sum of money changing hands or adoption workers' own misgivings about the market aspects of adoption, the initial goal of the information session is to firmly ground the practice as child welfare. One social worker stated, "There are so many children in the world who need families. That's why we exist. All of our practices are in the best interest of the child." At another session, the presenter told her audience, "We come to work for the children." Because the child is the central focus, many blithely state that they wish that they could "work themselves out of business" because it would mean that there was no longer a need for such services. At a conference for prospective parents, one social worker endorsed this party line, telling her audience, "We would love it if we could go out of business."

Other representatives also worked to assure potential clients that they were not in it to make money. For example, one presenter stated, "I tell all of the families I work with, the important thing is this is not a business." Similarly, a director of an adoption agency addressed her audience, "Adoption is about making a difference in a child's life. This is not a product; this is a human life. . . . I am not a traditional CEO trying to make lots and lots of money." In this regard adoption is positioned as distinct from the profit-maximizing model of the free market, with adoption professionals firmly grounding their work as social service.

The emphasis on child welfare was so strong that on several occasions adoption providers described instances when they deliberately persuaded applicants to drop out of the process. Under a purely profit-maximizing model, this behavior would not be rational, since turning away potential parents means turning down revenue. One social worker related how she tried to dissuade a potential client from moving forward: "One mother kept turning down referrals because she didn't think the child was pretty enough. I told her that she had to go to counseling before she could move forward." Another social worker spoke of denying an application from a sixty-five-year-old woman who wanted to adopt a newborn. These stories are telling because they illustrate how many providers are willing to adhere to high standards designed to serve in the best interests of children, even if it means losing business.

In another example, a social worker told her audience about a client who had very specific criteria for the child she hoped to adopt. This would-be mother wanted to adopt only a White Russian infant whose parents both went to college but died in a car accident. Although the social worker joked that she told the woman "to go away," she elaborated that she persuaded the woman not to pursue adoption. During the same session, the presenter later mentioned a case about a single woman who wanted to adopt a twelve-year-old from Russia but was not prepared for the realities of adopting an older child who had spent years in institutional care. The social worker told her audience that she "gave her a list of things to do before she could adopt in order to slow things down," hoping that the woman would drop out of the process.

The disapprobation against framing adoption in objectified terms is so strong that occasionally some adoption workers will police the language of their colleagues and publicly call them out should their terminology stray too far into market jargon. I witnessed this occurrence during one of the adoption conferences I visited. At a session on international adoption led by an adoption agency executive and a director of an adoption advocacy group, the adoption worker launched into her overview, providing an update on the demographics of children who would likely be available in the pipeline. Taking umbrage at the term available, the other speaker interrupted the first, admonishing her, "Children are not available for adoption. They need a family, and [the question is] do they have access to a family through international adoption?" This critique spawned a moment of awkward silence across the room, as it was clear that the initial speaker was not expecting this rebuke. Despite this aspersion, the speaker managed to curtly acknowledge her colleague's comment and continue the presentation.

As this interchange suggests, in private adoption the stakes are high, such that referring to children's availability raises the ire of some advocates. Although there are internal debates about language, as these disclosures indicate, at their professional core adoption providers see themselves as social workers and child advocates actively working to find parents for children. The child is positioned as their reason for being, and adoption representatives feel it is their duty to remind potential applicants of their allegiances. As one social worker explained, "We are a child-welfare agency. That means our client is the children." Another presenter emphasized her agency's child-centric orientation, articulating, "We are a unique agency in that the focus is the child. We view the child as our client." However, she amended her statement, qualifying, "Although obviously you are the client, and the birth parent is as well." At yet another session, the presenter used a similar strategy to emphasize that the child is the central client while intimating that the parents' needs would still be a priority. She asserted, "I just think that it's really important that we are viewing the child as our client." But then she rushed to continue, "And of course we want to support you and offer the best possible resources that we can both during and after placement."

Once providing the caveat that all of their policies are predicated on the child as the client, many presenters start to pivot their message, often painting their child-welfare foci as a potential customer service benefit. For example, at Statewide's information session, the presenter told her audience, "Statewide is considered one of the most experienced nonprofit international adoption and child assistance agencies in the U.S. Not only should that provide peace of mind to you as you begin your adoption process, but because of our history, you can trust that should any unexpected issues arise during your adoption, Statewide has likely handled these type of situations." The focus continued to migrate toward the prospective parents, as the speaker asserted that these vast experiences ensured that the agency would "know who to go to and how to address *your* needs as quickly as possible."

At China Heart, an agency solely facilitating international adoptions from China, the director was more blunt about what she called her "philosophy on customer service." She underscored how her staff would "hold your hand" and provide "that catering service," especially during the mandated overseas travel to meet one's son or daughter. My "agency is not about serving one family today," she proclaimed. "We are thinking about serving one thousand families tomorrow." Because the agency specializes in China adoption, she distinguished herself from her competitors, saying, "We do China only. China is our passion, focus, and specialty. We can keep the costs low, and our employees can give you our undivided attention." She cautioned that some other agencies with a full slate of programs lack the ability to provide catered services, warning attendees, "Some organizations have no idea what they are doing."

Whereas representatives from China Heart emphasized that their specialized approach to adoption is a consumer benefit, in contrast, those offering a multitude of programs framed their large roster as a positive for customers. As one speaker told her audience, "One of the reasons families choose our agency is we have been around a very long time, and we do have lots of different options." At Family Union, the speaker also highlighted their vast array of adoption programs, framing the choices they offer as beneficial for consumers:

> Many families choose to come to Family Union because of the wide variety of programs Family Union offers. We found over previous years a lot of adoption agencies specialized in working with one particular country to place children from. What happens is when that country process slows down or closes, . . . families are in a place where they're stuck. They have to choose another adoption agency or

start over in order to move forward with their adoption process. It's helpful as country requirements change or as adoption processes or time frames change, families are able to look at other programs through Family Union, and if they feel it is appropriate for their family, they can switch to another program without having to completely switch agencies.

The message in this statement serves a dual purpose. First, the tone underscores the consumer-friendly approach by emphasizing the many consumer choices this agency offers. Second, notice that the consumer option of switching programs is framed solely as a customer—not an agency—benefit. Yet as argued in Chapter 1, offering a myriad of country programs also helps protect the adoption agency, particularly when country programs close.

## Parents as Clients

Framing private adoption as an altruistic service pursued in the best interest of children is instrumental to the next phase of casting prospective adoptive parents as the good guys who are helping to alleviate the plight of parentless children. For example, at one information session held by Loving Family, a domestic adoption agency, the social worker positioned domestic adoption as helping to reduce potential foster care cases. She explains that during a birth, if there are "red flags" such that a mandated reporter might have to call in a state's child welfare officials, then these officials will "step out" if they know that the mother is making an adoption plan. According to the agency representative, these adoptions help prevent children from entering "the system" and "languishing in foster care."[30]

This strategy of equating domestic infant adoption as saving children from foster care may help to absolve clients' potential guilt over not choosing to adopt via the public foster care system in favor of adopting a child as young and as healthy as possible. Lindsay worked to ameliorate her clients' guilt about these choices, advocating, "The starting point should be what you want." Cognizant of these mixed emotions, at another information session the speaker acknowledged that private adoption is expensive, so parents should get their money's worth. Notice how she gives them permission to think about what will be easiest for them as consumers, contending, "You have to pay money to adopt, and [some] don't want to pay for a child with special needs that can be identified. Parents want something they feel will be easier, not a child with identified problems." Another presenter encouraged her audience to be forthright about their desires by stating, "You need to live through this [process] so you can parent the child." A third pronounced a blanket exemption, "*There is no right or wrong.* You are adopting a child who needs parents."

The message that there is no right or wrong gives prospective adoptive parents the permission to put their needs front and center. Emboldened by the assurance that they are partaking in an altruistic child welfare practice, they are relieved of the guilt associated with the inevitable winnowing process that adoption entails. True, adoptive parents *are* adopting a child who has been identified as needing parents. But in order to get to a desirable son or daughter, prospective parents have to bypass less desirable children also in need of parents. These are uneasy decisions, since they force applicants to grapple with whether they could handle adopting a racially different, older child with known medical issues. Since there is a relative shortage of healthy infants available for adoption, most of the children in need of families are likely to have some sort of special need. Conscious of the discomfort the process can generate, a presenter worked to relieve her audience members' fears by stating, "No one is going to make you adopt a child you don't want to adopt."

Given their competing priorities, adoption providers try to strike a balance between pitching adoption as social service and customer service. This balance requires a unique sort of emotion work that simultaneously discounts the idea that adoption has a commercial component while encouraging prospective parents to see themselves as consumers. For example, at a panel titled "International Adoption 101," at an adoption conference geared to prospective adoptive parents, I sat in a crowded conference center ballroom filled with an audience of mostly White attendees who were considering transnational and transracial adoptions. The presenter, a senior administrator at a large adoption agency, opened her presentation by directing the attendees to think of themselves as consumers but not necessarily as shoppers. She began, "Remember that you are a consumer. You are not a consumer of a product of a child, since children are not for sale. *You're not doing that.* You are a consumer of services."

This solicitation serves multiple purposes. First, the presenter assures audience members that children are not for sale, firmly situating adoption outside of the market realm. Many of these would-be adoptive parents were likely struggling to reconcile paying thousands of dollars in fees and were perhaps trying to figure out where the money was going. The statement exonerates these prospective clients, telling them they do not have to wonder whether they are engaging in some sort of commercial exchange. Second, the executive's statement basically implores audience members to take on a consumer mentality. Since she was coming from a position of authority, this entreaty gives parents permission to think of themselves as the consumers and the adoption providers as the purveyors of goods.

I witnessed a similar form of emotion work at an adoption information session when the social worker struggled to describe how to peruse her agency's website, which provides photos of children available for international adoption. When first introducing the topic, the speaker emphasized the consumer-friendly aspects of the process, encouraging attendees to go on-line to "click around and see the information available about the children." Should visitors identify a child who is appealing, she recommended calling her agency so that "the child can be put on hold" for applicants while they get their paperwork in order. She acknowledged the commercial nature of the transaction by saying, "I know it sounds kind of weird, like you are shop-ping." At this moment, the market metaphor seemed to go too far, and the audience bristled. The social worker then switched gears as the child advo-cacy role took over. She backtracked and commiserated with her audience: "I know. It doesn't sound good. This is how it works. But it is all done on the up-and-up." By acknowledging that the layaway metaphor "doesn't sound good," part of the social worker's job is to move the conversation firmly back into the realm of child welfare by persuading audience members that the process is honorable. Armed with reassurances that "this is how it works" and that everything is "on the up-and-up," applicants are given the implicit message that they can proceed with a consumer mentality.

The titles of some of sessions at adoption conferences underscore this parent-centered orientation. For example, I went to a presentation called "Deciding on the Type of Adoption That Works for *You*" and one called "Is Transracial Adoption Right for You?" Notice how these presentations frame the adoption decision-making process in terms of what works for the par-ents. Yet to uphold the discourse that adoption is solely about child welfare, adoption social workers cannot afford to crassly frame the decision-making process in terms of parents' desires and market realities. Imagine going to information sessions with titles such as "White Parents: Who Would You Rather Adopt, a White Russian Child Who May Have Fetal Alcohol Affect or an Asian Child Who May Not?" or "Do You Want to Adopt a Black Baby in Half the Time at Potentially Half the Price?" Articulating the adoption decision-making process in this manner would be unconscionable, since it veers too close to a commodified and calculated view of adoption. So instead of verbalizing decisions in this manner, these choices are often cloaked under the auspices of doing what is right for the parents. Thus the emotion work entails rebranding the adoption winnowing process in terms of the euphemism of finding the right fit.

## Finding the Right Fit

Repeatedly I heard presenters employ this strategy, urging parents to think about what "will be the right match for you and the right match for your family." For example, the presenter at Forever Family, a domestic adoption agency, chronicled the process in a judgment-free, neutral tone: "There are questionnaires that you are going to fill out about what type of child you are requesting and how that is going to affect your family, and what does this all mean, and how you are going to feel with the outside world, how they're going to view your family."

In this narration, euphemisms abound, cloaking issues surrounding potentially controversial topics like transracial adoption, open adoption, and the adoption of children with special needs. Certainly, from a social work perspective, parents should not adopt a child they are not prepared to parent. However, by framing the decision to choose one type of child over another as a matter of idiosyncratic fit, adoption workers give parents permission to bypass acknowledging these issues. The customer is not made to feel uncomfortable with his or her consumer desires since the tone of the word "fit" implies an innocuous individualized preference. In addition, the word is free of judgment and blame. So when a social worker tells her audience, "There really is a program for everyone. You just have to think of a country that suits where you're at," she implicitly gives parents permission to cast their decisions in a neutral way and to prioritize whatever suits their needs.

So what happens when prospective adoptive parents want to turn down a child who is not the right fit? As I learned from attending these sessions, adoption workers often communicate to potential clients that they will have the leeway to turn down a specific child or "situation" if it turns out he or she does not meet their aforementioned criteria. Because the processes of rejecting a child via domestic and international adoption are distinct, each of these practices is discussed separately.

## Turning Down a Situation in Domestic Adoption

In private domestic adoption, prospective adopters have the option of using an adoption agency or a private adoption attorney.[31] With an agency, the entire adoption process is curated by the organization. Agency employees conduct the home study for parents and organize parent trainings. Moreover, the institution recruits a pool of potential birth mothers and asks the pregnant women to choose among their registered clients. This takes the onus off of the prospective parents from having to continually place advertisements and field inquiries. If the adoption is an open one, the agency helps facilitate contact between the birth and adoptive parent(s) and handles the finalization of the adoption. In other words, the agency is more of a full-service model, whereas in independent attorney adoption the adoptive parents piece together services from multiple venues. One attorney glibly described the difference as "one-stop shopping" versus "ordering à la carte."

With the à la carte approach, parents have more consumer leeway but also face more risks because clients shoulder the burden of arranging and paying for advertisements to solicit prospective birth mothers. In my interview with Irene, an adoption attorney, I asked her what the typical budget looked like, and she replied:

> We've had clients who do it themselves and do it very minimally, maybe $300 to $400 a month. If you do it right, sometimes you can find all sorts of discounts, specials, and you know. So you can really put a lot of thought in how you spend your money, and you can really make your money go. There are some advertising specialists who say we recommend a minimum budget of $1,000 a month or $2,000 a month. There are some people who say, "You know, why are you going to do $1,000 a month and have to do it month after month. Why don't you just spend $10,000 or $12,000 and place sixty ads at once?" For some people it works; that's how you can have it that some people can have a placement immediately. If they are putting sixty ads in. But what if nothing happens? What I advise my clients is [that] you can spend that money, but you still have to have enough to do it again, and you still have to have enough to do an adoption.

While attorney-led adoption definitely has increased risks in terms of spending money without a guaranteed return, there are also benefits because the independent approach offers customers greater autonomy when recruiting and vetting potential birth mothers. At one adoption conference, the attorney was quite straightforward about these potential advantages, proclaiming, "With an agency, you are being chosen. With independent, you choose your own child."

Unlike adoption social workers who tend to eschew the shopping metaphor, or use it and then assure clients that they are operating aboveboard, adoption attorneys showed far less reticence employing the market metaphor. As Briggs's historical analysis reminds us, from the 1970s onward, adoption "became increasingly like a consumer market" for parents and less like a solution for children in need, particularly among attorneys and private facilitators capitalizing on the "free-wheeling, market-driven private system."[32] Casting themselves as the antidote to a broken public child welfare system, independent adoption facilitators framed their services as offering "a more efficient route to a healthy white baby."[33]

Emphasizing this consumer autonomy, at one information session a lawyer proclaimed, "When doing private you have a constituency of one." Another attorney spoke of the freedom prospective clients would have to continue infertility treatments (a practice that is often discouraged by adoption agencies) and still pursue domestic adoption. She said, "In private, you can do whatever you want. But agencies have different views about the practice. In private, it is up to you." In other words, independent private adoption attorneys frame their services through a free-market model, underscoring how a customer is always right approach may benefit prospective clients. As long as the courts certify that the parents have met the legal thresholds to adopt, the rest of the practice is "up to you."

In independent adoption, there does not appear to be the same struggle between balancing the child and parent clients. In fact, at a conference panel titled "Successful Domestic Adoption," one of the attorneys identified this single-minded focus as a benefit of independent adoption. She explained, "The agency represents the birth mother, the adopted child, and the adoptive parent," but in contrast, "the attorney represents only you, so there is no conflict of interest." She advised that if the prospective adoptive parents are the type of people who "know what we want, and we wanted it yesterday," then she advises that attorney-led adoption may be a better path.

In line with this customer-centric approach, several adoption attorneys emphasized the consumer latitude afforded by independent adoption. For example, during the question-and-answer session after a conference session on domestic adoption, one audience member asked whether the attorney had an age cut-off when taking on new clients. Recall how an adoption social worker disclosed that she turned down a sixty-five-year-old woman who wanted to adopt an infant, out of concerns for the child. However, age was not a factor for the attorney who responded that it was "not a problem." She then proudly spoke of helping a seventy-two-year-old man partnered with a forty-seven-year-old woman adopt a baby, continuing, "So if anyone is younger than seventy-two, it's not a problem."

Beyond assuring potential clients that age would not be an issue (at least for the attorney), during these sessions many underscored that in attorney-led adoption, prospective parents would be empowered to prioritize their wants. For example, several attorneys warned audience members that domestic adoption agencies often do not have an adequate supply of healthy White infants and that the waiting times can be excruciatingly long. In another session designed to explain the differences between independent and agency domestic adoptions, one attorney advised, "If you are working with an agency, it is important to find out: Do they place children that you are looking for? Do they place babies? Do they place White babies if that is what you are looking for?" Others emphasized that in attorney-led adoption there would be more latitude to turn down a birth mother situation. In contrast to the independent option in which the customer is always right, one attorney warned potential clients that they should learn an agency's policies before signing on: "If you're working with an agency, find out about their waiting list. Do you get put on the bottom if you turn down a situation?"

Imagine the following scenario when prospective parents might turn down a birth mother situation. A pregnant woman sees a classified ad in the newspaper placed by a would-be adoptive parent. The pregnant woman musters up the courage to call the 1-800 number listed on the advertisement. She and the hopeful mother have a short but pleasant conversation, and the pregnant woman decides that this is the family she would like to place with. Her heart becomes set on this family, and she starts to imagine her child growing up with them as parents. Later the attorney representing the prospective adoptive parents calls the woman and asks her to fill out an information sheet and sign the medical release forms. During the interchange with the lawyer, the pregnant woman discloses that she used heroin during the early stages of pregnancy before she knew she was pregnant. Knowing that this is a deal breaker for the adoptive parents, the lawyer tells the pregnant woman that the match will not work. The pregnant woman has to start over and reach out to another solicitation and risk being rejected again. The prospective adoptive parents do not face any repercussions for their decision beyond getting billed for the attorney's time, and they are free to wait for the next pregnant woman to respond to their ad.

Whereas adoption workers often try to juggle the multiple constituencies of children, birth mothers, and adoptive parents, the role of the adoption attorney is to solely represent the adoptive parents' wishes. One forthright attorney stated, "We encourage you to turn down a situation that is not right for you." Another cautioned that a downside of working with an adoption agency is that "some agencies think you should take whatever child is offered to you" and warned audience members that these agency representatives "may not do their due diligence, so to speak," and may overlook some potentially serious issues with the child. Echoing this consumer choice, another lawyer advised her audience, "You can turn one [birth mother] down without institutional wrath." One particularly vocal attorney reminded parents, "Remember, the agency works for the agency."

I spoke with Christine, an adoption attorney, about this scenario, and what happens should her clients decide to back out because of concerns about the child's medical profile. She describes how it is her job to call the expectant woman and decline the placement. She points out the irony that the clients who ask her to do this are often the same ones who will later "whine" to her and lament that they did not receive any responses from their advertisements. Christine elaborates:

Me: So medical issues are coming up more and more. Whose job is it to call the expectant woman and say, thanks but no thanks?
Christine: Mine.
Me: That must be a very hard conversation.
Christine: I hate it. The whining I-didn't-get-any-calls conversation is just distasteful. I really don't like having to tell birth mothers, unless she has come to the table with dirty hands. I feel badly but not as badly, [if she says something like,] "Right, I forgot to tell you I have been using methamphetamines for months." Unless

there has been a basis where she has been lying. What happens more often is that she has been really upfront and forthcoming, but then the adoptive parents freak out for some reason.

Even though private adoption attorneys are more likely than not-for-profit adoption agency employees to focus on clients' autonomy as consumers, agency workers convey a similar, albeit slightly watered down, message regarding turning down a situation. One adoption agency employee described the early stages of the application process as "working with you to design parameters and comfort zones" so the agency can "identify children who meet that criteria." Another social worker explained the process as, "You are going to talk with your counselor about what your comfort level is, and you are only going to be matched with children that match your situation." Likewise, at a third information session, the adoption professional also depicted the process in direct marketing terms. She emphasized that choosing her agency gives the parents access to their vast network, stating, "We can start marketing your profile to our network to locate birth mother situations for you." In this regard, adoption providers frame their roles not only as social workers but also as marketers and matchmakers who recruit expectant women carrying desirable children.

Although domestic adoption agencies frame the process as a client-centered and consumer-friendly process, prospective parents do not have the same leeway to turn down a referral as they would using a private attorney. But even using an adoption agency, prospective parents are assured that they will have some flexibility to decline a situation, especially if new medical information comes to light. During the question-and-answer session at an information session an audience member asked, "So say we are matched up with a birth mother and their family. And how do I say this? If they pick us, and we decide that they are not a good match for us, how does that work?"

The presenter responded:

It will depend on why you think she's not a good match. [When you sign up,] you are telling us what you are willing to accept in a birth parent's background. So when a birth mom picks you, all of those reasons should match up why she picked you. If you decide there is something there that she's not—that you're not connecting with, that is something that we address. But certainly as an agency we have a right to say, "You know what? It doesn't seem like a good fit for our agency, and you can't follow through with the adoption process anymore in general."

Perhaps most notable about the presenter's response is that she leaves open the possibility that the clients would no longer be eligible to adopt via her organization. If private adoption was solely based on maximizing profits, agencies would work with applicants regardless. But in this case, social workers negotiate between the needs of the prospective parents and the birth parents.

Continuing with her answer, the presenter finished her response by reiterating that applicants are given a good deal of choice at the start of the process, and these desires are honored, especially if new information comes to light. She continued, "If the birth mom [is] at the hospital, and it turns out that she smoked marijuana, and you were like, 'Hey, we didn't say that we would accept a birth mom who smoked marijuana,' that's a different scenario because it is not something that you agreed to in the beginning." So rather than being able to do "whatever you want," as in the case of private attorney adoption, adoption agencies provide a consumer guarantee such that prospective parents are given a great deal of consumer control at the beginning of the selection process, but once these parameters are set, parents are expected to abide by the initial specified criteria.

I want to emphasize that it is relatively rare for adoptive parents to walk away from a baby; it is far more common for a pregnant woman to change her mind once the baby is born. Since women cannot sign away their maternal rights until after the birth, there is the possibility that the adoption will fall through. In adoption circles, this is often called "a change of heart." At one information meeting the social worker estimated that about 50 percent of the pregnant women who contact the agency decide to parent, characterizing this figure as "the reality of domestic adoption." Because of the risks associated with a domestic adoption falling through, some prospective adopters lean toward international adoption. Cognizant of these concerns, some international adoption agencies play up the fact that children available via transnational adoption are legally free for adoption, meaning that the biological parents' rights have already been severed. For example, I attended one information session at Global Rainbow that purported that one benefit of international adoption was "all of the children are orphans without parents." A website of another China-specific adoption agency proclaims "100% of the children adopted from China are abandoned," and since "abandonment is illegal in China," biological parents do not leave any identifying information. The agency goes on to assure prospective parents that they will "acquire all legal rights for their child without worry that the birth parents will try to reclaim the child afterwards."

Although this aspect of international adoption is framed as a positive consideration, there can be additional risks to this form of family building since oftentimes there is little available social and medical history about the children. These risks are increasing as the demographic profile of available children shifts from healthy infants to children with greater medical needs. Thus, a greater number of prospective parents may be concerned as to whether they will be able to decline a referral. In the following section I describe how adoption workers discuss turning down a child and how they enact this type of emotional labor.

## Declining a Referral in International Adoption

In international adoption, rather than have a first mother/birth mother choose from a pool of parent profiles, parents and children are matched by a third party, either a government worker or an adoption agency employee. This process is advertised as being more fair and predictable since it is based on a queue, rather than the discretion of a woman making an adoption plan. One presenter emphasized the benefits of this more-standardized allocation process, describing the system as akin to standing in line at the deli counter. She said, "You get in a line, and when your number comes up, you go and get your child." Another underscored the egalitarian approach, stating, "You put your time in, you wait, and a referral comes to you." A third described it as "a matter of time before you're first on the queue."

When parents' "number comes up," they are usually given what is known as a referral. An adoption social worker explained what this entails: "In most countries, once a child has been matched with your family, you will receive what we call a referral for that child. And the amount of information you will receive about your matched child will really vary from program to program." She continued, "In general you can expect to receive, at the very least, a picture or two and recent medical records and just some basic information about your child's background."

Although the health information greatly varies depending on how much is known about the child's background, it often includes basic measurements on head circumference, estimated age, and height and weight so that parents can have these data evaluated by pediatricians specializing in international adoption for clues about the child's growth and development. Many international programs also test their children for HIV and Hepatitis B. The social worker assured her audience, "The testing is excellent. [We've] never had a child who is negative be positive."

At the "International Adoption 101" conference session, the presenter advised her audience that it is "important to have an idea where countries are trending," and she forewarned that for those interested in adopting a healthy infant girl from China, the wait time could now approach eight years. She then transitioned to talking about her organization's special-needs adoption programs by stating, "You are going to hear me talk a lot about older and waiting kids." Another said, "We ask families at the start of the process to think about their ability to parent a waiting child."

Often, adopting a waiting child is framed as a benefit to clients because they are able to adopt more quickly and sometimes for less money. A representative from Forever Family urged listeners to consider a waiting child, predominantly framing it as an expedient method of family building. She stated, "We really do encourage families to think about waiting children for several reasons. One is your own needs. If you want to become parents sooner rather than later, it is usually a much shorter process." Although meeting the needs of the parent-client is positioned as the foremost consideration, the speaker secondarily mentions that "it is usually the waiting children who are the most in need of families." Having grounded the issue as a child-welfare practice, she pivoted to reframe it in terms of the supply of children: "You just heard me talk about the very limited number of infants and toddlers in need of adoption. The need really is for older children, sibling groups, and children with a whole range of needs."

Although adoption providers emphasize the potential benefits associated with adopting a waiting child, international adoption agencies minimize their liability by recommending that parents have referrals evaluated by pediatricians specializing in international adoption. In some regard, these physicians perform a service that used to be left to the jurisdiction of adoption social workers who prided themselves on their ability to reduce the risk of an unsatisfactory placement by expertly designing kinship through testing and regulation.[34] However, with the referral process largely in the hands of overseas officials, a cottage industry has emerged. Kristi Brian describes this reliance on medical specialists who, for a fee of up to $600, will read the medical charts and watch any accompanying videos of the child and provide an assessment of the accuracy of the provided health information.[35] In this caveat emptor, adoptive parents are encouraged to see themselves as savvy consumers making informed consumer choices. For example, one presenter said, "You will have the opportunity to review all of the child's social and medical information thoroughly before making a decision. We encourage you to have the information provided to you evaluated by a physician familiar with international adoption. For referrals of special-needs children, we actually require this."

Some adoption agency representatives assure prospective clients that they will be given more than enough time to consider the referral before making a decision, even for programs known for placing healthy children. As Sara Dorow describes in her study of transnational adoption from China, the referral of a specific child to waiting families is the moment that "makes the child *real.*"[36] Receiving the referral also entails a decision: the prospective parents have to decide whether to commit to raising this specific child. This process can be understandably fraught, since "this often means scrutinizing the photo and the scant medical information for signs of trouble."[37] Dorow goes on to describe one couple, who after much agonizing, had turned down the first referral of a toddler whose head circumference was thought to be too small and was granted a second referral of a more acceptable child.

Although it is difficult to know how often this happens, anecdotally I have heard several parents describe having to make these agonizing decisions. For example, I once met a White couple at a playground who had adopted from Korea. Since our children were about the same age, we started chatting, and in the course of our interchange I disclosed that I too had been adopted from Korea. Even from our brief interaction, it was evident how much he and his wife loved their son. Somewhere in the course of the conversation we started talking about my research, which I broadly framed as the question, how are adoptive parents and children matched with each other? The father proceeded to tell me about how hard it was to qualify for the Korean program because of the country's rigid health restrictions and how they were grateful that they were able to apply. Perhaps feeling reflective that his son on the playground could have gone to another family had he and his wife not qualified for the program, the father told me that they had almost turned down the referral based on concerns about their son's head circumference. Watching the little boy play with my daughter, I could not help thinking that the process of making a transnational adoptive family was a unique mixture of fate and bureaucracy,[38] but the parent client ultimately has the final say as to whether to commit to the adoption.

Notably, during the information sessions, adoption workers affirm the mentality that prospective parents should feel free to prudently debate a referral. For example, during a presentation for Kid Connection's Ethiopia adoption program, the social worker promoted the country "as a great program in terms of the time and flexibility you have once you have been matched with a referral." Then she attempted to balance the conflicting needs of children and parents, stating, "Certainly, we consider the process in terms of wanting to do what's in the best interest of the child so having a family sit on a referral for four months while they consider whether that child is a good fit for their family is not in the best interest of the child." But in the next breath she assured prospective parents that they would be given ample time to make a decision, continuing, "However, if you do need several weeks to talk with your doctor to ask some questions and to find out that information before moving forward, that we definitely can do."

Although turning down a referral and essentially refusing to adopt a specific child can be an emotionally charged decision, social workers assure parents that it is an acceptable consumer choice. As Brian observed in her study of Korean adoptions, workers often assuaged prospective parents' concerns, underscoring that the adoption agency would not judge clients should they decide to pass on multiple children "until they found the one that seemed 'just right for them.'"[39] For example, the presenter from Baby Talk told her audience, "If you get the file of a child that has been matched to you and for whatever reason you or your doctors review it and aren't comfortable with something in the file, you are never required to accept the referral of a child." Similarly, the speaker at Synergy Adoption Services labored to shield attendees from any guilt associated with turning down a referral, comforting them by saying that should they have to refuse one child, in the end, "You get the child meant for you."

In other words, despite the tension between serving the child and the parent clients, adoption social workers seem to prioritize the market realities by guaranteeing a level of consumer choice to prospective parents. The take-away is that clients signing on with their agency will be able to exercise a good deal of autonomy and will not be required to adopt a child they do not wish to. This "customer is always right" mentality is delivered in a supportive tone as social workers soothe the concerns of audience members. For example, I was one of maybe a dozen people in the room who had taken the time on a Saturday morning to attend an adoption information session. After going through the different country programs they offered, the social worker discussed the referral process. She emphasized that, "For whatever reason, if it doesn't feel like this is a good fit, then you can say no." Her message was one of unconditional support as she managed the prospective parents' fears about adoption. "As hard as it is, as sad as it is to walk away," she continued, "if it doesn't feel right, it doesn't feel right. It is okay to say no. This is your life. This is your family. You have to decide if this is the child for you."

Not only do adoption workers employ a strategy of exonerating prospective parents of guilt should they decline a referral, but workers also stress that waiting clients will be unduly penalized. For example, one social worker said, "If your family chooses not to accept a referral, you will be placed back on the waiting list." Another reassured potential customers, "You don't go to the back of the line. You stay at the front of the line." A third emphasized, "You can always turn that file back in and get back in the queue to wait for another child to be matched to you. And you don't move to the end of the line; you go back to your place in line as far as waiting for that match." She continued, "If you get a referral that you are not comfortable with, and you choose not to accept the child, can you go back and wait for another child? That is definitely a yes." In other words, the presenters stress that even when turning down a child who is deemed unacceptable, prospective parents maintain their status as consumers who have the right to exercise a degree of autonomy without penalty.

The likelihood of turning down a referral was more prevalent for parents who were considering adopting from Russia and Eastern Europe.[40] One reason for this trend may be that children adopted from these regions face greater developmental delays.[41] Prospective adoptive parents and the physicians who evaluate the medical information in the adoption referral may be more aware of this phenomenon, potentially leading these parents to be more cautious and reject children that seem medically risky. Describing this situation, one agency social worker warned her audience, "Most of my Russia families turn down a couple of referrals. Some don't . . . but it is very common to turn down referrals, which is very difficult." A provider from a different adoption agency echoed this trend, stating, "Whoever is planning to adopt from Russia, be prepared that you may receive a referral that you have to decline. It doesn't happen all of the time, but it does happen." She continued by saying that should the prospective parents refuse to adopt the referred child, "You will simply wait for another referral."

By positioning the process of choosing or declining a child as simply waiting for another referral, adoption providers send the message that in this consumer process an identified child can be passed over in favor of a child that better fits the parents' criteria. One social worker even informed audience members that should they travel to a country to meet with their referred child and have second thoughts, they could potentially pursue adopting a different child on the same trip. She detailed, "After referral, you can go to the country if you want to go see the child before you say yes. Spend some time together. Maybe you go to see the child and see [another] one that meets your eye. That could happen too."

While some agencies have a more blasé approach to turning down referrals, other international adoption agency representatives clearly draw a line between acceptable and unacceptable reasons for doing so. For example, at one information meeting the presenter stated, "The only reason that you can decline a referral is for a medical reason. You can't say that you wish that he had blond hair or that her eyes were blue." Similarly, at another information session the social worker explained,

> It really depends on why you turn down a referral. If you turn down a referral because your doctor says it looks like this child has fetal alcohol syndrome or a heart issue, I think that is very legitimate. If you turn down a child because his skin isn't the right color or you just don't like the looks of him, the placement agency wouldn't be so happy. So as long as you have a real legitimate reason.

This explanation is telling for several reasons. First, notice how the presenter oscillates between the discourses of social service and customer service, explaining the differences between "legitimate" and "illegitimate" reasons for declining a referral. From a social service perspective, the presenter underscores that parents are not given absolute freedom to turn down a child. In other words, even though adoption providers frame the application process in terms of finding the right fit for parents, they also communicate they will impose limits on consumers' choices should the need arise.

## Money Matters

The moment when money changes hands can be particularly fraught with tension because it is during this instance that the line between child welfare and child commodification is the most blurred. Rather than frame adoption as paying upwards of $20,000 for a child, presenters often couch the costs of adopting in terms of paying for services. In light of these significant fees, one organization warned audience members to be wary of competitors who promise low fees or wait times because these are often "too good to be true." She assured prospective clients that their fees are "really in the mix of the rest of agencies." Another agent went as far as to disclose to audience members that her organization does its own reconnaissance to guarantee customers that their fees are in line with those of its competitors. She stated, "Once a year we survey the top ten agencies in the United States and take a look at the fees that they charge for the country programs that they offer. We make sure that we stay within that middle or lower middle range for agency adoptions."

Many presenters used the strategy of couching pricing discussions in terms of paying for services, so there is no association with baby buying. In domestic adoption, for example, prospective adoptive parents often pay some of the fees associated with the expectant woman's pregnancy, up to the limits allowed by law in the placing mother's state of residence. These fees can include not only prenatal care and maternity clothes but also lost wages because of pregnancy, rent, and groceries, adding upwards of several thousand dollars to the cost of the adoption.[42]

To prevent direct monetary exchanges between would-be birth mothers and adoptive parents, some agencies have parents pay into a general pool for the birth mother. One social worker explained this policy, stating, "You are not paying money directly to the birth parents. We feel that it is not a good thing to get money involved in that relationship." Another facilitator described how the adoption agency acts as the middleman to allocate the funds, emphasizing, "[We] don't want to appear to have a link between money and placement. No insinuations of baby buying. We want the agency to handle the disbursements." Even though adoption agencies charge thousands of dollars for the services, it is ironic that when it comes to giving money directly to women relinquishing children, money is not supposed to change hands.

International adoption agencies employ a similar strategy, acting as the intermediaries and shielding adoptive parents from monetary transactions that have the potential to insinuate baby buying. For example, parents adopting from China are required to make a $5,000 "donation" to the orphanage housing their child.[43] Some agencies have parents carry the cash in $100 bills directly to the orphanage the day they meet their future daughters and sons, but other organizations tout their practice of collecting the money up front so parents do not have to travel with so much cash or take part in a crude exchange of "donating" cash for their child. Describing this practice, one presenter stated:

With China there is a $5,000 donation fee. Whereas most families are required to bring that to China and carry that in cash on their person, we really think that makes families vulnerable. And we also don't want that transaction to be taking place when you are meeting your child for the first time. So we transfer all of that money to our office in China and take care of paying all of these fees so your first focus is on meeting your child.

As I was conducting my fieldwork during the height of the recession, the high cost of private adoption was even more of a concern. For example, during an information session at Statewide, when it was time to discuss the financial component, the social worker acknowledged that it is "no small section to go over." She said that most adoptions cost between $15,000 and $30,000 and that "this is a real challenge for some people." Another social worker attempted to soothe audience members' indignation as to why adoption is so expensive. Notice how she works to ground the transaction in child welfare in stating, "Before I started working here, I wondered why it was so expensive to adopt because there are so many children who need good homes and good families." She provided a breakdown of costs, making sure to frame the money spent in terms of the consumption of services, not the commodification of children. "I like this slide because it kind of breaks down all of these different areas of where you are paying. You are paying [for the] services of working with agencies, gathering information, mailing things to us."

Despite her attempt to delineate costs, it was evident that prospective parents were unclear about the breakdown in fees and that this information would be an integral criterion in their decision-making process. For example, at one information session on transnational adoptions an audience member was trying to get a handle on the out-of-pocket costs and trying to discern what was included in the multithousand-dollar program fee for each country versus additional travel costs. He inquired, "I am a little confused. I was looking on your website. The adoption from Uruguay[44] says $14,000, but you said it can range to $35,000." The social worker responds that the $14,000 is just the program cost that "goes for the program itself. Care in country, proper legal process." The interlocutor followed up, "So in other words, we need to figure in for airfare for two of us to go over, three of us to go back, plus all lodging and etcetera in country." One could almost see him doing the mental calculations in his head as he asked, "But the interpreter in the country is included in the international program costs?" At this point, the presenter was a bit flustered as she searched for the information but failed to find it in her notes. Before she could respond, another audience member piped up with an additional question: "We are going to adopt a waiting child. There is an additional donation to the orphanage. Does [the program cost] include this as well?" A third chimed in, wondering whether a hypothetical child with a lazy eye "would be fast tracked."

One thing that is so interesting about this exchange is that it shows that solely framing adoption costs in terms of a child-welfare process is an inadequate marketing strategy. Prospective adoptive parents take the time to attend these sessions because they are seriously considering adoption, and they need all of the relevant information about characteristics of children, waiting times, and costs before they can select a provider and move forward. So when agency representatives are unprepared and uninformed, the strategy can backfire, as seemed to be the case when the speaker was caught off guard. She dodged these questions by saying, "That is one of the nice things about our agency. We are a pretty big agency, so we have staff members who specialize in each area."

These applicants are about to embark on an arduous and expensive process, and many audience members were clearly frustrated with such a noncommittal response. It would have likely been a more effective marketing strategy to position these audience members as autonomous consumers and to arm them with the information they wanted. These prospective parents would then have had license to prioritize their needs and move forward with the decision-making process. Only at this juncture can would-be parents sort through their many options, weighing the age, race, and health characteristics of available children with concerns about costs, waiting times, and openness. As the next chapter details, these questions are not easy, and adoption providers recognize this. Rather than overwhelm potential paying customers on their first meeting, many spokespersons allude to these decisions in terms of "fit." This euphemism does the emotion work of assuring would-be adoptive parents that their wishes will be respected and honored.

But what happens when prospective adoptive parents are encouraged to see themselves as consumers? How does this mind-set shape how they approach winnowing the field from all available children to a suitable son or daughter? As one social worker advised her audience, the chance of being successfully matched with a child in a timely manner depends on "how open you are to risk and race." Another encouraged prospective parents to consider "what country is right for you," elaborating that the decision often "depends on what you are looking for in a child. What you are looking for in a culture, in race, in the risks that we talked about." The next chapter unpacks this connection between race and risk, arguing that adoption providers push White parents toward transracial adoption by framing it as a savvy market strategy.

# 3

# Transracial Adoption as a Market Calculation

I am at an information meeting sponsored by Statewide Adoption Agency, a large placement agency that facilitates domestic and international programs. Besides me, there are five people in attendance: two heterogamous couples and the single woman that I mention in Chapter 2. As is often the case, I am the only non-White person present. The social worker asks us to introduce ourselves and share whether we are leaning toward a particular adoption program. At the time of my fieldwork, Statewide offered nine programs including Russia, Kazakhstan, Ethiopia, and a domestic infant program, so this information is helpful so that the presenter can cater her pitch to prospective clients.

One of the women, Lydia, introduces herself, saying that she and her male partner are "leaning toward Ethiopia." However, she qualifies this statement, lamenting, "but our options are limited." Later during the question-and-answer session, I learn that Lydia is forty-seven years old, and she and her forty-six-year-old partner are long-term cohabitants but not legally married. They want to adopt internationally, but their relationship status makes it difficult, since many countries have marriage requirements. They disclose that they were advised by another adoption agency not to get married, because some countries impose a minimum threshold for length of marriage before they can adopt, and they are likely to age out of eligibility if they wait that long. Since Russia and Kazakhstan were still accepting unmarried applicants, it is notable that they had ruled out these countries, even though through these venues they could presumably find a White child who would racially match them both.

Lydia and her partner's decision to "lean toward" Ethiopia brings up the question of why White parents adopt across race. Moreover, how do adoption workers help prospective adoptive parents arrive at this decision? Transracial adoption renders families' adoptive status immediately visible and creates complex issues of racial identity and belonging.[1] It would make sense that White prospective adoptive parents would want to avoid this public scrutiny and the additional responsibilities associated with raising children of color. From prior research, we know that few non-White adoptive parents cross the color line when adopting, and these parents instead opt to create same-race families.[2] So why does the proportion of White transracial adoptive parents continue to grow and what is the role of the adoption worker in advocating for these types of placements?

Some attribute the rising number of transracial adoptive placements as evidence of altruistic benevolence on the part of White parents who were moved by the plight of orphaned children, beginning with transnational adoption from Korea. Anthropologist Eleana Kim argues that the circulation of these children served as potent symbols of "depoliticized figures of humanitarianism," noting that "Korean orphans provided opportunities for intimate diplomacy through international adoption."[3] Likewise, historian Arissa Oh traces the rise of intercountry adoption, outlining how Americans' enthusiasm for overseas adoption stemmed from a mix of idealistic and altruistic motivations. She writes, "Generally speaking, adoptive families adopted for religious or humanitarian reasons" and notes that Korean adoption was seen as the embodiment of a virtuous practice and "an affirmation not only of the adoptive parents' Christian goodness but also of their Americanness."[4]

However, even with its humanitarian roots, Kim argues that "stratifications of race and gender are unmistakably reproduced in transnational adoption," stating that adoptions from Korea grew in popularity because they filled a niche for racially flexible Asian children.[5] Oh details how, as demand for overseas adoption grew, the success of the 1960s Korea program "provided a template of sort," as adoption agencies "expanded their operations to other countries by replicating or adapting the methods they had devised there."[6] While Oh underscores that it is an oversimplification to say that Korean adoption "originated as a humanitarian movement and then transformed into a market," she argues that, "by the 1970s, it had become an industry that had largely moved from supply-driven to demand-driven."

Building on the previous chapters where I argue that private adoption serves as a type of marketplace where child welfare and child commodification have an uneasy coexistence and that adoption social workers use strategies of emotion work to ease parents into a consumer mind-set, in this chapter I argue that the push for transracial adoption among workers can be better understood in the context of market demands. The chapter is organized around three central themes. The first section examines how adoption workers categorize their clients' motivations for adopting. They detail how infertility and, more broadly, fertility barriers are the usual catalysts for adoption-seeking behavior. Considering that many applicants may have first tried to conceive a biological child, adoption workers recognize that many prospective clients start out wanting a baby.[7] But since White babies are in limited supply,[8] adoption workers must help guide prospective adopters through uncertain terrain, urging them to reconsider their priorities—and that they may have to give up some of them—to obtain a son or daughter.

The goal of the second section of the chapter is to deepen the nuance of the market metaphor by illustrating how the adoption market is an assortative process that ranks applicants by their family structure. Adoption workers have the distressing assignment of communicating the bad news that not all applicants have the same choices available to them. Based on country-imposed restrictions, White heterogamous married couples tend to have the most options, but even these high-status adopters are further winnowed by their age and health.

While family structure is a key variable in terms of whether prospective parents even qualify for a program, as I learned from adoption workers, it is just one of the many other factors at hand in determining the eligibility and allure of an adoption pathway. Thus, the third part of the chapter identifies and details the other market variables that come into play. Adoption practitioners "sell" or advocate for transracial placements because they see race as a variable to be ranked, prioritized, and flexed. In terms of domestic placements, adoption workers convey the message that transracial adoption can be an expedient choice that improves parents' chances of being selected by a prospective birth mother in a timelier fashion. Additionally, social workers communicate that overseas transracial adoption can be a strategy to maximize the likelihood of receiving a healthy infant or child.

## Coming to Adoption: The Next Step Along the Way

Throughout my interviews with adoption social workers and attorneys, the connection between infertility and adoption was ever-present. Erin confirms this correlation, detailing, "Without a doubt, most families in my experience, do not come simply because they want to supply a home for a child." Similarly, Abigail testifies that most of her clients first try to have children "the old-fashioned way." Jennifer, an adoption caseworker who has worked in private adoption for well over a decade, reiterates the association between infertility and private adoption. She attests, "I think that we've been pretty safe in saying that over the years, 80 to 90 percent of families have an experience with infertility."

For heterogamous couples, if they have the financial resources,[9] many devote a lot of time and money riding what Sylvia calls the "IVF train." Having built a counseling practice working with infertile couples, she describes clients' mind-sets as they come to adoption: "Most people will continue going and going and going, and after they have been through all of the different things they have been through, they are burned out." Perhaps having read and evaluated fertility clinics' reports and filled out reams of health insurance paperwork, by the time that some parents enter the adoption marketplace, they are looking for quick results. Sylvia recounts, "They want to be told to go here and press this button, so to speak, and you'll get a kid." She continues:

> People see adoption as getting the kid. They don't see it as this lifelong family-building alternative, which has some extra layers, some predictable kinds of experiences. What people do, in my experience, is they have this idea of the [biological] child they are going to have, and then they move away from that in what's the next closest thing, what's the next closest thing, what's the next closest thing. At a certain point, often when they turn to adoption, it is often that all bets are off, and [they think], "Where are the kids, and how can I get one?"

Once these potential customers arrive at the door of the adoption agency or the lawyer's office, many adoption professionals tread lightly, engaging in a form of emotion work geared at helping prospective clients wrap their heads around adoption. For example, at Baby Talk's information session, the presenter acknowledged how the stress of infertility seeps into the adoption process. The speaker informed her audience that they would have to come to terms with their losses before fully immersing themselves in the process. She stated, "Adoption may not be your first choice, but it doesn't mean it's second best. Home study is an assessment for readiness, especially for those who have spent a lot of time in infertility treatments. You have spent a lot of time, a lot of money. I know that it is emotionally draining, financially draining."

Research shows that infertility is often a source of acute stress and shame for women who report feeling like failures in their quest to conceive and carry a child to term.[10] As Sylvia puts it, "People are feeling very wounded that they have to pay for what people do in the back of a car and have throwaway unwanted pregnancies." Michele, another clinician who specializes in working with infertile couples, describes how advances in assisted reproductive technologies (ARTs) incentivized her clients to exhaust their medical options before pursuing adoption. She states, "People have been staying in treatment longer, and I think they're more battered when they come in the [adoption agency] door." Echoing this thought, Lindsay, another adoption social worker with decades of experience, bluntly sums up her clients' predicament: "The majority of couples who come off the infertility [treatments], they are often going through hell."

Acknowledging the impact of infertility treatments at the information meetings, adoption social workers urge attendees to reconcile their feelings before they "come to adoption." With this in mind, the presenter at Baby Talk asked her audience to consider, "Are you really ready to adopt? Have you grieved your infertility? Are you excited about adoption?" She warned prospective applicants, "I can usually tell within the first ten minutes of a meeting [whether clients are ready]," admonishing them that they cannot have the attitude of, "Well, fertility [treatments] didn't work; this is kind of the next step along the way."

Despite this pep talk, it was clear that many social workers were cognizant that they faced an uphill battle getting clients to embrace the adoption process. Prospective adopters were impatient to become parents and wanted to adopt as quickly and as inexpensively as possible. When I asked adoption workers what prospective adoptive parents want to know when they first approach an agency or attorney, without fail they discussed parents' initial focus on costs and duration. Christine, an adoption attorney, summarizes her clients' mind-set, saying, "So now they are even older and have spent more money and are perhaps more anxious." In addition, Patricia, an adoption social worker, discusses this phenomenon: "Their initial questions on the phone are how much is it going to cost and how long will it take." Echoing these sentiments almost verbatim, Nora states, "They want to know how much it will cost and how long it will take."

Although adoption professionals may see adoption as a separate process with its own time line, for those who just went through the ordeal of infertility, the two processes are not so easily compartmentalized. Patricia describes her clients' state of mind when they first come through the door:

> I think what we find is families are lumping all of their experiences together. They don't necessarily realize they are doing that, but they will begin to panic or have lots of anxiety. Let's say their home study has been approved for maybe three months, and they are very anxiety ridden. And when we talk to them it's, "But I went through five years of infertility." So they lump it all together.

Perhaps aware of how assisted reproductive technologies may have failed some of their potential clients, during the information sessions many alluded to adoption's "100 percent success rate" as a selling point. For example, Tracy describes to me how she emphasizes at the information sessions that adoption can be more of a sure thing:

The majority of our families have gone through the infertility process and have been through the maybe–maybe not, 50–50 chances.
They come to an information meeting, and we go, "There is a 100
percent chance that at the end of all this, you will have a child." And
they hear that statistic and they say, "You know what, I am done with
the shots; I am done with the invasive procedures. I don't want to be
told where, how, and when to do it. I am done with this road."

The expectation that prospective adoptive parents had undergone infertility treatment was so strong that some adoption professionals were skepti-
cal of preferential adopters who wanted to adopt for reasons outside of
fertility barriers. Many caseworkers in charge of screening initial applications spoke of "red flags" that went up when prospective adoptive parents
mentioned other reasons for wanting to adopt such as a religious motivation
or wanting to "rescue" a child. For example, adoption social worker Penelope
discusses her experience approving new applicants, stating, "Among some
people on the committee there was this disbelief about people who just
wanted to adopt who didn't come from infertility. There was this suspicion:
Why would they want to do that? That's weird." Whereas it was seen as
"weird" or potentially suspect to want to adopt for ideological reasons, in
contrast, infertility was positioned as the most valid and common motivation for adopting.

It is important to note that some prospective adoptive parents who may
not have diagnosed impaired fecundity in the medical sense also face substantial barriers to biological reproduction.[11] Gay male couples and single
fathers by choice face inherent obstacles to fatherhood since they do not have
uteruses and therefore cannot gestate a baby on their own.[12] Additionally,
lesbian couples, older women with "aging eggs," transgender women, single
mothers by choice, and those with complex medical histories hindering biological reproduction also face what I broadly refer to as fertility barriers.
Along with infertile heterogamous couples, people in these categories are the
bread and butter of adoption providers.

While single applicants and homogamous might not fit the medical definition of impaired fecundity, because of their limited choices, many adoption providers often speak about single applicants and same-sex couples in
the same breath, equating them to heterogamous couples experiencing infertility. For example, in one interview Alyssa equates infertile couples with
nontraditional parents, stating, "I would say three-quarters of them fall into
the camp of we are gay or lesbian, so we can't conceive ourselves or we are
having issues with infertility or secondary infertility—or single people."

Similarly, I spoke with Irene, an attorney specializing in private infant
adoption, about her clients' motivations. Trying to get a handle on the
proportion of prospective adoptive parents coming from a background of

infertility, I asked her about her clients' motivations. Most notable about the exchange is that Irene characterizes infertility beyond the medical definition, expanding the diagnosis to encompass prospective parents who are too old to get pregnant without intervention and those for whom it would be medically inadvisable to try to conceive:

> Me: Would you say that infertility is one of the major drivers for why people come to see you?
> Irene: Yes.
> Me: Would you say more than half?
> Irene: Yes.
> Me: Close to all?
> Irene: Sometimes people don't try. I have a couple right now who came to me. She's forty-nine; he's in his fifties. I don't think they are even trying. Sometimes they have a biological child who has a genetic problem. Sometimes someone has a history of breast cancer or ovarian cancer who didn't even try to conceive because they know their medical history prohibits it. So there are a lot of people like that. A lot of breast cancer survivors. They know adoption is going to be the route for them.

Irene does mention that occasionally she works with clients who want to adopt "just because," but she qualifies this statement adding that "generally those people adopt through the foster care system."

Irene's comments underscore how foster care is seen as a different entity spurred by different motivations. Since the average age of a child waiting to be adopted from foster care is seven-and-a-half years,[13] this segment of the adoption marketplace tends to attract a different demographic. Analyzing data from the National Survey of Adoptive Families, Hiromi Ishizawa and Kazuyo Kubo find that these foster care adoptive parents are more likely to be lower-income and have families blending biological and adopted children.[14] The latter suggests that infertility may not be a driving factor, and indeed, foster adoptive parents are the least likely to say that infertility was a motivation for adoption.[15]

Reflecting the inexorable link between fertility barriers and private adoption, many agencies have explicit policies requiring prohibiting the simultaneous use of ART and adopting. For example, the social worker at Loving Family told her audience, "We believe that in order for a successful adoption to occur, each family must go through a mourning process—mourning the loss of the dream of conceiving and having a biological child." Similarly, at Baby Talk's information meeting another social worker echoed the sentiment that to adopt, would-be parents have to be ready to move on from trying to have a biological child. "We really want you to choose adoption," she told her audience. "You need to be ready to go with adoption. You need to be done with your grieving. We want you to be 100 percent excited about adoption. If you are not excited, I think that you are probably not ready to move forward at this time."

Despite these rules, some of the social workers I interviewed shared their suspicions that clients often defy their guidelines. Olivia confides, "This has happened to me at least two or three times. People get pregnant during the process. Not all of my families are honest. I just found out that one of my families is pregnant. She didn't tell me, but I am pretty convinced that it is through treatment." While adoption professionals urge prospective parents to wholeheartedly "choose adoption," they do not have much leverage to prevent clients from using a two-pronged approach. Certainly, adoption workers can silently fume when applicants blatantly defy their policies, but as customer service representatives in a down market, they cannot afford to burn bridges. Olivia explains how there is little recourse should clients get pregnant: "We put them on hold just to make sure that it is a healthy pregnancy."

With the uncertainties that private adoption entails, it makes sense that some hopeful parents may try to hedge their bets by concurrently pursuing adoption and in vitro fertilization (IVF). Although IVF is expensive—with one cycle, without using donor eggs or sperm, costing about $12,400—and has only about a 30 percent success rate,[16] it can be cheaper than private adoption. In addition, White parents using ART do not have to contend with transracial adoption, since sperm and eggs from White donors are readily available.[17] Last, IVF allows hopeful parents to enter parenthood in a recognizable and uncomplicated way, uncluttered by having to contend with potential issues such as racial differences or open adoptions.

It is worth repeating that parents (like myself) who are able to conceive and carry a baby without intervention have the utter privilege of avoiding these expensive and draining processes. Even though many hopeful parents are emotionally fried and would like to push a button and "get their kid," to adopt they must enter into a new arena for kinship that requires, as Barbara Katz Rothman describes, "an exercise in thoughtful comparative shopping."[18] In other words, prospective parents are put in the position of de facto consumers in the adoption marketplace, tasked with gathering information to choose among services and programs with vastly different costs, waiting times, and profiles of children. Yet not all parents have the same market options, since the adoption marketplace stratifies not only children available for adoption but also the prospective parents looking to adopt.

## The Assortative Adoption Marketplace

From the 1940s on, modern adoption practice was stratified as social workers developed a canon of best practices to evaluate the fitness of prospective adoptive parents. These guidelines favored some applicants while excluding others. According to historian Julie Berebitsky, social workers held the belief that adoptive families "should parallel the 'natural' family as closely as possible," leading professionals to privilege married applicants in their twenties and thirties. These young married couples that could not have biological children were viewed as the most legitimate prospective parents, such that "by 1945, infertility became virtually the only readily acceptable reason for adopting a child."[19] This preference for younger applicants meant that older couples were at a disadvantage since social workers were reluctant to match them with a baby. Berebitsky describes how individuals over forty "were repeatedly urged to consider older children," since an older child would more closely mirror the child they would have had on their "own" had these late-in-life parents started their families at a more natural phase in the life course.[20] While this policy was grounded in social workers' deeply held philosophy about the importance of matching adoptive families according to the as-if-begotten model, as Berebitsky notes, the policy had useful practical implications since it funneled less desirable parents toward hard-to-place children.[21] The end result was that a stratified marketplace was created, where the most deserving parents got the most adoptable children.

If older married couples were at a disadvantage during this era, single applicants were even more so. Interestingly, single adoptive motherhood was more accepted in 1915 than in 1945. In the post–World War II era, the dominant ethos was that women (especially the White middle-class women that made up the bulk of adoptive parents) should focus on being wives and mothers. Single women who wanted to adopt were viewed with suspicion and were often castigated as "man haters" or lesbians and were "pushed from the ranks of adoptive mothers."[22] Notably, social workers relaxed their standards when single parents wanted to adopt older children or children with special needs who were previously considered "unadoptable," thus creating a two-tiered adoption system whose remnants are still visible today.

In the contemporary adoption marketplace, a prospective adoptive parent's relationship status remains the defining variable shaping one's eligibility and access to adoption. Married heterogamous partners have the most options, followed by single female applicants (less so single men). Homogamous partners, regardless of their marital status, maintain the least number of options. Mississippi was the last state to abolish laws prohibiting adoption among openly gay applicants, and currently no state statutes explicitly prohibit homosexuals from adopting.[23] But in spite of a legal pathway toward adoptive parenthood, these couples often face additional barriers, especially when seeking infants.

Several adoption providers I interviewed were adamant that maximizing one's chance for a baby was the main priority for most prospective parents, regardless of whether they were single or partnered, or in a homogamous or heterogamous relationship. Nora, a social worker who works for an adoption agency with long-standing advocacy ties to the LGBT adoption community, argues, "They are like anyone else. The gay community is no different than the straight community. They want babies like everybody else."

Although single and same-sex prospective adoptive parents may begin the adoption process wanting "babies like everybody else," they face greater barriers obtaining them. These restrictions have become especially cumbersome over the past decade, as prime sending countries incrementally changed their policies, making it harder for nontraditional applicants to procure a baby. Whereas China once had one of the most flexible programs,[24] the country now imposes strict requirements regarding applicants' income and net worth, age, and body mass index.[25] *how is this even a thing?*

In addition to openly gay and lesbian adopters, single women and men are often relegated to the second tier of transnational adoptions—that is, if they are allowed to adopt at all. Jennifer explains how this two-tiered status curtails single applicants' options. At the time of the interview, her agency still maintained a roster of country programs, but there were few attractive options among them. She states:

> We are working actively with eleven or twelve countries at a given time, and five or six of them are open to singles, which is not too bad at first glance. Then you look and realize that singles are exempted for older children and children who have special needs only. I don't mean to imply any negative attitude in stating it that way; it is simply that most singles, like most couples, are interested in adopting as young as possible and healthy. So while they have a number of programs they qualify for as singles, the types of children that are eligible to be adopted by them are going to be kids who are going to be older and have special needs.

Beyond relationship status, some countries have implemented strict eligibility restrictions, barring applicants who are overweight or have ever been treated for depression. At Baby Talk, the presenter explained these requirements to potential clients, stating, "Countries are being a little bit more restrictive on who can adopt, especially the Asian countries. South Korea and Taiwan, China, they now have restrictions on BMI. If you are a little overweight, they don't like that. If you are on any type of psychotropic medication for bipolar or anxiety, they are very against. So if you are on any of these kinds of medications, that would not be a country for you. Ethiopia, Russia, they are still very open with that."

As the person tasked with answering the intake phone lines, Jennifer is often the worker charged with keeping up-to-date on these ever-changing rules and explaining these new parameters to prospective customers who are often unaware of these modifications. She describes callers' reactions, stating, "There is a certain indignant response when you are telling them they are not going to be able to [adopt]," especially "when they are quite successful in their lives and have all of the resources to parent a child, particularly a child who needs their care desperately." She tries to deflect callers' anger away from her agency and toward the sending countries, making sure to communicate, "These are the children of the country, and to speak quite frankly, they make the rules."

It is interesting to note that Jennifer grounds single-parent adoption firmly within the narrative of finding parents for children, positioning single applicants as figures who can step in to parent children "who need their care desperately." But a few moments later Jennifer contradicts herself, describing how there are ample applicants who want to adopt young, healthy children without compelling sending countries to have to accept less-desirable applicants. She attests, "The other reality is, and it is hard to hear for these callers, but there are enough families in the queue for adoption that don't have any kind of special circumstances, that don't require any exemption, that the countries don't have to look for singles because there are enough couples." In other words, since the demand by high-status applicants already exceeds the supply, it may not be true that these children are desperate for care, since the reality is that there are more than enough applicants to go around.

Jennifer is not alone in her attempt to inform prospective clients that they are not the ones setting restrictive policies. At an information session sponsored by Family Tree Adoption, the presenter was quick to emphasize that eligibility impediments are external, forced on them by the sending countries. She said, "It has gotten more difficult for single applicants. It is not because of us but because of what other countries impose."

Before Russia banned overseas adoptions to the United States, the country was one of the few that did not have a two-tiered program. It allowed single applicants the same access as married applicants, but for many prospective parents the program was financially out of reach, since the process required two separate trips to Russia. Ironically, applicants with the most insurmountable fertility barriers—that is, single persons and same-sex couples—tended to have the fewest options. Summing up this sellers' market, at one adoption information session a single woman took stock of her predicament and commented, "It is almost like the eligibility sets the path." She likened her options to a "Catch-22," because singles are the "most likely to be able to afford a cheaper program—but it is not open to singles."

Whereas single applicants have limited options in the international adoption marketplace, openly gay and lesbian applicants—regardless of whether they are single or married—have few, if any, options in the international market.[26] Many readers may be surprised to learn that openly gay and lesbian applicants are unable able to pursue overseas adoption, because for a time international adoption served as a refuge for same-sex couples. Dorow describes how this used to be the case in China, summarizing that there once "was a tacit 'don't ask, don't tell' collusion between some U.S. adoption agencies and parent applicants—and perhaps even officials in Beijing who turned a blind eye" to same-sex applicants and facilitated their approval.[27] During this era, some adoption social workers did more than turn a blind eye by deliberately coaching applicants how to depict their household composition without setting off potential warning bells. For example, Nicole recalls this practice, explaining, "I remember one woman who was adopting from Guatemala, and we had to call her and tell her you can't butch it up so much in your photos and have so many lovey-dovey photos with your housemate."

This strategy was short-lived as major sending countries like China and Guatemala effectively changed their "don't ask" approach to a "must ask" policy. Danielle describes how new rules required Guatemala applicants "to sign something to say that you weren't gay or lesbian." Although prospective parents may have felt so desperate to adopt that they would be willing to perjure themselves by signing an affidavit lying about their sexual orientation, sending countries also required agency representatives to authenticate the veracity of these statements. "We had to write in the home study that you weren't [gay or lesbian]," Danielle recalls, detailing how these new laws greatly affected their social work practice.

She elaborates that before the ruling took effect, "we wrote your home study as a single but included your female partner in all other aspects of the process: domestic violence, health, security of the child." But this transparent approach had its drawbacks once sending countries tried to winnow out lesbian applicants. Danielle describes the wave of panic that went through her agency during this inquisition: "I remember very clearly when China caught on that lesbians were adopting, and we got a fax saying please tell us that the following clients aren't lesbians. Essentially naming the clients. These were home studies of single women living with other women. Nothing was said about their sexual orientation." She continues that this seeming witch hunt was "terrifying because in some cases we had coached these women to be out because that is the best practice, social work–wise, to know both parents." With these disclosures, social workers were in an untenable position, since they could not feign ignorance about their clients' relationship status despite the fact that "China was saying [to] cut people out if they are [lesbians]."

In response to this crackdown, her agency grappled with how to handle these requests. On the one hand, many employees firmly believed that gay and lesbian applicants had the right to adopt and did not want to participate in any discriminatory behavior. But to knowingly deceive sending country officials carried big risks in terms of potentially jeopardizing their standing and their supply of children.[28] Danielle continues:

> So five or six years ago we had a big powwow here at the agency about what can we do. Can we take gays and lesbians at the agency? Even if they hadn't done a Guatemala, signing the affidavit, it has to be in the home study that they were heterosexual. And we decided that we couldn't. We couldn't represent people as straight to other countries that we knew to not be.

While most of the international adoption social workers I interviewed were adamant that they no longer blatantly encourage same-sex applicants, there was one interesting outlier at one of the adoption information meetings I observed. The presenter delivered the news that homogamous couples could not adopt, but with a wink and nudge. First, she covered her bases by informing her audience, "No country works with homosexual couples," but then she dramatically paused, putting her hand up to her face as if telling a secret she did not want you to hear, and continued in a mock whisper, "But let me qualify that by saying singles can apply."

Although this agency sent a mixed message about the feasibility of inter-country adoption for gays and lesbians, at a preadoption conference session specifically geared toward gay and lesbian prospective parents, the overarching takeaway was to avoid this path. The presenter told her audience that pretending to be single is essentially "off the table." There are inherent dangers to this tactic, since applicants have to swear that they are not gay or lesbian. She warned that "the only thing that can overturn an adoption decree is fraud, so it is not a good idea to lie." Driving home this point, she added, "This is not the foundation for your family."

Because of these restrictions, many adoption professionals work to guide homogamous couples toward private domestic adoption. During my interview, Abigail explains, "Our agency perspective is to help guide them to domestic adoption, because you want to adopt somewhere that is going to be approving of who you are as a person." Similarly, the presenter at Forever Family—an agency exclusively devoted to private domestic adoption—informed her audience, "We are open to every family. It doesn't matter whom your family is composed of; that is not important to us. We don't have any quotas for adoptive parents. We take all families, and we don't have a cap because we want a birth parent to have every possible option when they are looking at that book [of parent profiles]. So we really accept all families."

While Forever Families was willing to continue to accept applicants into their pool, other agencies impose a hiatus on new applications if the numbers get too unwieldy. For example, at Cornerstone's information session the presenter detailed, "Our domestic program does place with gay couples as well as gay singles—although I should mention, we are not able to take new applications from anyone right now." The very fact that adoption workers have to restrict applications from potential paying customers looking to adopt babies is telling. While agencies would presumably want to increase their revenue by collecting more application fees, they also have to manage the customer experience of those still waiting for a match. Prospective parents who are already in the pool might not appreciate having additional competition. These considerations and competing priorities serve as a powerful reminder that the demand for healthy infants far exceeds the supply.

Even if prospective parents do make it into the pool, since the number of applicants vying for a baby outnumbers the number of infants available, there is no guarantee that applicants will be chosen by a pregnant woman making an adoption plan. I argue that to increase the odds of getting a healthy infant, adoption workers direct hopeful parents toward transracial adoption. For single and homogamous couples confronting additional hurdles, there may be an even greater motivation among practitioners to float the idea of transracial adoption. This strategy makes sense considering that single parents and homogamous partners are often quoted longer waiting times. Patricia elaborates:

> We definitely give them [gay and lesbian couples and single applicants] a different time line. People are making adoption plans because a lot of times they are single. So they are not necessarily looking for a single parent for their child. And a lot of people are not open to same-sex lifestyles [because] they either don't know much about families like that or they grew up not accepting families like that. So they definitely have more of a challenge when adopting through domestic infant [programs].

Alyssa explains the uphill battle that nontraditional applicants encounter, considering that the women she works with "want two people to raise their baby because otherwise they'd raise their baby. So single people always wait the longest unless you have these extraordinary qualities that are so appealing to this potential birth parent." Describing the additional barriers, she attests, "I'd say the truth is half of our pregnant women are not even interested in looking at a profile of a family that is not married and heterosexual. Single people wait longer than even gay or lesbian couples." Based on these sobering statistics, she describes how "some families know [the odds] . . . [and say,] 'Well, I should be open to all races because otherwise I am never going to get chosen.'"

Knowing the odds, independent adoption attorneys often couch their approach as advantageous to single and same-sex prospective parents. Since clients who use direct advertising to solicit a pregnant woman are not necessarily being compared to multiple hopeful families, one lawyer suggests that attorney-led adoption works better for marginal applicants, since they "are not competing with a pool." This message was echoed at a forum for prospective adopters when an adoption attorney warned the audience that an agency "might have fifteen to twenty other families, whereas in independent [adoption] you can distinguish yourself."

During my interview with Christine, she reiterated how the independent method can be advantageous for nontraditional applicants because they can distinguish themselves by forming a relationship with a potential birth mother. She explains, "The way that most agencies work is when a birth mother comes, in order to match them, they present profiles to the birth mother." While this approach gives pregnant women greater options, Christine indicates that the method has negative ramifications for nontraditional families. She continues, "If you stand five profiles [of prospective adoptive parents] next to each other, and three of them are heterosexual couples and one of them is a same-sex couple and one of them is single, the direct comparison puts [nontraditional families] at a disadvantage."

The direct advertising model works in her client's favor because if the birth mother sees a newspaper solicitation, and "she sort of connects with her [the prospective parent], with the single mom, or whoever it may be, they [expectant women] don't need to go any further. They are not 'forced' to look at other couples who are the two-parent families, picket fence, and the dog."

While single applicants or a lesbian couple might face greater obstacles to be chosen by a birth mother, according to Irene, "I think gay men have it okay." Surprised at this assessment, I asked her to elaborate. She explains, "I think—and other people I have heard say it—I think that there is an element in which the pregnant woman, a birth mom, gets to think, 'I am still the mom.' And she gets to be the only female and maternal figure in the child's life." Irene goes on to explain how many of her gay clients tend to be more willing to maintain open adoptions.[29] "A lot of same-sex couples," she states, "especially male same-sex couples, are very open to having open [adoptive] relationships. And they see the benefit of having that female role model, and that can be a really wonderful option for a woman making an adoption plan that she can be encouraged to have a relationship." Adding credence to this assessment, a few months later I heard a similar sentiment during the conference session focused on gay adoption. The presenter echoed Irene's words almost verbatim as she told her audience, "Gay men seem to have more relaxed feelings on openness. Also, the woman feels that she still gets to be the mom."

Another likely reason why gay men "have it okay" may be that they are more willing to widen their net and consider transracial adoption. Since international adoption is now largely unavailable to openly gay and lesbian applicants, their only recourse for a baby is domestic adoption. Yet same-sex prospective parents must "compete" with several opposite-sex couples also vying for a baby. Given these longer odds, domestic transracial adoption becomes a market calculation.

Wanting to understand the role of the market in shaping nontraditional parents' decisions to adopt across race, I asked Lindsay point-blank, "Would you say that same-sex couples are more open to transracial placements?" Her response is telling, since she discredits the idea that homogamous couples are vastly more predisposed to transracial adoption. Instead, she attributes the higher rates of cross-race placements to the market realities, stating, "I would say that singles and same-sex couples—not all [*pauses*]—probably are more open just because their chances will be greater. The broader your parameters, the better your chances of a quicker placement. But are they any less prejudiced than anyone else? Maybe that plays into it as well. I do think that people are realistic."

As Lindsay puts it, lower-tier parents have to be realistic consumers and utilize strategies that widen their chances of being selected by a would-be birth mother. In my interview with Tracy, a domestic adoption social worker, she walks me through this calculus:

> They are seeing that this [Caucasian] program has one hundred families in it and this [African American] program has thirty-five families. And of those thirty-five families, only half will accept full African American. So [they think,] "If we are okay with a full African American, we are probably going to be one of fifteen, maybe twenty, profiles to be shown to a birth mother, whereas in the other program, we will be one of one hundred."

Since the sheer probability of being chosen increases with widening one's parameters, transracial adoption gets perceived as an expedient market strategy. This reasoning applies not only to homogamous couples. Irene espouses how single men often follow the same strategy, describing how one of her single male clients pursued transracial adoption as a means to fatherhood:

> I have a single male client, and this is not the gay thing, but he is a single male. He is White from a very prominent and financially secure family. And he adopted an African American little girl. And the biological mom has other children, and they all go to the fancy house at the beach at some incredibly exclusive area where the entire birth family goes frequently throughout the summer. And he sort of welcomed them, and I think there is that role. And she is not the mother, and he is the only parent. But [there is] recognizing that

this is another person who can provide something of value to my child.

Later I asked Patricia, a social worker specializing in domestic adoption, why she thought so many single and same-sex parents adopt across race. Her response points to how their lower status in the adoption marketplace shapes these patterns. Patricia explains:

> Their choices are limited as well. . . . I think the same-sex community and the single-parent community have done a tremendous job in stepping in to parent children that other people would not even have considered parenting and done an amazing job. But I think it is because they have been limited as well. There are a lot of agencies who will not work with same-sex couples. A lot of single applicants will wait twice as long. So I think it is a "we need each other, so let's get together" type of thing.

Patricia's comments illustrate the crux of the assortative adoption marketplace. Notice how she describes the sorting process in market terms, summarizing the trend of nontraditional parents adopting non-White children as "we need each other, so let's get together." In other words, because single and same-sex prospective parents have limited (if any) choices in the international adoption marketplace, on the domestic front they are the most likely to try to expand their pool of potential birth parents by being willing to adopt transracially.

To summarize, so far I have shown how adoption workers characterize the mind-set of clients that seek out private adoption. These social workers and practitioners detail how most prospective applicants come to private adoption having faced significant barriers to biological reproduction. Thus, they enter the process often wanting what parents of biological children usually get—a healthy infant who racially resembles the parents. But given the stringent guidelines and the decreased likelihood of being chosen by a birth mother, single applicants and homogamous partners are relegated to the second tier of choices.

This leads me to the last section of this chapter, where my aim is to describe how adoption workers advise prospective parents to weigh their choices and potentially use transracial adoption as a means to improve their chances of getting a younger and healthier child. Abigail describes how few parents are able to capitalize on every variable. Thus for applicants, deciding which ones to prioritize can be an excruciating process of mindful evaluation. "Nobody is able to come in and say I want A, B, C, D, and E, and F," she declares, emphasizing that would-be adoptive parents still need to make concessions and "rank their priorities and see which ones can be flexed."

## Ranking Priorities and Flexing Market Variables

At the early stages of the adoption process, adoption workers ask parents to decide the characteristics of the child they hope to adopt and how much they are willing to endure to ensure this outcome. Do they want the youngest and healthiest baby they can find, or do they want to adopt an older child with known medical issues? Do they envision having a son or a daughter? Do they want to be in an open adoption or a closed one? How long are they willing to wait to locate a child who fits their desired profile, and how much are they willing to pay? Are they willing to take the risk that the adoption could fall through? To maximize their chance on one variable, applicants may have to compromise on another. In the following pages, I discuss these variables in turn, detailing how adoption workers depict each of these considerations.

### Time

For those who come to adoption after facing fertility barriers, waiting times are an important variable as prospective parents understandably want to get on with their lives as parents. Lindsay, a social worker who routinely conducts home study evaluations for prospective parents, describes this urgency: "The impulse is to adopt and to adopt quickly." She continues, "They can probably tell you every little bit about infertility drugs, but when it comes to adoption, they don't want to know about it. They just want to adopt. They just want to have a baby. They've been through this torture, and their notion is 'let's move on, and we'll have a baby.'"

When "moving on" to adoption, Lindsay summarizes how most of her clients initially see themselves emulating the as-if-begotten model, in which the adopted baby could pass for a biological child: "Most of them want an infant, a newborn, and White if they are White." She explains this preference, stating, "Adults, especially if they didn't have adoption in mind to begin with, want to look like their child on some level. . . . That is another motive for adopting a same-race child. They want to be seen as homogenous like everyone else."

While White parents may initially begin the adoption process hoping for a White newborn, since the 1970s, the number of available White infants has precipitously declined. Access to contraception and abortion, coupled with the decreased stigma for single motherhood, vastly reduced the supply of these babies.[30] Whereas before *Roe v. Wade*, one in ten unmarried White women relinquished their babies for adoption, nowadays less than 1 percent of women regardless of race choose adoption.[31] As Sylvia puts it, "The explosion of adoption was in the seventies." Although there are still plenty of prospective adoptive parents hoping to adopt White healthy newborns, there are fewer babies to go around. Wanting to verify this market imbalance,

I asked Christine whether there were more families looking to adopt healthy infants than those being placed for adoption. She forcefully replies, slapping the desk in front of her for emphasis, "Definitely. No question. Like multifold."

The relative demand for White babies is so great that some adoption agencies still abide by the antiquated practice of rationing them out, reserving them for applicants that they deem as the most deserving—that is, heterogamous married couples with documented infertility. For example, the website of a faith-based agency informs interested applicants, "Due to the limited number of children available through domestic adoption services, only couples who have experienced infertility will be accepted. Childless couples or those with only one other child are eligible to work with this program." Notably, the organization loosens their draconian restrictions for clients interested in adopting lower-status children. The agency offers this caveat: "However, this requirement does not apply to those adopting internationally, and those adopting minority children or children with special needs."

Religiously affiliated adoption agencies are not the only ones to impose this criterion. The website of a secular adoption agency also abides by a similar policy. It states, "Currently there are less available Caucasian infants than there are families requesting to adopt them. Therefore [name of agency] will not be accepting applications for our Caucasian adoption program from families who are able to conceive a biological child." In other words, given the shortage of sought-after White babies, these children are reserved for those deemed the worthiest—the White would-be parents who cannot produce a child of their "own." While White babies are held on reserve, the agency relaxes its regulations for lower-status children, informing parents, "However, there is a need for families for African-American children in the US and many international adoption programs that allow families with children to adopt."

While the practice of withholding White babies seems to apply to only a handful of adoption agencies, many others will allow qualified applicants into the pool and then warn them it could take years for a match to come through. For example, the website at Coordinated Care informs viewers, "At this time, the wait for a Caucasian infant is unpredictable, as the birth parents generally request profiles of waiting adoptive parents and select the family they feel is best to meet the needs of the child. However, generally speaking, most families receive a child in approximately 2–2½ years."

However, waits are usually shorter for Black children. Coordinated Care's website goes on to tell their readers, "The waiting time for bi-racial and African-American children varies, but is often less than that of a Caucasian youth." Along the same line, at Loving Family's information session, the presenter told her audience, "If you want a Caucasian infant with no medical problems, the waits can get closer to eighteen to twenty-four months." Yet she offered participants a lifeline, detailing, "The wait time will vary according to what you are open to. If you are open to a Black, African American, Jamaican, or Haitian child, the wait will be shorter."

Whereas in domestic adoption one's flexibility on race tends to drive the extent of the waiting times, in intercountry adoption the age of the child is another variable. At Kid Connection's information session, the representative explained this trade-off to her audience: "Most people coming to adoption want the youngest child they can get. They put their ticket over here. The more tickets in each pile, the longer you are going to wait." She continued, "If you want a child zero to twenty-four months, it will be a twelve- to twenty-four-month wait." However, this waiting time is significantly reduced "if you just expand your age limit a little bit, [and request] a two-and-a-half to three-year-old, that will shorten your wait." Similarly, at Baby Talk, the presenter espoused a comparable strategy, advising listeners: "Usually there is a wait in international adoption; there is also in domestic. And depending on how open you can be on age and how flexible you can be on medical risks, the waits will go down."

For country programs like China, where there is a backlog of applicants, being flexible on these variables is one of the few ways to assure adopting. For example, the presenter at Coordinated Care explains the difference between the waiting and traditional China program: "Waiting times are going to move faster if you are open to a waiting child. So instead of waiting that five to seven years, you could potentially complete an adoption within a year or two, depending on the age of child you are open to."

Given the seemingly interminable waits, I asked whether any prospective adoptive parents were even bothering to apply to the "traditional" China program known for placing healthy infant girls. One social worker informed me that the only people applying were Chinese Americans who qualified for a fast-tracked placement. These parents did not have to make these trade-offs, since there were still young healthy girls available. Yet White parents do not have the same luxury, and consequentially, these applicants have to make a different calculus.

## Tolerance for Uncertainty

In addition to deciding how much time they are willing to wait to adopt, prospective parents also must evaluate their thresholds for risk and uncertainty. Although it can be maddening to wait as one's dossier snakes it way through the bureaucratic maze of international adoption, there is an ordered certainty about the process. Recall from Chapter 2 how one presenter likened the process to waiting in an especially long line at the deli counter, since sooner or later, "your number comes up."

In contrast, in domestic adoption—whether through an agency or an attorney—nowadays the expectant woman making an adoption plan is empowered to choose the family for her child. Instead of a long but orderly queue, success in domestic adoption is largely out of the control of prospective adoptive parents and those advocating on their behalf. According to Kiera, the ambiguity is a significant factor that pushes some of her clients toward international adoption. She states, "So especially for families who have dealt with so much infertility, the idea of—even with all of the risks with international adoption—they have a basic time line. And at the end of the day, there will be a child that they will be parenting." Kiera continues, "With domestic, it is kind of the luck of the draw. You are ready, your paperwork is in, and you could be called tomorrow. Or you could wait for years or never be called at all. So for a lot of families, that is not something they are comfortable with."

The risks are especially heightened when pursuing an independent attorney-led adoption since the advertising is completely up to the prospective parents. Even though attorneys specializing in this field have a keen sense of which newspaper advertisements yield the greatest success at soliciting pregnant women looking to place, there are no guarantees. Irene describes how she is always forthcoming with potential clients about the temporal and financial risks associated with independent adoption: "With a newspaper ad, if the right person picks it up, it could happen immediately, or it could happen never. You could put out thousands and thousands of dollars and no one ever calls."

Wanting to get a sense of how much money clients typically devote to advertising, I asked Christine about the usual budget. She is honest in her assessment that the cost can be a real hardship for clients, stating, "It is very hard. You need to be prepared. The ads cost a lot of money; they really do." She continues that she tries not to give people a set number but advises them to "start with four states." The amount of money spent really depends on the clients' resources. She explains, "It is a budget item. How much can they afford? Some people have lots of money, and they will put in $10,000 to $15,000, and other people will put in $4,000." But the amount of money does not always guarantee results. Christine elaborates, "There is no rhyme. Some people could get a response in their first ad, and other people could put in $10,000 and not get very much back. It is very troubling and very unpredictable."

For prospective adoptive parents unable to stomach or afford this unpredictability, domestic adoption through an agency can slightly reduce the risks since the agency has its own resources to recruit a pool of birth mothers. This can be a real selling point for agencies as they can market themselves as a safer option. Even though the ultimate selection remains up to the pregnant woman, at least clients signing on with an adoption agency know that there are pregnant women walking through the door. From the questions posed by information session attendees, it was clear that many were drawn to this business model. For example, at one session a male attendee posed the question "Do you have adoptive families who just aren't picked? That never get picked?" In response, the social worker assuaged the fears of the questioner, underscoring that the agency option ameliorates some of the risk, since, "We have the philosophy [that] if you stick with us, we'll stick with you."

It is interesting to note that the social worker frames this sort of fidelity to their clients as a benefit to applicants, but this philosophy also benefits the agency. While many collect fees as they go in terms of processing the application and administering the home study, the largest sum is due at the time when a match is made. So it makes fiscal sense that workers would want to help get clients to this point by encouraging them to stick with their agency, rather than take their business elsewhere.

Importantly, the uncertain amount of time and potentially money it takes to solicit a potential match is just the first component of the potential hazards involved with private domestic adoption, since the pregnant woman maintains the right to change her mind until after the birth of the child. The social worker at Baby Talk tried to manage prospective applicants' expectations, communicating that a sizeable number of expectant women ultimately decide to parent. She estimated that this occurs "about 20 percent of the time," adding the warning that "until that paperwork is signed, she can change her mind, which is called a change of heart. It does happen."

Since the possibility of a change of heart is inevitable in any domestic adoption, agency representatives will often play up the fact that their approach at least minimizes parents' financial risks. For example, at Forever Family's session, the presenter described how the agency's pay-as-you-go model provides an additional layer of consumer protection, detailing, "The money goes into an escrow account, and we don't deem it earned until a placement actually occurs." So if there is a situation where "a birth mom changes her mind before a baby is born, and she decides that this adoption is not what she thought it was going to be, and she wants to parent," the money will be returned. She stated, "What will happen is all of the fees will be returned to you, and you will get all of that money back."

The presenter elaborated how these policies also protect prospective parents against the nightmare scenario of a disrupted adoption, which she described this way: "If you are picked by a birth mom and—God forbid— a disruption happens. A disruption is when a baby is placed with you in your home, in your care and custody, and then the birth mom changes her mind and decides that she wants to parent that baby." Under these circumstances, there is still a layer of consumer protection for the clients, since, "We don't return the placement fee to you, but the next time you are picked by a birth mom, you're not submitting that money all over again."

I asked Christine about the percentage of expectant women who change their minds, and we had the following exchange:

> Me: What percentage of expectant women would you say change their mind before labor and in the hospital?
> Christine: Hospital, 10 to 15 percent, and before labor, much less.
> Me: So they are going along making this plan, and in the hospital—
> Christine: That's your moment of truth. Can I really do this?
> Me: 10 to 15 percent—that's a lot.
> Christine: It's a pretty good percentage, it really is. It feels like a lot, if you are one of those parents, but if you are doing something, and your risk is 10 to 15 percent, that's pretty good.

Given these figures, Irene describes how she tries to self-manage the risks by persuading the pregnant women who are working with her clients to agree to counseling in order to minimize the risk of a change of heart after the birth. Moreover, Irene performs her own risk assessment on behalf of her clients, trying to evaluate the likelihood that a placement will actually occur. She describes this appraisal as asking, "Does she have goals and aspirations? If she is a young girl and in college, and she is studying to be a clinical social worker and has worked really hard and now she's pregnant?" According to Irene, these women are more likely to follow through with the adoption plan, since "it is less likely that she wants to parent because she will have all of these plans that will be put on hold." But on the other hand, Irene states, "If she doesn't have any plans and all of her friends are having babies and are single moms on public assistance, she may say, 'Oh, I'll just do it.'"

Despite the fact that Irene is diligent about making an "assessment of what the risks are," she acknowledges that "there are always surprises." She recalls a change of heart that occurred a few months prior, when "I represented a fifteen-year-old girl, and no matter how many times I tried to get her to counseling, she was absolutely adamant that she was going to place." The day of the birth the new mother was still planning on moving forward with the adoption plan. Irene recalls, "I saw her the day she delivered, and she was adamant that she was going to sign." Abiding by the state's revocation laws, the woman had another day before she could legally sign away her maternal rights. Irene recollects, "And I told her, 'Okay, I will come back tomorrow. I don't want you to sign today.' And the next day she said, 'I am keeping the baby.'" Caught up in the story, I asked her what she told the adoptive parents, who had flown in from out of state desperately hoping that this would be the day they became parents. Speaking from experience she testifies, "There is nothing you can say to make that better."

While the aftermath of these situations can be heartbreaking for prospective adoptive parents, Irene contextualizes these risks are inherent to any private adoption. "There is no getting around it," she concludes. "That can happen when adopting from an agency, too." She acknowledges the perilous nature of the domestic adoption process but counters that foster care and international adoptions also have their drawbacks. While international adoption used to be seen as the less risky pathway, since the children were legal orphans, she points out that this market segment is no longer as attractive, stating, "Look at the unexpected changes that can occur internationally. It is hard." She maintains that those who want to obliterate the chance of a woman changing her mind can adopt "a child from foster care who is already [legally] freed" from biological parents but impresses that these parents would have to be willing to compromise on other market variables, stating, "That child is going to be old—we're talking six, seven, or eight."

## Gender

Gender is a market variable unique to adoption because it is one of the few instances when adoptive parents have more say than biological parents, who presumably do not get to choose whether they have a son or daughter. Yet the idea of choice is elusive, since adoptive parents overwhelmingly prefer girls, and thus, adoption workers have to manage these requests by letting clients know that there are not enough girls to go around. Unlike in domestic adoption, in which placing mothers may not necessarily know the gender of the baby they are carrying, in international adoption—since the child has already been identified—it would be possible to request a girl over a boy. Thus, at a conference session focused on transnational placements, the speaker communicated this shortage by emphatically stating, "If you are open to gender, you are going to get a boy. The wait for girls is double."

Intrigued by this gender preference, I later spoke with Danielle, asking her why she thought adoptive parents wanted daughters over sons. She associates the preference for girls as the manifestation of the bias that adoption is second-best to having one's own progeny, elaborating:

> After fifteen years of thinking, here are my reasons. Women are often the motivators in the family for adoption, and the husbands are coming along gradually, and women have a stronger pull to raising daughters. I think this is a trickier one. I think the people . . . are not passing on their genes, and there is a thing about not passing on your genes to a boy, but for a girl there is not the same thing. So people do not have a strong preference for a girl with a biological child. So with the boy, carrying on the family name, I think that there is a little bit

of adoption discomfort there. You can take someone else's girl, but someone else's boy can never be yours.

With this in mind, many agencies no longer allow applicants, especially those without children, to request a particular gender. The presenter at Family Union explained this policy: "What we found with families that are applying to adopt internationally is that the majority of families who come to us initially start the process wanting to adopt a healthy infant girl." She adds that this preference creates an imbalance between supply and demand. "And with most of our country programs, even when there are an equal number of boys and girls available, if families state their preference, we are always going to be able to match girls faster, and there are always going to be boys waiting for families with no families in process waiting to accept them. So when both boys and girls are available, we oftentimes have a requirement regarding what gender families can specify."

Other international adoption agencies are more willing to entertain parents' gender preferences but warn them that they are likely to wait longer for a referral. For example, at Kids Connection, when their Russia program was operating, they allowed applicants to choose whether they would adopt a son or daughter. The social worker told her audience that there were temporal drawbacks to requesting girls, warning, "Today, as of now, in Russia you could wait twelve to eighteen months for a young girl." But if parents were willing to acquiesce their priorities, "for a boy who is eighteen to thirty-six months, you could get a referral in less than six months." Similarly, for their program in Ethiopia, the social worker informed attendees that there was no wait to be matched with an older boy—that is, age four and up. Yet for an older girl, the wait was six months to a year. In other words, for those pursuing international adoption, the more parents can be flexible on age, the more their gender preferences are likely to be taken into account.

## Open Adoption

Open adoption is the term used to describe adoptive families who maintain contact with their child's first mother or birth mother. The trend toward open adoption is a fairly recent phenomenon. Characterizing this evolution, Barbara Melosh writes, "The shift to open adoption in the 1980s was driven by birth mothers themselves. By meeting and choosing their child's parents, relinquishing mothers assuaged their fears of consigning their children to an unknown fate. Their control over placement also overturned old relationships of dependence and expertise, in which social workers or other mediators called the shots."[32] In contrast to domestic adoptions where openness is increasingly common, for intercountry adoptions geographic and language barriers, not to mention the secrecy that tends to enshroud transnational placements, often preclude the possibility of openness. In line with this trend toward closed adoptions, according to the National Survey of Adoptive Parents, only six percent of intercountry adoptive families had any contact with members of their child's birth family.[33]

Sylvia describes how the guarantee of a closed adoption served as a huge draw for prospective parents, stating, "Many times they want to do an international, intercountry adoption because they feel that there is a cutoff with the birth origins. They have this idea that all American birth mothers are going to come in and take their kid away someday, and they are just going to have been babysitting. They are terrified that the bond won't be strong enough, and they'll lose this kid. That the kid won't really be theirs, and the kid won't really be connected and will dump them."

Playing off of parents' fears, adoption providers often tout the closed nature of international adoptions as a benefit to prospective parents. During one information session, the presenter stated that closed adoptions are "one of the great appeals of international adoption," because "you don't have to worry about birth parents coming back once the adoption is finalized." Likewise, another social worker assured her audience, "The possibility is very, very small of finding birth parents."

Many international agency representatives urge applicants to embrace "the spirit of openness" by keeping their son or daughter connected with his or her birth country. But this brand of openness is likely far more palatable than the potentially daunting task of forging a relationship with the woman who relinquished her child to you. With this in mind, another presenter assured potential applicants, "You aren't going to have a direct open adoption relationship."

Similarly, at Cornerstone the presenter explained to her audience, "Openness is something new we are talking about in international adoption but really very valid. Some programs are giving us the opportunity for greater degrees of openness." Notably, she underscored that open international adoption does not necessarily entail contact with the birth mother. She listed what this form of contact may look like, stating, "Sometimes ongoing contact with their community, sometimes that means their foster family, sometimes it means their extended biological family."

In contrast to international adoptions where open adoptions are few and far between, about two-thirds of domestic adoptive parents report that they have some form of ongoing contact with birth family members.[34] With this in mind, the speaker at Kid Connection told prospective clients that "long gone are the days when you can pick up a child and the birth mother doesn't know anything about you." She further warned, "Some women will say that they don't want to have any contact, but that is very rare." Instead, "what we see more and more is that the birth mother wants nonidentifying information." Describing what this relationship might look like, she elaborated,

"Maybe you'll share photos at the child's birthday or more, starting when the child is six, twelve, eighteen, and twenty-four months and every year after that." The speaker assured her audience that they would be able to maintain their confidentiality, detailing how "Kid Connection is the intermediary. We gather pictures and letters and pass them all on."

Most adoption providers attempt to frame the trend toward openness in a positive light. For example, the presenter at Adoptions Associated spun open adoption as "more people who love your child." However, a few outliers assured prospective adopters that the commitment would probably fade. For example, at an adoption conference session one prospective mother asked the presenter about the level of openness she would be expected to maintain. The speaker hinted that birth mothers tend to cease contact as the grief of relinquishment and the chaos of their lives take their toll. She intimated that in this day and age, it would be nearly impossible to set up a closed adoption because "there are few and far between closed adoption agencies." However, she diminished the commitment of open adoption by relaying the consolation that "more often than not, after a few years, the birth mother moves." The speaker was quite callous about breaking off the relationship, framing it as "at least you tried" and "you can tell [the] child that you tried."

As this woman's comments indicate, adoption workers have to navigate the tension between wanting to advocate for open adoption while also assuaging prospective customers' fears about openness. While many social workers embrace the idea that openness can often be in the best interests of adopted children, they have to balance this message with the work of ensuring that clients do not seek out a different provider who will accommodate their desire for a more closed adoption. This tension can be fraught, especially considering that not only is openness in domestic adoption the new normal; it is also becoming legally enforceable. In twenty-eight states there are enforceable postadoption contracts that can mandate visitation rights even after the birth mother has rescinded her maternal rights.[35] Tracy, a domestic adoption social worker who divides her caseload between pregnant women and adoptive parents, describes the benefits of these agreements. She details how such documents provide an additional layer of security so adoptive parents do not "run for the hills and never see [the birth mother] again."

Understandably for prospective adoptive parents who may still be coming to terms with not being able to have a biological child, having to share their long dreamt-of son or daughter with another woman who has legal visitation rights may be terrifying. With this in mind, at an adoption conference one attorney cajoled her audience: "I always say that the hypothetical birth parent is a lot scarier than the real birth parent."

Yet these assurances did little to comfort the White couple in their early thirties at the next table from me at a conference session called "Successful

Domestic Adoption." Later in the presentation, the speaker (an adoption attorney) informed her audience that in her state, postadoption contact agreements are not legally enforceable if using a private adoption attorney. Upon hearing this, the wife looked up from her notes and made eye contact with her husband sitting next to her. Heartened by the news that she would not necessarily be held to a visitation agreement she signed in good faith with a birth mother relinquishing her child to their care, the woman pumped her fist and definitively whispered, "Check." Although this couple was in the early stages of their adoption decision-making process, from her outburst it was clear that openness was a concern and mitigating the risk a priority.

Whereas many adoption workers performed the emotion work of managing prospective adoptive parents' fears about open adoptions, there were a few outlier agencies that prided themselves on a higher level of openness. For example, the presenter at Loving Family explained that as opposed to serving as an intermediary helping adoptive parents and birth parents exchange photos and letters, the agency's model is to share identifying information, including e-mail addresses and phone numbers. "You have direct access to them, and they have direct access to you," explaining that it would be typical for the adoptive mom to call the birth mom and say, "I was just thinking of you. The child did this and made me think of you. Let me e-mail you some photos of it. His birthday is coming up. Are you coming to the party?"

The agency recognizes that this type of open relationship is not for every prospective adoptive parent. At their information session, the speaker warned audience members that they would turn down applicants who did not seem like a good fit. Upon hearing this, one audience member asked what would disqualify someone from being a strong candidate, and the presenter answered, "Someone who is trying to make the process go faster and agrees to send photos without really understanding implications. Someone who is not invested in establishing a relationship with the birth parents."

Alyssa, a strong advocate for open adoption, shared how she routinely turns away three-fourths of her applicants who are not good candidates for open adoption. Upon hearing this startling figure, I commented that it is not a very good business model to turn away three out of four paying customers. Alyssa responds, "I shouldn't say that I turn them away outwardly. I turn them away with the way that I talk. But when I pitch who we are, they self-select out." She goes on to describe how if prospective parents say things like, "I hear that most birth moms go away anyway. All my friends have open adoptions; their birth moms are gone, so I am really good with this," she tries to steer them away. Another red flag is when applicants seem resigned to open adoption and say things like, "I hear this is the way it is nowadays, so we're good with it, whatever."

Alyssa's statements remind me that adoption workers are not solely interested in pushing forward their bottom lines by selling more adoptions.
Some are more than willing to see paying customers go elsewhere, veering
toward protecting the rights of birthmothers over acquiescing to the desires
of clients who pay the fees. But maintaining this balance can be difficult,
especially when considering the costs of doing business. It is worth repeating
that the intent of this book is not to vilify adoption workers (or the parents
they serve) but instead to draw attention to the complex matrix of the adoption marketplace that leads adoption workers to sell the idea of transracial
adoption as a way to navigate the age-race-health comparison.

## The Age-Race-Health Comparison

Let us return to Lydia and her partner, the cohabitating couple introduced
at the beginning of the chapter. They were "leaning toward Ethiopia," and
thus a transracial adoption, albeit with limited options. At Statewide's information session, Lydia reported that they hoped to adopt a healthy child as
young as possible, "under age three—ideally under two." In other words, to
maximize the likelihood of adopting a young, healthy toddler, they were
willing to be flexible on race. Since Ethiopia was one of the few countries still
offering a pipeline of young, relatively healthy children available for adoption
and was one of a handful of programs that accepted unmarried applicants
in their late forties, she was able to maximize several variables (age, health,
and a closed adoption) and be flexible on race to achieve parenthood.

The idea that one variable has to be sacrificed so another is gained is so
ingrained that adoption workers routinely frame adoption as series of trade-
offs. For example, I attended an adoption information session titled "Making
the Age/Race/Health Comparison in Adoption." Intrigued by the notion of
making a market calculus, later I asked Amanda how prospective parents
evaluated these factors. Her words echo these implicit compromises in the
adoption decision-making process, stating, "[Families] do have to make decisions about age. They do have to make decisions about race and assessing
their community. They have to make decisions about the medical needs of
the kids."

Clearly Lydia and her partner were not the only ones willing to be flexible on race by adopting from Ethiopia. In fact, during the time I conducted
my fieldwork, adoptions from Ethiopia were booming. At an information
session offered by Family Union, the social worker explained the popularity
of the program in the context of other market variables: "We have gone from
placing sixty kids to one hundred kids [a year], and that number is going to
keep growing." She continued, "A lot of qualities are very attractive" about
the Ethiopia program, elaborating that the "children can be relatively young"
and that the "overall process for Ethiopia is twelve to eighteen months. We

have been receiving a steady stream of kids and are very quickly moving through our cases." At Statewide, the presenter offered an almost verbatim assessment of Ethiopia's popularity, summarizing how the process allowed families to maximize several market variables. "Families are drawn to Ethiopia; the adoption process is a tried-and-true one," she attested, continuing, "We have seen relatively healthy kids. The process can be a little faster. The fees tend to be a little less. I think overall, there is a lot of attractive things about Ethiopia."

Throughout my conversations, adoption professionals continually emphasize that the age and health of the child tend to be the most "attractive" market variables. The majority of parents want to adopt healthy babies and if healthy babies are not available, then the next preference is for healthy young toddlers and so on. For example, I asked Abigail how many parents want to adopt a child younger than two, and she laughs, responding, "All of them." Echoing this finding, in another interview Lindsay states that the hope for a young child "is the biggest motivating driver right now; it is not older child adoption." Danielle reiterates the demand for babies, stating, "There is a lot of focus on where can I get a baby. There are not babies available for international adoption like there were ten years ago. So ten years ago the questions were very different."

Over the course of a decade, the supply of children available for international adoption radically shifted. Moreover, prospective parents became savvier consumers who were more aware of the risks associated with adopting from certain countries. For example, in the early part of the millennium, thousands of White adoptive parents had flocked to Eastern Europe to adopt White infants and toddlers from Russia and the former Soviet bloc. Sylvia explicitly discusses this trend as a market strategy for getting a same-race adoption, stating, "Up until recently all of the White people were going to Russia." However, in the span of five years, fewer parents chose this region because of the concerns about the health profiles of children available for adoption.[36] Partially in response to the highly publicized case of an adoptive mother returning her son to a Russian orphanage,[37] the Russian parliament passed a law banning foreign adoptions to the United States,[38] effectively cutting off a major supply of White children in the adoption pipeline.[39]

But even before the ban on Russian adoptions was ratified, many prospective adoptive parents were reticent about adopting from Russia and Eastern Europe in general. Nicole spoke of an increased awareness among adoptive parents and adoption professionals regarding the health issues facing many Russian children available for adoption. She says, "I have been to a billion of those medical-issues-in-adoption seminars, and pediatricians are basically like, 'Don't adopt from Russia.'" Echoing this sentiment, Abigail discusses how savvy prospective adopters deliberately eschew Russian and Eastern European adoptions because of these health concerns. "There is a stigma about Eastern Europe," she says. "Some families come in and won't even think about Eastern Europe because of the alcohol abuse, so then they're looking at different countries based on that."

Erin discusses how Korea emerged as a favorite country for eligible adopters because it allowed them to maximize two out of three variables. She summarizes that many parents pursued Korean adoption to optimize health and age, continuing, "I think that's why the program in South Korea is so popular. The children typically are getting good medical care, and the children are typically young when they are referred to families. And I think that's what the majority of families are hoping for."

Under these constraints, race becomes the most malleable criterion, especially for those who prioritize getting a baby. Danielle attests to the necessity of these trade-offs, surmising, "For people with race flexibility, domestic is a good option. You have to have race flexibility to adopt a baby anyway." Similarly, in a conversation with Lindsay who routinely conducts adoption home studies for parents working their way through the domestic adoption process, I asked her why her clients pursue transracial adoption. She responds, "It is interesting to answer your question about this racial thing. These are families who basically move from infertility to adoption. They don't start out by saying, 'We want to adopt.'" Notice how Lindsay directly connects infertility and "this racial thing," making an explicit link between the market and transracial adoption. Her clients do not start out by intending to adopt, but once they come to adoption, many try to maximize their chances of adopting a healthy infant in the shortest amount of time.

Cognizant of these trade-offs, many domestic adoption social workers advise their audience members that they can maximize their chances of being chosen in a timely manner by widening their net. For example, during the Q&A at Kid Connection, an audience member asked about the current time line for domestic adoptions. The adoption worker responded, "It can happen very quickly, or it can take two years. The more open you are to communication [with the birth mother] or are open to race and ethnicity, the faster it will take." Being open to a transracial adoption can pay off, and conversely, "the more narrow you are in terms of what you are choosing, the longer it is going to take." Similarly, a website of another domestic adoption program advises readers that their flexibility will determine how long they will wait for a match:

> Factors that affect waiting time include how flexible you are with respect to the child's race, ethnicity and medical condition, whether you will accept a history of high-risk behavior, substance abuse, medical and/or mental health issues on the part of the biological parents, and/or your willingness to have an open relationship with the biological family.

Since among White parents, there is a lower demand for Black children than White children, adoption workers usually quote vastly different waiting times for Black babies and frame adopting a Black child as a fruitful strategy for minimizing one's wait. At Cornerstone, the social worker explained that there was likely to be a shorter wait for Black babies placed via domestic adoption, detailing, "Currently there is a high need for families willing to adopt African American or biracial newborns. If you are interested in this type of placement, the process may be quicker."

While the social worker at Forever Family did not explicitly state that the waiting times could be shorter for prospective parents considering the adoption of a Black baby, she informed her audience that they would be competing among fewer families. "So in our Caucasian program," she stated, "there are probably between 110 and 120 families, give or take." But in contrast, "in our African American, African American mixed-race program, we actually have 35 families in our program right now. So that kind of gives you an idea of where we are."

Patricia testifies that these increased odds of being chosen often factor into her clients' calculations:

I think when families realize that if they are open to a child of color, they are likely to get placed faster, . . . suddenly they would like to adopt a child of color, whereas it was never something they had considered doing before. But they found out that "if I am only open to a Caucasian, I might wait two or three years, but if I am open to African American, I could be placed in six months."

Michele also discusses how the possibility of shorter waiting times motivates some White parents to pursue transracial adoption, elaborating:

It comes back to flexibility on race. We do see families who are limiting themselves to a child as healthy as possible, Caucasian or Hispanic, in a relatively closed adoption. . . . Realistically they will be waiting three plus years in order to be successful in adoption because there are so few opportunities.

For some prospective parents, being flexible on race is more palatable than entertaining the risk that their son or daughter may have significant medical issues. Although the movie *Juno* popularized the narrative of the free-spirited but responsible White teen birth mother who receives excellent prenatal care before making an adoption plan,[40] this type of woman is harder to locate in reality. While some prospective adoptive parents may initially stake out the position that they only will adopt a healthy White baby born to a birth mother who took prenatal vitamins, did not smoke, and did not consume drugs or alcohol throughout the pregnancy, these children are in short supply and great demand. Explaining this conundrum, a friend of mine who has been working in adoption for years once told me that women who invest this much in motherhood tend to keep their babies. These birth mothers are few and far between, and many prospective adoptive parents are likely vying for this type of placement. Thus, to widen their chances of being selected, prospective parents have the option of being flexible on the health profile of the expectant mother.

At their information session, a representative from Forever Family explained the agency's system of asking prospective parents to fill out a checklist so their file can be shown to women carrying children who fit their specifications. She elaborated: "The checklist is what you are telling us is okay in a birth parent's background." Applicants are asked to consider the following questions: "Are you okay with a birth mom who drank alcohol socially in the first trimester? Are you okay with a birth mom who smoked marijuana throughout the pregnancy? Are you okay with a birth mom who maybe had some mental health issues like schizophrenia or bipolar or just depression?" By setting these parameters, the social worker detailed, "it breaks it down for us. You are able to say, 'This is what I am okay with in a birth parent's background. This is what I am not okay with.'"

It is worth repeating that these are not abstract conversations about a hypothetical child. Rather, this paperwork represents a type of covenant that potentially commits parents to raising a child with these characteristics. Just as parents who are open to gender will get a boy, those who are open to these conditions are likely to be placed accordingly. Once agreeing to these conditions, it is difficult to back out once the pregnant woman selects the particular family. The speaker at Kid Connection reiterated the significance of this commitment, explaining that once setting their criteria, applicants "can't meet a pregnant woman and say, 'That is not the person for me.'"

Many agency representatives advise hopeful adopters to widen their net and loosen their parameters to maximize their chance of getting selected in a timely manner, or at all. The presenter at Forever Family detailed, "We do not have an average wait time for how long families [wait]. A lot of it depends on what birth parents are looking for, since they are the ones who are going to be picking you." Despite being subject to the discretion of the pregnant woman, the presenter assured her audience, "you'll have control over some things in how open you are in your profile key and how not open you are in your profile key." These decisions will affect "how many birth parents will be able to see you" and thus applicants' likelihood of becoming parents through adoption.

Although the focus of this book examines transracial adoption from the perspective of adoption providers working with hopeful parents, it is important to note that birth mothers are often the most marginalized members of the triad, and birth mothers of color have even fewer options. A White birth mother carrying a White baby may have over one hundred families competing to adopt her child, and she can literally handpick the family and circumstances under which her child is adopted. On the other hand, given the current private marketplace, in which most prospective parents are White, a Black woman has fewer options. If a disproportionate number of families open to Black children tend to be single and gay parents, these pregnant women may have to resign themselves to picking a nontraditional family, even if it is not the birth mothers' first choice. Describing these odds, Patricia explains, "Typically you go and meet with a woman and her family, and she is Caucasian, and the birth father is Caucasian, and, you know, you may have twenty families who are open to the placement. But you meet with a Hispanic woman or a woman who is Black or African American, and she may have two or three." In other words, the market calculation often increases single and homogamous partners' chances of becoming parents, but it is at the expense of first mothers' options.

Although I argue that adoption workers frame transracial adoption as a market calculation, again I return to the knowledge that as much as adoption can be read as a story about markets, it is also a story about love and the irrevocable bond that adoption can form. One of the things that makes adoption such a sociologically meaningful site of inquiry is that family making is facilitated by workers who are often placed in the untenable position of balancing competing clients and contradicting demands. On the one hand, workers have to get potential customers excited enough to "come to adoption" and embrace this still-stigmatized form of family building. To foster this customer relationship, workers must assure clients that adoption is a viable option while conveying the disappointing information that there may not be enough high-demand children to go around, especially should applicants fall outside of the heteronormative ideal of the nuclear family.[41] To meet client demand, many adoption workers will couch transracial adoption as a feasible strategy to obtain a healthy and young child.

While greater proportions of White parents are willing to adopt across race, research examining adoption patterns from the U.S. Census shows that the majority of transracial adoptive parents adopt Asian or Hispanic children.[42] In other words, they are more likely to adopt children who could be categorized as "honorary white."[43] In the next chapter I explore how adoption serves as a window into the color line and as a vehicle to understand how race and nativity intersect. This distinction helps us understand why Lydia, along with thousands of other adoptive parents, chose to pursue the adoption of a foreign-born Black child over a native-born Black child.

# 4

# "And You Get to Black"

*Racial Hierarchies and the Black–Non-Black Divide*

Latino, Hispanic, and Asian: they seem to be the more
preferred minorities.
                          —GRETCHEN BISHOP

Gretchen Bishop is a licensed adoption social worker in her early thirties who has worked in private adoption for the past five years. She got her start in social service as a college student interning at a not-for-profit organization dedicated to child welfare. There, she contributed to a project establishing after-school programs for foster care youth. "This led me to become more and more interested in adoption and second families," she explains. "So whether this is a child being raised in a kinship situation by a grandparent or an aunt or uncle, or whether that be a foster care situation, or an adoptive placement. So I became really interested in what a first family versus second family relationship was like. . . . That is what led me to be very thrilled to accept my position at [my agency]."

Early in the interview Gretchen spontaneously mentioned her concerns about transracial adoption and how her clients tend to focus on the practicalities of the application process rather than the implications of raising a child of color. "You know, it's interesting," she begins, "sometimes parents, by the time they are getting to me, they can be in a variety of different places in terms of how they are feeling about adoption and their next steps." Underscoring the strong link between infertility and adoption, Gretchen elaborates, "The vast majority of parents who are coming through are those who are unable to have a biological child or have decided to discontinue trying." She discusses her clients' state of mind at the start of the process: "Okay, so how does this work? How much does it cost? Am I required to travel and for how long? What is the overall time frame of the process?" In other words, these families are concerned with what Gretchen calls "very practical things. Very few families are asking questions about, 'Okay, how can I handle transracial adoption? Is it right for me?'" She laments that an unrealistic ethos of color blindness can saturate adoption, leading many of her families to downplay the role of race. Voicing her concerns, Gretchen states, "I have just heard far too many times families say things like, 'Well, the most important thing is that we are going to love, honor, and cherish this child. That is the most important thing.'"

It is not surprising that many of Gretchen's clients hold this quixotic color-blind view, since transracial adoption is often positioned as the personification of a postracial society. During national adoption month, memes like "Our skin may not match, but we match hearts," and "You may not have my eyes or smile, but from the very first moment you had my heart" abound with the message that love sees no color. Given that transracial adoptive families are so conspicuous and at times still stigmatized, the allure of slogans that celebrate adoption's irrevocable bond is understandable. While upbeat quotations have their place, these oversimplified messages can diminish the gravity of what transracial adoption entails.

Mainstream publications on adoption also uphold these color-blind sentiments. For example, in his book praising adoption, NPR reporter Scott Simon declares, "Race, blood, lineage, and nationality don't matter; they're just the ways that small minds keep score. All that matters about blood is that it's warm and that it beats through a loving heart."[1] Granted, Simon published his book in 2010, the heyday of a post-racial wave of optimism heralded by the Obama presidency. During this color-blind era, Eduardo Bonilla-Silva and David Dietrich argue, "A mythology that emerged in post–civil rights America has become accepted dogma among whites with the election of Barack Obama: the idea that race is no longer a central factor determining the life chances of Americans."[2] Given this wishful albeit erroneous context, Simon's prediction that his Chinese daughters will grow up thinking "people come in different colors and it is no big deal,"[3] can be read as an offshoot of this palpable desire to have transcended race.

Simon is not the only adoptive father to write about race and adoption in this manner. In *Adoption Nation*, Adam Pertman argues that adoption in the United States is undergoing a "revolution," such that "after decades of incremental improvements and tinkering at the margins, adoption is reshaping itself to the core."[4] Part of this metamorphosis is due to the explosion of modern families so that "single women, multiracial families, and gay men and lesbians are flowing into the parenting mainstream." He adds that another improvement is "middle-aged couples are bringing a rainbow of children from abroad into their predominately white communities."[5]

What is so striking about Simon's and Pertman's passages is the way that race is minimalized. These publications ignore what scholars of race have proven time and time again—that race serves as a master status that powerfully shapes the opportunities and privileges bestowed on people.[6] The authors' approach diminishes racial difference, equivocating race to mere crayon hues such that children who come in "a rainbow" of colors will be seamlessly moved into predominately White communities, making racial difference "no big deal."

But as this chapter shows, transracial adoption is not color-blind; rather, race and racial boundaries are indeed a big deal. To investigate the question of how racial boundaries are drawn in adoption, it is important to reiterate that a key focus of this book is to investigate the role of the racial color line in America. As several scholars have argued, the racial landscape of the United States is changing such that light-skinned, and racial minorities of high socioeconomic status, like some Asians and Latinos, may inhabit an "honorary white" status.[7] But this boundary relegates Black Americans to the other side of the color line. While there may be room for some darker-skinned racial minorities to cross over into honorary White status, the color line is never fully dismantled.[8] As Lawrence Bobo writes, "In America we remain immersed in a culture of contempt, derision, and, at bottom, profound dehumanization of African Americans, men and women, but especially of young black males."[9] Although this grim racial hierarchy gets played out in adoption, it is important to keep in mind that the Black side of the divide is not a monolithic category. Rather, I argue that the adoption color line can be narrowed to an even more specialized division between those who are "full" African American and those who are not. To support this claim, I offer two test cases illustrating how some Black children are seemingly bestowed a more privileged status compared to their monoracial African American counterparts.

## Transracial and Transnational Adoption

Although foreign-born children of color adopted by White parents technically fall under the umbrella of transracial adoption, scholars have noted that these placements were symbolically and ideologically different from placing native-born minority (usually Black) children. As Barbara Melosh states, "At home, the reaction against transracial adoption signaled the limits of American pluralism and the constriction of adoption itself. Yet at the same time, the steady growth of international adoption—often transracial— suggested just the opposite response."[10]

This distinction between transracial and transnational adoption was magnified in the 1970s when community members came out strongly against the outplacement of Black and Native American children in White homes. These social movements resulted in the passage of the Indian Child Welfare Act (ICWA) and the publication of the National Association of Black Social Workers' statement in opposition to transracial adoption.

Although ICWA was not enacted until 1978, its roots extend back a decade to a 1968 press conference held by the American Association of Indian Affairs, which called attention to the long-standing discriminatory policies that removed American Indian children from their families.[11] These concerns led to ICWA's passage, a law that delineated a preference, in descending order, to keep Native American children with their biological families, within extended families, and within the tribe.[12] Tracing the history of ICWA's genesis, Laura Briggs reminds us that "ICWA was about sovereignty—about the self-government of tribes or Indian nations as such, distinct legally from the larger United States," and as such, the law was "defined by the nature of their political and legal status, not 'racial,' status."[13]

Briggs argues that ICWA's campaign to bring attention to "the increasingly visible resistance of tribal peoples in the 1960s and 1970s to losing children to adoption by Anglo families" may have influenced the decision of the National Association of Black Social Workers (NABSW) to issue its own statement.[14] This powerful document decried the placement of Black children in White families, arguing that transracial adoption robbed children of their racial and cultural heritage. Moreover, providers argued that these cross-racial placements were unnecessary since there was an abundance of Black families eager to adopt Black children.[15] The statement itself drew considerable public attention, but it is important to keep in mind that there was never any legislation passed outright banning these placements. Yet the controversy that ensued was effective, as it curtailed the pace of Black-White placements,[16] pushing prospective adopters toward international transracial adoption.

The expansion of the Korea adoption program correlated with the decline of transracial adoption in the late 1970s and early 1980s. Historians of adoption estimate that the transracial adoption of American-born Black children reached a peak in the early 1970s, with 2,574 placements a year.[17] As domestic transracial adoptions declined, international adoptions from Korea skyrocketed. As several scholars of Korean adoption have noted, the earliest cohorts of children adopted from Korea consisted of mixed-race children fathered by American GIs.[18] But by the late 1970s, the demographics of children shifted as greater numbers of Korean babies were born to unwed mothers who faced intense stigma and lack of financial and social support, leading them to place their children for adoption. By the early 1980s more than 6,000 Korean children, predominantly infants, were arriving in the United States each year.[19]

Describing this push-pull phenomenon, Kim Park Nelson argues, "Ironically, it was criticism from African American and Native American communities that pushed the adoption industry to pursue sources of children outside the United States at a time when Asians were broadly understood in the American mindset to be largely exempt from racial subjugation that affected other people of color."[20] Likewise, Arissa Oh asserts, "American preference for a foreign non-White child over a domestic Black child became firmly established during the 1970s. Unable to obtain a White child, and unwilling or unable to adopt a Black child, Americans turned to Korean children: a 'racial middle ground' that did not require white parents to cross the highly charged black-white divide."[21]

The extent to which the cross-race adoption of Asian children was seen as distinct from the cross-race adoption of Black children is also evident in the adoption terminology used to describe these placements. Reviewing the literature, Mia Tuan describes how "the term 'transracial adoption' is typically reserved for those adoptions involving the domestic placement of African-American children with White American parents, while 'international adoption' or 'inter-country adoption' refers to foreign-born Asian or Latin-American children adopted by White American parents."[22] By linguistically separating Black children from Asian and Hispanic children, adoption social workers implicitly reinforced the racial hierarchy and sent the message to their White clients that overseas placements provided a more palatable form of transracial adoption. Park Nelson describes this calculus: "Since the anti-transracial-adoption positions of the NABSW and in the ICWA emphasized histories of racial discrimination against African Americans and American Indians, the perceived absence of racial discrimination against Asian Americans made the transracial adoption of Asians into White homes appear safe in comparison to domestic transracial adoption."[23]

Although there is a general scholarly consensus that the greater willingness among White parents to adopt Asian and Hispanic children must be triangulated against the aversion to adopting Black children,[24] studies suggest that few White parents are willing to frame their decisions in such calculated terms.[25] Instead, Kathryn Sweeney describes how the White adoptive parents she interviewed "talked about race without directly doing so," especially "when rationalizing the decision to not adopt a Black child."[26] Similarly, Khanna and Killian detail how White adoptive parents often rely on coded language, using terminology such as it would have been "too much" to adopt a Black child, explaining that this reasoning was likely a euphemism for it would have been too "undesirable."[27]

Because of the reticence that adoptive parents may feel when talking about the racialized decisions that ultimately led to the construction of their families, hearing from adoption workers provides an underutilized perspective. Using a frontstage and backstage approach, I examine how adoption agencies frame and publicize their racialized policies in their promotional materials during their information sessions. This analysis is complemented by my backstage approach where I interview adoption workers, asking their thoughts on racialized practices like charging discounted fees for darker-skinned children.

This chapter is divided into three broad sections. The first describes how the racial hierarchy in adoption places White children at the top, Asian and Hispanic children in the middle, and Black children at the bottom. However, my goal is not merely to corroborate what other scholars have found before. In the second section, I argue that these divisions are not just reflected in adoption workers' insights, but they are actually *perpetuated* by their policies and practices. I show how racial pricing and the language used to describe Black children reproduces and widens the racial divide. Yet two important counternarratives suggest that the Black side of the Black–non-Black divide is not a monolithic category. By focusing on the discourses and policies surrounding the transracial placement of biracial Black and foreign-born Black children, I argue that there are exceptions to African American exceptionalism. This has troubling implications for the color line, moving it toward a monoracial-African-American–not-monoracial-African-American divide.

## Less of a Transracial Adoption: Asian and Hispanic Children

In line with prior research, throughout my interviews, many adoption professionals spoke of how White parents seemed more willing to adopt Hispanic and Asian children than Black children. Sylvia references how the minority stereotype surrounding Asians made these children seem more desirable compared to the negative stereotypes surrounding brown and Black children. She attests, "As I am sure you know, there are lots of stereotypes around Asians. Asians are preferable to African American and Latino. They are sort of lower down. There is a pecking order."

The acknowledgment of the racial "pecking order" was widespread. Gretchen elaborates on this spectrum, referencing almost verbatim Bonilla-Silva's delineation of the tri-racial divide that situates Whites at the top, honorary Whites in the middle, and members of disenfranchised groups as part of the collective Black at the bottom:

> There definitely seems to be a spectrum of race and culture as it relates to our society in terms of White being on one side and Black being on the other side. And then there's a spectrum of all of the other races in between. I would say maybe it goes White, Hispanic, maybe a variety of Asian cultures. And maybe kind of a big jump to maybe a more browner skin and Middle Eastern and Indian. And maybe another big jump and you get to Black. I am not saying that's okay, but it is a pretty reasonably understood spectrum.

The effect of the racial hierarchy is especially evident when taking into account White parents' preferences, whether they are adopting domestically or transnationally. Alyssa, the director of a domestic adoption agency, describes how these desires play out, stating, "We have twenty-five families. Say, probably about twelve are open to babies who are Hispanic or Asian, and probably only four are open to babies who are African American." Following a similar ranking, Gretchen notes that among her clients adopting from overseas, "I think that many Caucasian families feel prepared to parent a child who is from Asia or maybe from Latin America more so than they might a child from Africa." Reinforcing this delineation, Erin details, "By and large, we are working primarily with Caucasian families who are adopting Asian babies." She continues, "For whatever reason, there is some kind of perception that adoptions from Asia are less—again, this is my feeling—that people perceive it as being less of a transracial adoption."

Abigail offers her insight as to the popularity of adoptions from Asia, subtly equating Asian adoptees as the next-best market option given the shortage of White children. She explains, "A lot of families may want Caucasian kids. And a lot of people may feel more comfortable with Asian adoptees because people have been adopting from Asia for decades now, so it is something they are more familiar with—and their friends are more familiar with—so it doesn't feel so foreign to them."

It is interesting that Abigail uses the descriptor "foreign" to discuss the experience of adopting a Black child versus an Asian child. Although children born in Asia are undoubtedly from a foreign country, these adoptions are seen as familiar, comfortable, and relatively low risk.[28] This characterization of Asians as familiar and non-foreign stands in direct contrast to contemporary racialization theory that positions Asians as "forever foreigners."[29]

But as Sara Dorow argues, Asian adoptees embody a flexible foreignness which marks them as exotic but worthy of rescue because of their ability to assimilate. She states, "Chinese children become flexibly rescuable, then, *in contrast to* a continuity of abject (black, older, special needs) and unattainable (white, young, healthy) children at home."[30] In other words, "healthy Chinese baby girls are 'needy enough' and 'different enough,' but not so needy or different that they are beyond desire and revaluation for white American families."[31]

In her research on Korean adoption, Kristi Brian details how adoption facilitators play up the allure of the Korean adoption program, describing how facilitators "often characterize it as one of the safest, easiest, and quickest routes to a young, healthy baby."[32] Danielle, one of the social workers I interviewed, echoes these sentiments, describing how many prospective parents self-select into various adoption programs and—within limits—are flexible on race. She states, "Korea was the most—and I am not trying to be offensive—Korea was the most white-bread program. People who felt that they didn't have any other flexibility would adopt from Korea."

It is worth unpacking Danielle's statement that Korean adoption was the most "white-bread" program and what it means to refer to Whiteness in this capacity. Ruth Frankenberg argues that descriptors like white bread and mayonnaise used to define Whiteness as a processed and bland food can signal the absence of culture: "The linking of white culture with white objects—the clichéd white bread and mayonnaise, for example . . . connote[s] several things—color itself, . . . lack of vitality (Wonder bread is highly processed), and homogeneity." Frankenberg states that this rhetorical strategy effectively turns Whiteness into "an unmarked marker," perpetuating the invisibility of White privilege.[33] With this in mind, Danielle's characterization of Korean adoption as white bread likens it to a raceless transracial placement in which difference is rendered absent and unmarked. She continues that another perceived benefit of adopting from Korea was that parents could have their child delivered to their regional airport. "They didn't have to travel. The kids came with very good medicals. . . . It was largely closed. . . . it was very comfortable."

Compared with so-called honorary White Asian children, the racialization of foreign-born Black children stands in stark contrast. Danielle juxtaposes Korea's comfortable white-bread program with Africa's unknowns: "Africa is the opposite of that. No medical information, not great family background information . . . and race [*pauses for emphasis*] a very full presence." Thus, according to Danielle's assessment, for White parents, Asian transracial adoption is configured as "very comfortable," but African transracial adoption elevates the significance of race to "a very full presence."

Although some adoption workers were uncomfortable with prospective adoptive parents' characterizations that Korea offered the superior program, it is important to underscore that social workers bolstered this idea during information sessions. For example, at Baby Talk the presenter declared, "I think that South Korea is my favorite country because it is very Western. The medical care they get is very Western. The health information is very detailed and very good. It is probably the country where the kids are the healthiest." Additionally, a social worker at Family Tree portrayed the Korea program as "one of the most appealing programs," detailing, "The children are young. They tend to do really, really well." She then added, "Last year one of our interns was a Korean adoptee. The kids just do remarkably well. The children are in foster care and receive high-quality medical attention."

This statement deserves unpacking on several levels. First, notice how the Family Tree social worker puts forth the message that Korean adopted children have the potential to grow up to be productive young adults and they can follow a trajectory of success, presumably graduating college and acting as interns. Second, she offers an implicit reassurance that these children will grow up to be so comfortable with adoption that some will even pursue careers endorsing the practice. Third, this brief statement provides a window into attitudes toward foster care abroad compared with attitudes in the United States. The speaker frames the fact that the children are in Korean

foster care as an advantage, because they are cared for in small group settings rather than a large institutional orphanage. The fact that these children
are valued because they are in foster care stands in contrast to the negative
associations often characterizing racial minority foster-care children in the
United States.

## Pricing Priceless Children: The Dark-Skinned Discount

The idea of attaching a price tag to a child often elicits strong feelings of
discomfort, since the act of commodifying a human life provides a painful
analogy to the slave trade where children were brutally auctioned, bought,
and sold.[34] But as Viviana Zelizer argues, there is a key difference between a
black market, "defined as a degrading economic arrangement," and a "legitimate market," which "exists for the exchange of children."[35] Charging a
fee does not make adoption a pernicious baby trade. To sustain this legitimate marketplace, fees must be charged to cover the overhead and costs associated with legally transferring parental rights to a child from the birth
parents to the adoptive parents. Although some social workers remain uncomfortable with the pecuniary aspects of the exchange, many are reconciled to the fact that, similar to other professionals who charge a fee for
service, the revenue is critical to keeping them afloat. Beth, an adoption social worker, declares, "Fees have to be charged; there is no way [otherwise].
No lawyer will do any job unless they decide to do a pro bono case without
charging a fee for their service. I think that it is unrealistic to think that
adoption agencies shouldn't charge." Of course, it would be unrealistic not
to charge since these monies cover the vital child welfare work of conducting
the home study certifying that the adoptive family can provide a safe habitat
for a child, legal background checks, birth parent options counseling, and
the like. In other words, it is not the fact that adoption providers charge a fee
for their services that is sociologically interesting—it is the variation in the
fees they charge.

It makes sense that prices could vary *from* agency to agency to account
for regional differences that affect staff salaries and state-imposed caps on
how much financial aid birth mothers can receive in supporting the pregnancy. However, one would expect that types of children would be priced
fairly equally *within* the same agency, especially for the same type of adoption. It is understandable that government-subsidized foster-care adoptions
would incur fewer out-of-pocket costs and that fees for international adoptions may vary since the travel requirements vastly differ by country. However, the cost of a private domestic adoption should be rather stable at each
agency.[36]

The fact that there are different fees in private domestic adoption provides an interesting test case as to how race shapes the price of a child. Age

and nationality variables are somewhat controlled for, considering that—by definition—domestic adoption agencies specialize in placing U.S.-born infants. Since prospective adoptive parents can delineate what medical risks they are open to in their profile key, the health variable is somewhat controlled for as well. Thus, differences in price serve as an acute indicator of the racial hierarchy and the color line. Under a truly color-blind system, the fees would be the same for every domestic infant placed by an agency. But that is often not the case, since many private agencies abide by a variegated pricing structure that systematically discounts darker-skinned children.

Some adoption providers justify the existence of a two-tiered system with the explanation that minority children are harder to place. Because they are less in demand, especially among agencies' predominately White clientele, the fees for these children are lowered to align with their perceived market value. Yet as scholars have pointed out, there is a flaw in the logic that harder-to-place children should be priced lower. If agencies set their fees commensurate with the amount of work it takes to place a child, then children who are seen as harder to place should command more in fees, since it presumably takes more man-hours and hence greater operating expenses to match these children.[37] However, when agencies implement tiered pricing schemas, it is never the "easy-to-place" White children who cost less; instead, they cost more—a *lot* more.

Family Tapestry is a private domestic adoption agency with a long history of placing U.S.-born infants with families across the country. Like many other adoption agencies, they use a two-tiered fee structure. Although the agency charges a flat fee for conducting the home study and obtaining fingerprints and background checks, it lowers its program fees considerably for Black children. Its promotional materials state that the program fee for White children is $22,000, but in contrast, it discounts the fee for Black children to $14,000.

Tracy's employer also institutes a similar policy that I call the "dark-skinned discount." During the interview, she attests how supply and demand shape her agency's decision to lower its fees for Black children to move them through the adoption pipeline. I asked her, "What do you think is the draw of the biracial African American program?" and she hypothesized, "I am going to say the majority of it is probably the fees. They're drastically different; it is almost cut in half. . . . And that is because we need families for the program, so we subsidize programs, one for the other." She conjectures that the two-tiered pricing motivates clients to adopt transracially, especially if they can get a (presumably lighter-skinned) biracial child at a discounted price. "I think fees have a lot to do with it. So they are looking at the fee schedule and say, 'This [White baby] adoption could be anywhere from $35,000 to $40,000, and this [biracial] one is going to be around $20,000 to $25,000. Sometimes, I feel like that's what it comes down to, and that is a sad fact, unfortunately."

Adoption agencies like Tracy's employer and Family Tapestry are not anomalies. The practice of charging less for Black children is an open secret in private adoption. Barbara Fedders argues, "The laws regulating private adoption grant agencies much discretion in how they set fees, and a significant number of agencies charge prospective adoptive parents a higher fee to adopt a White infant than to adopt a Black infant."[38] But it was not until NPR ran its Race Card Project broadcast that the general public became aware of the practice.[39] Since that broadcast and the outrage that followed, racial pricing seems to have gone more underground. It still happens, but researchers now have to dig a little deeper to uncover this fee structure. For example, many of the agencies that I included in my study no longer post their fee schedules online. Luckily, I was conducting my fieldwork before the NPR story aired, at a time when adoption agencies were less reticent to publicize the practice, especially to potential clients at their information sessions.

What is so interesting about Family Tapestry's pricing structure is how it treats "middleman" racial minorities (e.g., Hispanics and Asians) who are not White or Black.[40] Notably, they are not included among the Black children and discounted accordingly, and the agency does not create a mid-tier pricing category reflecting their in-between status. Instead, Family Tapestry positions and prices these children on par with White children. As the promotional materials for its domestic program state, "Children in this program are of Caucasian, Latino, Asian, and East Indian heritage." While Latino and Asian children are literally afforded an honorary White status, in contrast, Family Tapestry abides by a policy of hypodescent, effectively characterizing and pricing any child with one drop of Black blood as Black. For example, its information describes this discounted program this way: "Children in this program are of either full African American heritage or other races mixed with African American."

The practice of pricing Asian and Hispanic children on par with White children may stem from adoption workers' awareness that these children are perceived as a second-best option, given the shortage of White infants in the domestic market. Irene details how her clients are willing to adopt non-White children, but within a narrow scope: "I would say that most of our clients are White. And not all—we definitely have African American and Hispanic clients—but I would say that the vast majority of them are White. And most of them are hoping to adopt a White child or a White/Asian child or a White/Hispanic child."[41]

Although it is sociologically interesting to examine how U.S.-born Asian and Asian multiracial infants are priced as honorary White, in reality it is somewhat of a moot point considering that only half of one percent of domestically adopted children are Asian. In contrast, the pricing structure for Latino children has important implications because 17 percent of domestically adopted children are Hispanic.[42] So the fact that they are categorized and priced on par with White children can greatly shape the revenue stream of some agencies. However, not all Hispanics are afforded an honorary White status. In a marked departure from the practice of classifying Hispanics of any race as Hispanic, Family Tapestry would categorize and price Black Hispanic children as Black.

Family Tapestry is not the only adoption agency I came across that follows these practices. Baby Bunting is another private domestic adoption agency that separates out its Black adoptions via what it calls its Marshall Program.[43] Located in an urban area, Baby Bunting places an array of children from different racial backgrounds. The presenter explained to her audience, "Like I said, [our city] is very diverse. About 30 to 40 percent of our placements are through the Marshall Center, 40 percent roughly are Caucasian, and about 20 percent are Hispanic with room for other ethnicities. But in the [urban] area, the main three [races] are Caucasian, Hispanic, and African American."

Similar to Family Tapestry, Baby Bunting charges an identical flat fee for its home study services regardless of the race of the child being adopted. Yet the corresponding program and placement fees associated with adopting a White versus Black child greatly differ. For White children, the program and placement fee outlay totals $35,000, while the fees amount to $15,500 for Black children. Baby Bunting opts to charge the full fare for Hispanic and Asian children, but following the one-drop rule, it relegates "multiracial African American" children to the lower-tier program.

During Baby Bunting's information session, some audience members were curious and slightly taken aback by the racialized pricing. The presenter explained the origins and rationale behind the program: "[Marshall] is a program where you know your child is going to be at least part African American. The program is focused on placing infants who are really more difficult to place, which are the African American infants. So you know if you do Marshall, your child will be at least part African American."

Later during the session, the speaker circled back to the segregated Marshall program and struggled to justify its existence. Notice that the presenter did the emotion work of couching this practice as child welfare, assuring prospective customers that the fee structure is about taking care of, rather than discounting, children. She began by framing the program as a child welfare strategy initially created to find homes for children traditionally seen as harder to place: "Just a little bit more about our Marshall Center. Each year we receive many more phone calls from birth parents interested in placing an African American child than we do from parents interested in adopting an African American child." However, the speaker then paused and backtracked as she thought out loud, stating, "Although I think that has changed a little bit now." She let slip that it is erroneous to say there is a shortage of adoptive families for healthy Black infants, articulating, "Well, in both programs, we have more parents than we do children." Perhaps recognizing that she had gone off-message by admitting that healthy Black infants may not be so hard to place after all, she sort of stumbled and paused. Taking a breath, she continued, "But the African American children need to be adopted just as much as the White children need to be adopted, so it is a great program." She concluded her explanation by firmly couching two-tiered pricing as child welfare, pronouncing that, "The Marshall Center is our special effort to make sure we have homes for all kids entrusted in our care."

Although racially segregated programs are well established, other adoption social workers were adamantly opposed to what they considered to be a demeaning practice. For example, I asked Patricia whether her agency had separate fees for White versus non-White children. She forcefully responds, "We do not. And intentionally we do not." She goes on to elaborate how this practice not only demeans Black children but also reeks of baby buying:

> We really feel that, since adoption is not about buying a baby, there should not be different pricing dependent upon what race child families are open to. Families are paying for a service, and all of our families receive the same service, so we feel that our fee schedule should reflect that. To our thinking, it feels a little demeaning to have different pricing for different babies.

While she opposes two-tiered pricing in principle, Patricia admits that she and her colleagues have considered implementing these policies in hope of recruiting more families of color to private adoption. She continues, "But it is something we have talked about because we probably don't have a large number of families of color in our program because of that. So we have to figure out how to be able to balance that to have families of color in our program while not sort of doing what we think is not appropriate."

Patricia's logic is interesting in that she assumes that it is socioeconomic status that prevents families of color from pursuing private adoption. There is some sociological support to this deduction given that demographic data have long showed that the Black middle class tends to occupy the lower end of the income spectrum.[44] However, there is a growing proportion of Black upper middle class as well.[45] If agencies truly wanted to be affordable, they could enact a sliding scale based on income. But even this measure might not work in terms of recruiting families of color. Adoption scholars and child welfare advocates have reported that non-White prospective adoptive parents often feel marginalized when working with agencies that are predominately White.[46] Perhaps feeling unwelcome, these would-be adoptive parents may decide to sign on with one of the few agencies dedicated to serving racial minority adoptive parents, rely on informal adoption, or eschew adoption all together.[47]

The exclusion of Black adoptive parents is nothing new. Tracing a history of adoption, Herman argues that White social workers "rarely treated African American applicants as equal partners in family making, defensively guarding their own prerogatives instead."[48] She describes a report from the 1960s blaming White social workers for failing "to understand that blackness was not only a matter of skin color and hair texture but also a cultural and sociological identity." The report asserted, "These social workers were confused by the spectrum of color—white to black and everything in between—that existed within many Puerto Rican families. They worried too much about 'lowering' standards for black adopters when they really needed to accept 'the socio-economic realities in which people must live, and where we find them.'"[49]

Responding to these criticisms, social workers of that era argued for the implementation of a two-tiered pricing schema so that the adoptions of Black children were more affordable for Black parents. Herman describes how this practice took shape:

> Social workers knew that rigid adherence to the material standards of White middle-class families amounted to a policy of racial exclusiveness. This became an increasingly pressing policy issue during the civil rights era. Some argued for standards that were more culturally sensitive and realistic about African Americans' socioeconomic standing, such as accepting maternal employment or relaxing requirements about income and age. To be flexible in these ways was not to lower standards or sacrifice the emotional welfare of minority children, they hastened to add.[50]

To recruit greater numbers of Black adoptive parents, Beth describes how, years ago when she worked in domestic adoption, her agency followed a similar practice of lowering the fees for Black adoptive parents, using an informal sliding scale based on ability to pay. She states, "The agency I was working for [pauses]—to help African American families adopt, so money wasn't an issue, they waived the fee for [them]." She continues, "And if the White families were also not able to afford it, their fee was waved." But this rarely happened, since White clients tended to pursue intercountry adoption, and in those cases they did not have the same discretion. She remarks, "In general, most of the White families were adopting foreign, so the fees couldn't be waived as easily. But for families adopting African American [children] going into African American homes, there were no fees charged."

However, this practice raised the ire of some of the workers at peer institutions who may have been concerned that they were losing market share to agencies with more generous policies. She recalls, "I remember another agency in the area was outraged by that. [They would say], 'Hey, if Whites have to pay for their adoption, so should Blacks.' And there was a huge discussion if Black Americans aren't motivated to pay the money, then they shouldn't be allowed to adopt." But rather than couch the race-based payment system as unfair to White customers, the naysayers framed their critique as a concern for the children's welfare. Beth continues on how opponents raised the argument: "If they do not have the money to pay for the adoption, they don't have the money to raise a child." She interjects that this "wasn't a very good argument, but that was an argument that was raised. . . . There was no money exchanged, but the other agencies didn't appreciate that fact."

Even though two-tiered pricing policies were initially created to recruit greater numbers of Black families who would otherwise not be able to afford it, the population-based data reminds us that White parents remain overrepresented in private adoption.[51] Compared with foster care, where 64 percent of parents are White, almost 80 percent of private domestic and almost 90 percent of international adoptive parents identify as White.[52] During one of my interviews, Tracy confirms that her clientele is homogenously White: "I would say that the majority of couples are Caucasian couples and we have a few biracial couples in the book and maybe one full African American couple." Similarly, Jennifer attests that her organization serves a predominately White clientele. For example, when I ask, "Are the majority of parents White Caucasian?"[53] she answers, "It is safe to say 90 percent."

Considering that private adoption agencies tend to have a customer base that is disproportionately White, it seems that the two-tiered pricing strategy failed to accomplish the original goal of recruiting more adoptive parents of color into the private marketplace. Sylvia characterizes this racial segregation, stating, "Most families doing private adoption—domestic intercountry, [domestic] agency, [domestic] lawyer—are White. They're White. It is very different if you look at foster care." Noting this imbalance, Patricia discusses how she wishes there was a greater push to attract Black clients and the frustration she feels about "the lack of outreach to African American families." She describes how there is "the assumption that African American . . . or Hispanic families don't want to adopt, or only want to adopt from foster care because it is free or no cost." Poignantly, Patricia states that she wishes people would realize "that race is still an issue in this society. . . . I think those are probably the most frustrating things."

Several other women I interviewed were also opposed to the practice of racialized pricing, especially if it meant discounting Black children. They cited how it was insulting to pregnant women and to the adoptees themselves who would grow up knowing they were "worth" less on the open market. For example, Nora responds:

Personally, I feel that it plays into devaluing the placement of African American children, which essentially it is. . . . I can't imagine being an expectant parent [with] a child who has been placed through domestic adoption and knowing that was something that had happened. It doesn't personally sit right for me, but I haven't given it tremendous thought in terms of whether other agencies shouldn't be doing it.

In her answer, Nora does allow some latitude for other agencies to formulate their policies as they see fit, despite her personal convictions that racialized pricing devalues African American children. She expresses a great deal of confidence in the judgment of her peers, believing, "They are advocating for the children that they need to place." Confident that her contemporaries are acting in the best interests of the children they represent, she excuses their segregated approach, arguing, "For whatever reason, they have come to the conclusion that [this] is one way to do it to help them find the permanency of a family in a reasonable amount of time. We haven't just faced that dilemma."

Alyssa also comes out strongly against charging less for Black babies, testifying:

I know why agencies do that, because we have a harder time finding families open to adopting African American babies. Because we want these adoptions to happen, because we want to provide this service for a birth mom, to have options for her. You lower your fees, and then you'll attract more people. . . . But for us, we just see it as the exact same amount of work for us to provide services to birth parents. We, of course, don't like the way it looks that you are paying less money to an agency to adopt a child of color. That bothers us, and we don't get it. . . . I think mostly it just feels icky to make a child worth less.

I followed up with Alyssa, asking her if she wished that other agencies would stop the practice, thinking it would reduce the risk of losing business to competitors if everyone had to follow the same guidelines. However, she defends her colleagues. "I know where it came from, and it comes from a good place: to find and make homes readily available." But she does interject, "It [the pricing] has gotten so insane, so distorted, that this is okay." Alyssa continues that she sees her work as being "a part of the movement—not the movement but a part of the team—that says we provide just as many services, and sometimes even greater, to an African American woman. And since we charge for our services, why would we charge less?" Firmly grounding the money her agency charges as a fee for service, not a fee for a child, she proclaims, "We don't charge to buy babies. We charge for services. Our services are the same no matter what race the baby is."

Whereas Patricia, Nora, and Alyssa were vocal about their opposition to discounting Black children, other women I interviewed had reconciled themselves to the practice, stating that the result justified the means. Lindsay describes how her agency instituted a three-tiered pricing schema, with White children commanding the highest price, and Black children the lowest. "They used to have three different fee schedules: one for the Caucasian children, one for the biracial, and one for the Black," she states, continuing, "I was never opposed to that because what it did was—the assumption was it encouraged White people to adopt across racial lines." This economic motivator was important, Lindsay explains, because it provided an additional incentive, ultimately placing more Black children in permanent families. She attests:

> That was one thing that they were doing [to encourage placement], and if the families were comfortable, I didn't have a problem with it, because Black children are harder to place. The reality was, if it was the same [price] for everyone, White people were only adopting White people and stretching their budget as much as they could, just to adopt. If they were happy adopting a Black child, and the money thing worked for them, and there were more families for Black children, I thought it was a good thing.

In line with previous generations of social workers, Lindsay justifies this differential pricing as a strategy to attract Black clients: "The other thing it did [was] it opened up—because you don't have as big of a Black middle class, because of lower socioeconomic circumstances—it also opened the door to Black families. You had more Black families to adopt, and it was creating parity with the White families." While these workers theorized that the racialized pricing would incentivize Black parents to use the predominantly White agency, in practice this fell short of their professed goal. When I asked her whether the majority of her clients were White, Lindsay concedes, "Yes, the majority. Some are interracial, but mostly White."

Immediately after couching the two-tiered fee structure as an incentive to recruit Black families, Lindsay pivots back to transracial adoption, passionately defending the pricing schema as a well-intentioned social welfare strategy. She acknowledges that it may not be a politically correct (PC) approach but insists that her colleagues' motives are pure:

> So I never had a problem with that program, and it was never a reflection on the children. It was a social issue, and it was a financial

issue, and it was a practical issue. If they were placing with White families who didn't want them, then I would have a problem with that. But it was just to encourage them to think about it. I never had a problem with it. It wasn't a political issue. It was made into a political issue—was it PC or un-PC? I saw it more as a hurdle to be overcome financially. If it is less practical to adopt across racial [lines]—and it is always less practical to adopt across racial lines— and if you get people to think about it because it met their pocketbook more [*trails off*]. This world is guided by money, and it is a consideration in any darn thing, so it is a consideration in adoption.

Other agencies I came across did not run their own two-tiered programs; instead they subcontracted with placement programs that routinely discounted Black children. For example, I attended an information session about one agency's African American Infant Program. It is worth emphasizing that this agency did not have a "regular" domestic infant program, so the African American Infant Program was the only venue for adopting a newborn. Notice how the very title of the "infant" adoption program supports the argument that transracial adoption can serve as a market calculation, as the program signals that parents will be able to leverage their market priorities by being flexible on race to adopt a baby.

During the agency's information session, the presenter stated that working with the African American Infant Program could offer a benefit to prospective adoptive parents because they would be able to network with multiple placement agencies without individually contacting and applying to each one. "Families can work with many of our network agencies without paying multiple application and processing fees," she stated. "Families are encouraged to work with as many agencies as possible to maximize their opportunities."

Unlike Family Tapestry and Baby Bunting, who charge a set price by race, fees at placement agencies tend to vary. The presenter explained, "These fees typically fall between $15,000 and $23,000." Notably, the price not only varies among placement organizations but oscillates depending on the racial composition of the individual child. These race-based fees are likely similar to the ones profiled on NPR's Race Card Project, which featured a screenshot from a placement agency website listing the fee for a Caucasian baby as $29,000, the fee for a biracial White and African American baby girl as $25,000, and the fee for an African American baby girl as $17,000.[54]

Later in my research I had a chance to speak with a social worker from the agency with the African American Infant Program about the variations in fees. She recalls how she was shocked when she first learned that "the race of the father makes the price go up or down." Under these parameters, children with a greater proportion of Black heritage cost less than White children. Thus, children who are "full" African American garner the lowest fees. As children move up the hierarchy in terms of having more White ancestry and presumably a lighter skin tone, they command a higher price. "It is more expensive if you are Hispanic," she notes. The difference in cost for an African American child compared with a Hispanic child was significant. She attests, "I was blown away. It was a lot of money." It was evident that the social worker was uncomfortable with the hierarchical pricing. She goes on to describe how she asked the placement agency about the policy but was unimpressed by the answer: "We asked them, 'What do you tell people?' They gave us back some stupid thing that they say and tell families. That is supposed to make them feel better?"

Despite her personal misgivings about the practice, the agency itself went along with this racialized pricing. By agreeing to these terms, this agency implicitly endorses that lighter-skinned children embody a greater social and economic value. Notably, even though some workers disagree with the idea that Black children should cost less, the overarching message still gets structurally embedded when workers go along with racialized pricing by discounting darker-skinned children.

Nowadays, few placement agencies make their individual fees publicly available, lest they end up featured on NPR or a similar media outlet. However, several adoption agencies continue to actively publicize their available adoption situations with information that includes the specific racial composition of available children. These racial designations also serve as a powerful reflection of the racial color line. For example, Born in My Heart Adoption Agency (BiMH) routinely updates a list of its current adoption situations. Children who are Black are routinely referred to as "full African American." The website lists one situation this way: "Birth mother from New Jersey working with licensed [state] agency will consider home study–approved families from the Eastern Region of the United States to adopt her full African American baby boy." Notably, the label Caucasian is reserved for "full" White children, but these children do not suffer the indignity of having the crude prefix attached to their racial composition. For example, one situation states, "Birth mom, N.D., has contacted BiMH adoptions to assist her in making an adoption plan for her Caucasian baby girl."[55]

Following the legacy of hypodescent, a child with "one drop" of non-White blood is no longer considered White. Yet there is a hierarchy of mixed-race children as well, depending on the child's composition. Notice how the adoption agency endeavors to be as explicit as possible about the child's heritage, specifying whether the child is part White or part Black. For example, one listing states, "BiMH is assisting birth parent W with selecting adoptive parents for her baby boy. . . . Birthmom's ethnicity is Native American and African American and she reports the birth father as Hispanic." Another details that "BiMH is helping terrific birthparents, M&P, with an open adoption plan. M&P have signed irrevocable relinquishments and are looking for an open adoption for their Hispanic/Caucasian/Native American baby girl." If the child is part Black, the wording makes sure to signify this fact: "BiMH has been contacted to help find a family for a Caucasian/African American baby boy that is due in June." These explicit racial descriptions stand in sharp contrast to the message that "love sees no color."

## Biracial Babies: A Lighter-Skinned Alternative

Although the one-drop rule historically allocated a person with "one drop" of Black blood as Black,[56] in adoption there are finely graded distinctions between monoracial and biracial Black children. It is important to note that in the context of adoption, "biracial" usually connotes that the child shares Black and White heritage. Of course, one could argue that most African Americans are multiracial since scholars estimate that between 75 to 90 percent of African Americans have some sort of multiracial White heritage.[57] But biracial in adoption means something very specific—that one of the child's birth parents is assumed to be "fully" White. Even though sociologists of race and ethnicity would classify a child born to a Black mother and a Black Hispanic father as a biracial or multiracial child,[58] in adoption this child would not be counted as biracial because he is not part White.

In private adoption, it is the child's part-White heritage that elevates his or her status and desirability. In the following exchange, Patricia explains her agency's internal debate as to whether to cede to clients' exact racial specifications by allowing White parents to insist on a White mixed-race child.

Me: What issues do you discuss?
Patricia: Whether a family should be able to say that they just want to adopt a child who is biracial Black. Do they need to be open to a child who is fully Hispanic, or can they be open to a child who is biracial Hispanic?
Me: Meaning part White?
Patricia: Yes.

Notably, while Black—and to a lesser extent Hispanic—children are relegated to what Eduardo Bonilla-Silva calls the "collective Black" side of the color line, for those who are mixed race, their White ancestry elevates them above their monoracial counterparts.[59] Drawing on interviews with transracial adoptive parents, Sweeney shows how White parents differentiate among biracial and "full" Black children because they assume "that the experiences of a multiracial person are less raced than a Black person in the United States and they were therefore comfortable enough to adopt a multiracial child but not a child perceived as Black."[60] Although White parents may endorse this market calculus, prior studies have shown that biracial transracial adoptees face nuanced challenges associated with their mixed-race status.[61] Calling attention to implications for child well-being, Sweeney argues, "Agency practices of distinguishing multiracial children may also perpetuate the idea that multiracial children are 'near-White,' and will not face racism in society."[62]

In spite of these warnings, from my research it was evident that many adoption agencies were active colluders in perpetuating the idea that biracial Black children were distinct from monoracial African Americans. Purveyors of adoption pushed forth this message in two key ways. First, many agencies kept separate placement statistics on the number of monoracial African American children and biracial children they place to assure White potential adoptive parents that biracial children are available. For example, one agency lists its yearly statistics, reporting that it placed forty-eight Caucasian, twenty African American, and twelve biracial babies. While keeping separate statistics on biracial Black children is telling, the mid-tier status of biracial infants is even more evident when taking into account that some agencies permit White parents to request a biracial child as opposed to a monoracial African American child. This request means that the family's profile would be shown only if one birth parent was White and the other Black.

Like the decision to adopt transracially, the willingness to adopt a biracial child but not a fully Black child must also be analyzed within the context of the racial hierarchy and colorism.[63] Given the shortage of White babies, Lindsay details why a biracial placement may be seen as an acceptable compromise to White parents: "Those families who thought they'd have a birth-child and that child would be White will sometimes say, 'We will do a biracial child as opposed to a full African American child.'" When I asked Lindsay to elaborate on this trend, she replies, "I do think it is an issue of color, and there is the assumption that those children are going to be lighter skinned, and lighter skinned is more desirable. So there is that social value and that's a piece of it."

In some respects, given the body of research on skin tone stratification within the Black community,[64] the preference for a lighter-skinned Black child is not surprising. Lighter-skinned Blacks are often perceived more positively compared with their darker-skinned counterparts.[65] However, it is surprising that some adoption agencies will acquiesce to colorism and allow White parents to stipulate they want a lighter-skinned baby. Over the course of the interviews I asked adoption professionals working in domestic adoption their thoughts on the practice. Interestingly, both proponents and detractors of the practice couched their decisions within the amorphous conception of what would serve in the best interests of children.

During to my conversation with Lindsay, I ask her, "What are your thoughts on policies that say it is okay to for parents to be open to adopting a biracial Black child but not a full-Black African American baby?" Like in her discussion of racialized pricing, Lindsay situates this practice as a child welfare strategy, rationalizing that allowing White parents to be that specific ultimately serves in the best interests of children:

> To me, you are always going to be the best parent to the child that you want to raise. I always tell parents that this is not the time to be politically correct. If you want a White child, you adopt a White child. People agonize. A lot of time they are aware of their prejudices, and things they didn't give much thought to come up during the adoption process. They say, "I should be able to adopt a Black child." I say, "Unless you have a few years to work through whatever it is and you can get to the other side and feel comfortable, adopt the child you are comfortable with, because you are not doing anyone a favor to adopt a child that you don't have an affinity for." I don't want that for a child.

While mandating parents to adopt across race is certainly not sound adoption policy,[66] it is not clear whether allowing White parents to pinpoint a child's racial composition to such a degree serves in the best interest of a child. Notice how Lindsay begins the process with prospective adoptive parents' racial preferences and assumes that child welfare will naturally flow out of these affinities. Rather than questioning whether a White parent who is only comfortable adopting a biracial Black child is truly prepared to adopt across race, the decision is framed as a consumer choice in which the parent has the latitude to determine his or her boundaries and adopt accordingly.

Similarly, Tracy draws on the argument that acquiescing to clients' comfort and consumer autonomy will ultimately serve in children's best interests:

> As an agency, I think that the theory is that we want them to be comfortable with the child. And if they are not comfortable with those things, it probably is not the best situation to put the child into. I think that as an agency we firmly believe that it is about what is good for the child, and allowing adoptive parents to be that picky is in the best interests of the child. And that being said, as a social worker I fully know that a biracial child can be as dark in color as a child that is full African American, and this is part of the counseling we do. And the meeting, and the talking, and all of the groups that we do, and the educational courses are so we get families to the point when they say, "You're right. You're very right." It is sort of sad, but we get families who say, "We want them to look like Beyonce."

Interestingly, Tracy positions her agency's position as racially progressive, emphasizing that her White clients have to be "all in" for a biracial child, regardless of the baby's actual pigmentation. She minimizes the fact that some of her clients may be selecting a biracial child to increase their chances of getting a lighter-skinned baby, stating, "It is an all-or-nothing type of program. You are all in for a biracial child who may look African American." She draws the line at allowing prospective parents to specify that the eventual son or daughter would need to be lighter than a paper bag, emphasizing that it would not be fair to the pregnant woman to impose such explicit specifications. "There's no shades," she responds. "That's not fair to a birth mother. She doesn't know. Ultrasounds are great nowadays, but they are not that great. And I always say to imagine how it is for a birth mom. The fact that she got to a place where she is ready to make the adoption plan and to take that hit is devastating to the birth mom, and I will never put a birth mom in that situation." Having drawn the line, Tracy positions her agency as racially enlightened, contrasting it with other agencies. "There are places, maybe other agencies, who believe race isn't such an issue. . . . I see it every day. It is definitely an issue, and it is definitely something that you have to be willing to talk about with families and be open and honest about it."

Despite the assertion that allowing parents the consumer option of selecting a biracial Black child was a progressive child welfare strategy, other women I interviewed were adamantly opposed to the practice. When I asked Fiona about pinpointing such preference, she was reluctant to endorse it, recognizing that it often serves as a market strategy for White parents to obtain a presumably lighter-skinned child. "For two White parents, I think that I would have a hard time with it. I don't like that. I feel like you want the child to be a little bit more like you and [have] whiter skin. And I would question, what is that about? Are you embarrassed? Are you looking for a lighter shade?"

Likewise, Amanda was very vocal in her opposition. She viewed these concessions as drawing a "ridiculous" line that gives in to consumers' desire for lighter-skinned children:

> We will not allow a family to be open to biracial only. We will not do that. Philosophically, we feel that if you are prepared to adopt a child who is half African American, you need to be prepared to adopt a child who is African American. That is a ridiculous line to draw because if you are prepared to support the child's identity, you have to be prepared to support the child's identity. . . . If our role, or part of our role, was to determine if they would be able to support a child of a different ethnicity, there is no amount of logic that would say to me that supporting half that identity is feasible. We know what's behind it: "I can parent an African American child as long as they are light-skinned."

Although this policy continues to be debated among adoption workers, I discuss the practice not to argue the merits for and against these placements. Rather, the key sociological takeaway is that extant adoption policies not only follow but also perpetuate the prescriptions of a Black–non-Black divide. It is important to remember that the Black side of this divide is not a monolithic category.[67] Just as there are divisions on the non-Black side regarding how Asians, Hispanics, and Whites are racialized, distinctions are drawn on the Black side as well. When White social workers emphasize the relative attractiveness of biracial Black children and allow White parents to be picky in their specifications, it has the unintended consequence of further refining the racial color line. When adoption practitioners implement practices that separately count, preferentially request, and accordingly price biracial African American children, they further segregate monoracial African Americans.

To further support my argument that domestic adoption policies move the color line toward isolating monoracial native-born Black children,[68] in the next section I investigate the rising popularity of adoptions from Africa and the Caribbean. There is an interesting paradox in this distinction because unlike biracial Black children who may be lighter complexioned, these African and Afro-Caribbean children are likely to be as dark as—or darker than—native-born Black children. Thus it appears that there is something else at play besides a pigmentation hierarchy driving the exponential growth of transnational adoptions of Black children, particularly from Ethiopia.

## Blackness of a Different Color: Foreign-Born Black Children

In *Whiteness of a Different Color*, Matthew Frye Jacobson traces how non–Anglo Saxon nineteenth-century immigrants like the Celts, Slavs, and Iberics, and from the Mediterranean were once seen as "distinct white races."[69] He shows how these immigrants were relegated to a different and less worthy "shade" of Whiteness and how their rising numbers among American immigrants "posed a terrible threat to the well-being of the republic."[70] But over time they assimilated and these "swarthy" White ethnics were able to claim a common identity as members of the "Caucasian race."[71] Jacobson's work is useful because it shows how variegated distinctions can exist among subgroups largely considered to be the same race. Just as Celt and Mediterranean Whites were presumed to be Whites of a different color, there are also distinctions between African immigrants and African Americans who embody Blackness of a different color.

There is a growing sociological literature showing that Whites tend to hold Black immigrants in higher regard than their native counterparts. This is especially apparent when examining the labor market. In a review of the literature, Mary Waters, Philip Kasinitz, and Asad Asad conclude, "Whether due to simple racism, the perception that immigrants make better workers,

African Americans' less effective use of social networks, or employers' perceptions that immigrants are more exploitable, the preference for immigrants seems quite consistent."[72] For example, Waters' research on Black immigrants shows that White employers often have more positive associations toward foreign-born Blacks because they too are immigrants "just like you and me." She finds, "In effect these whites saw themselves in the immigrants even as they saw American blacks as 'the Other' or people who shared none of their values and characteristics of their families."[73]

In line with the favoritism in the labor market for Black immigrant workers, I argue that in the adoption marketplace there is a consistent preference for Black immigrant children. Although there are multiple sending countries in Africa such as Liberia, Nigeria, and Ghana that have each placed over a thousand children in the United States, Ethiopia had been the driving force in African adoptions. Between 1999 and 2016, Americans adopted 15,317 children from Ethiopia—more so than the rest of Africa combined.[74] In the previous chapter I showed that part of the allure of adopting from Ethiopia was that relatively young children were available. In this section I expand on this market calculation, paying particular attention to how adoption practitioners and the parents they serve differentiate between native-born and foreign-born Black children.

While it was fruitful to use domestic adoption fees as a window into the color line, this approach is flawed for comparing the relative value of children sent via intercountry adoption because there are too many contingent factors. We know in general that intercountry adoptions are the most expensive form of adoption. According to the National Survey of Adoptive Parents, 93 percent of international adoptive parents report that it cost more than $10,000 to adopt their child.[75] In likelihood the total outlay was much higher, considering that a recent study found the median price of an adoption was $34,000.[76] But one cannot do a direct cost comparison of fees since sending countries impose different travel requirements (e.g., one trip versus two trips) and the strength of the U.S. dollar varies. For example, one agency estimates that it costs up to $46,000 to adopt from Korea while the total fees are $42,500 to adopt from Ethiopia.[77] This price difference does not necessarily indicate that Korean children embody a higher status than Ethiopian children. It costs a lot less to hire caregivers in Ethiopia than South Korea, so it makes sense that the fee for service would be considerably less in one country compared with the other. These contingencies are beyond the control of adoption agencies, so a direct cost comparison cannot really tell us how the racial color line is enacted and perpetuated. Since this mode of inquiry is bound to give us limited results, in the following section I draw more heavily from the perspectives of adoption workers to understand the ways in which African and Afro-Caribbean children are promoted as embodying a more positive type of Blackness.

Like transnational adoption in general, the fact that Ethiopian adoptions are largely closed remains a significant factor contributing to the country's popularity. Notably, Ethiopian adoptions are more open than other international adoptions from countries like China or Korea since families adopting from Ethiopia are often given the chance to meet with birth-family members during their travels. But the level of contact does not nearly approach what is mandated via domestic adoption. So while international adoption workers encourage these families to "embrace the spirit of openness," in my interview with Fiona she notes there is a big difference between domestic and international openness. She contends, "There is open and *open*," elaborating how the gulf of geography, language, and resources mitigates adoptive families' fears about the birth family and contributes to the allure of intercountry African adoptions:

I also feel like adopting an Ethiopian child rather than an African American child over here, . . . parents have the feeling that "if I adopt an African American child from over here, that means that their family might come with it." And they are [geographically] closer. The family in Ethiopia is not going with it. They are still open, but there is open and *open*. . . . What's the likelihood that a family from Ethiopia is going to get on a plane? I am thinking pretty low.

Danielle also mentions how parents' concerns about openness fuel their decision to pursue an Ethiopian adoption:

I always ask people who are adopting from Ethiopia why they didn't do domestic. The reason I ask this is that domestic is becoming more and more open, and if someone is choosing Ethiopia because they didn't want the openness in domestic, I challenge them a little bit. We talk about what about the openness in domestic bothered you? You know, it is not exactly the same. In domestic there is the possibility that maybe you'd see this person. Maybe you'd have annual meetings. Maybe they'd run into them at the grocery store. Africa is pretty far away. That is not going to happen.

Despite the fact that the White parents adopting from Ethiopia had similar motivations for adopting abroad as parents choosing children from Latin America and Asia (e.g., a relatively young and healthy child in a semi-closed adoption), many of the social workers I interviewed implicitly differentiated between the transracial adoptions of African versus other foreign-born children. For example, Heather discusses the new challenge of vetting families who adopt Black children, stating, "The biggest recent change has been the shift to Africa. And that brings up new issues in terms of race and finding the right families." The fact that some social workers differentiated between White families adopting African versus Asian children underscores the effect of the Black–non-Black racial divide. Olivia muses about this difference: "If they are adopting an Asian child or a Hispanic child, I can see how they may not think this is as big of an issue." However, she compliments the White parents choosing Africa, stating, "I do think that families who are adopting from Africa are more thoughtful."

Recall Danielle's classification that parents without flexibility tend to seek out adoptions from Korea. She refers to these parents as "white bread," juxtaposing their desire to minimize risk and race with those adopting from Africa. Whereas the former transracial adoptive parents are painted as risk-averse and inflexible, she characterizes the latter as "really comfortable with the idea of being a conspicuous family." The idea that transracial adoption of a Black child makes one "a conspicuous family" while the transracial adoption of an Asian child is "less of an issue" or "less of a transracial adoption" is notable because in both cases White parents adopt non-White children. But even though these pairings are all technically transracial adoptions, it is clear that Black children occupied a separate status.

As the supply of young children from other sending countries dwindled, African adoptions attracted a wider range of parents who may not have been as "thoughtful" about race. Danielle muses, "I would say that distinction— initially when those [other] programs were up and running we found that parents who were prepared to parent a Black child had the most comfort with race. So they weren't trying to say, oh everybody loves Asian kids. Asian kids are so smart, or they will look almost like me." Yet as parents' consumer options declined, she details how Ethiopia rose in prominence. "But with Guatemala being closed, with Korea being almost closed, with China being almost closed, essentially Ethiopia is getting in the mainstream." Similarly, Nicole's assessment of how the rise of Ethiopia stemmed from depleted market options is almost verbatim to Danielle's characterization: "I think that China slowed down, Guatemala opened and closed, Korea slowed down. It was sort of the perfect storm." She continues, "Ethiopia is now getting in the mainstream." Lindsay echoes these sentiments, detailing how she has seen a "flood of Ethiopia adoptions" among White parents. She follows up, underscoring the explicit connection between the popularity of Ethiopia and the availability of infants, remarking, "Those children are under a year, which is part of the deal."

Ethiopia became so mainstream that some parents who were caught in a seemingly never-ending wait for a Chinese infant girl opted to switch programs and adopt from Ethiopia. Erin told a story about calling her clients to let them know about the possibility of changing programs and adopting from Ethiopia instead of China. Presented with the opportunity to adopt a relatively healthy infant girl in less time, some families were willing to switch and traverse the Black–non-Black divide, but others were far more hesitant. "We brought up the idea to a lot of China families because we wanted to let them know their options," Erin reports. But for some applicants, the Black–non-Black color line was too wide to cross. She details how one family declined this offer, recalling, "And one of the families I was working with, their biggest concern was they lived in the suburbs somewhere and not having a very diverse neighborhood. [They asked,] 'What will we do in terms of connecting this child to this community?' I was like, 'The onus is really on you to do that.'" She continues that her agency accepted the clients' decision "without any judgment on their part," and she praised the family for their honest assessment of their capacities, stating, "I think that it is great that they were able to realize that before the child is in that situation."

This story deserves further analysis on several levels. First, it is important to underscore that this White family had already committed to a transracial adoption when deciding to adopt from China. Even though this family "lived in the suburbs" and did not have a "very diverse neighborhood," the parents (and the social worker who approved the home study) were seemingly not as concerned about what that would be like for a Chinese child. In this regard, perhaps they saw the adoption as less of a transracial pairing. Yet the idea of bringing a Black child into the same neighborhood raised concern because in their eyes, a Black child, as opposed to a Chinese child, would need a more diverse neighborhood. Put another way, racial diversity, and perhaps race itself, was seen as less of an issue when transracially adopting a Chinese child than when adopting a Black child. Rather than raise a potential red flag that her agency had approved a family that did not live in a very diverse neighborhood, Erin lauds her clients for their self-awareness that an Asian child would be acceptable, but a Black child would not.

Second, although this particular family opted not to switch to the Ethiopia program, several adoption social workers told me that many of their clients did move to the Ethiopia program once they discovered that relatively healthy infants were available in a much shorter time frame. Faced with seemingly unending waiting times for the China program that stretched years beyond what parents had imagined, several families decided to switch into the Ethiopia program. These are the same families who invariably passed on the option to domestically adopt an African American infant in favor of adopting from China. In response to this calculus, Beth concludes, "I think some of them have the idea that it is easier to get a Black child from Africa and raise that child than it is to get an African American child." This brings up the question: What makes the adoption of a foreign-born Black child a more acceptable market option than the adoption of a native-born Black child?

I spoke with Patricia about this phenomenon. She reveals her frustration that prospective adoptive parents often have the misperception that adopting from overseas will be easier. She states:

> It is also very interesting that people will adopt internationally an older child and not domestically an older child. And [they] don't really understand orphanage care, institutionalization. I find it very interesting that someone would say, "Well, I could adopt a four-year-old from Costa Rica," but if you asked them to adopt a four-year-old from the U.S., people are like, "What?" I don't know if there is a fantasy in their mind [that] the child is going to come as a blank slate. No child ever comes to anyone with a blank slate.

Barbara Yngvesson writes of the allure and the fallacy of the clean break, noting how the practice of labeling children available via intercountry adoption as social orphans, regardless of whether they had known living birth families, promoted the "centrality of the child's orphan status—the legal clean break that is required to make him or her available for adoption."[78] Similarly, Dorow notes that Chinese girls were especially sought after precisely because they were thought to come with "light baggage" or, in other words, the "racial flexibility, good health, young age, distanced birth mothers."[79] She continues, "Factors of race, gender, age, and health play into the narratives of choice that imagine the possible relocation of some children, and not others, into adoptive homes."[80] Bestowed with a racially flexible status and seemingly unburdened by ties to biological family, these children were seen as distinct from other racial minorities and immigrants.

Whereas internationally adopted children are afforded this racial distinction, transracially adopted domestic minorities—especially via foster care—are not granted a similar dispensation. Anna Ortiz and Laura Briggs argue that one reason why foster care is seen as so undesirable is that it gets coded as poor and African American. They connect the messages put forth by influential studies such as Oscar Lewis's "The Culture of Poverty" and Daniel Moynihan's "The Negro Family" (also known as "The Moynihan Report"), which set the foundation such that "race emerged sharply as a term to characterize pathology."[81] Ortiz and Briggs trace how these negative stereotypes dominated domestic adoption policy, eventually creating the "crack baby crisis." They show how these narratives, taken together, created "a biologically suspect and racialized U.S. 'underclass'" which "rendered its members—and particularly its children—intrinsically pathological and completely irredeemable."[82] Despite policy interventions designed to move greater numbers of foster care children into adoptive families, many White parents deliberately eschewed the foster care system as "dealing with poor and traumatized kids," and turned to "the private system being the source of ($30,000) White infants."[83]

In paradoxical contrast to "the exceptional undesirability of U.S. foster care children," Ortiz and Briggs argue that foreign-born children available for transnational adoption—even those who are older and presumably have been exposed to neglect in institutional care—were able to escape the label of being "damaged goods."[84] Confirming this sentiment, Nicole reflects how "it became very trendy to adopt from Ethiopia. Part of the reason is that these children are not coming from histories of abuse and neglect. They are coming from poverty and disease. That feels a lot more comfortable to families [than it] might be adopting domestically from the foster care system, where there is a history of abuse and neglect and the child's parents have had their parental rights terminated."

Conscious of the fact that most of her clients were averse to foster care, Beth (somewhat mischievously) describes how she purposely asks new clients applying to Ethiopia whether they considered adopting from the foster care system. Even though she is aware that many of her clients assume that "children of African American descent . . . are born with drugs in their system and they come from a much more volatile background," she still asks them, "Why not do U.S. adoption? It costs you a lot less, and it is right here, and we have just as many children in need." According to Beth, the most common answer she receives is, "Those kids are usually drug-addicted, and their risks are high," underscoring the extent of negative connotations surrounding foster care.

It is not solely prospective adoptive parents who buy into these characterizations. Occasionally during the interviews and information sessions I observed, I witnessed how adoption workers perpetuated these distinctions, subtly communicating the message that adopting an African American child from foster care carried too many risks. For example, during an information session at Kid's Connection, the presenter assured her audience, "In Ethiopia, drugs is never the issue." Additionally, during my interview with Lindsay, her comments highlight the assumption that there are elevated risks in foster care. This exchange came about when I asked her whether parents are typecasting an American birth mother versus a foreign birth mother. She does qualify this distinction, stating, "[In] Russia you have the fetal alcohol syndrome, and people are very wary of that." But she adds that these children can be identified and possibly winnowed out of the pool because, "That is very identifiable. A lot of times it is apparent in their physicals." Lindsay attests that prospective parents "are just as afraid of fetal alcohol [as] they are of drugs. Culturally *there* [Russia], you are more likely to have fetal alcohol." Unlike fetal alcohol effect, which can be presumably identified with the medical screening such that prospective adopters can decline a referral, Lindsay states that would-be parents worried that they would not be able to identify crack exposure in time. "*Here* you have drugs, crack cocaine," she states, detailing, "The crack epidemic, there was a great fear of it." Elevating the risks of drugs over alcohol, Lindsay defends the fears of adoptive parents as legitimate concerns, contending, "Do I feel that they are maligning birth mothers? No, because it turns out that is a real risk."

If a racialized fear of African American birth mothers serves as the push factor moving prospective parents away from foster care, the allure of an exotic child contributes to the pull toward Africa. Along this line, several adoption workers credited the growing number of celebrity adoptions from Africa as adding to the exotification of these children. Abigail states, "Right now a lot of families are interested in adopting from Africa because that is the place where a lot of celebrities are adopting from." Nora specifically cites the publicity that ensued when Angelina Jolie adopted from Ethiopia and Madonna adopted from Malawi, adding, "I think that there's a glamour to it."

Playing up these supposed distinctions between glamorous African-born children and underclass native-born African American children, some adoption agencies and workers propagate finely tuned distinctions between these groups. For example, I conducted an interview with Carolyn, a social worker who had worked in international adoption for over a decade. At one point in the conversation she describes White parents' interest in Ethiopia, mentioning that Ethiopian children have "a different look." She emphasizes that Ethiopian children "do not look like African American children." Although Carolyn was hesitant to go into further specifics as to how Ethiopian and American Black children may differ by phenotype, her statement that Ethiopian children "do not look like African American children" suggests that these children embody Blackness of a different color.

Beth passionately and angrily discusses how some adoption professionals explicitly differentiate between native-born and foreign-born Blacks. She describes this phenomenon: "Other agencies started getting into Ethiopia and putting on their advertisements . . . 'We have a program in Ethiopia. These children are not African looking; they do not have the big lips or the wide nose. And their skin complexion is'—I was irate." Beth states that upon hearing about this, "I just hit the roof."

The extent to which differences between Ethiopian and native-born African American children are calculated and characterized harkens back to the historical practice of making distinctions between White ethnicities. Jacobson describes how "these new White races were subject to the new epistemological system of difference—a new visual economy keyed not only to cues of skin color but to facial angle, head size and shape, physiognomy, hair and eye color, and physique."[85] Notably, this eugenic practice ceased as Whites were able to coalesce around their imagined identities as Caucasians. However, these cues still retain their currency when distinguishing between Africans and African Americans.

In addition to perceived phenotypical differences, another potential benefit of international adoption was that it gave White parents the leeway to draw on the narrative of engaging in a humanitarian act. The fact that poverty and disease are seen as more "comfortable" factors for White parents echoes Dorow's assessment of how rescue serves as a redeeming narrative in transnational adoption. As Dorow argues, "saving" children "served as a complementary justification. Humanitarian rescue discourses helped distinguish international adoption from domestic adoption options."[86] In line with this assessment, Beth contends, "With Africa there is this whole rescue mentality. We are saving poor African children from really bad situations." The cache of the rescue narrative was especially potent after the devastating 2010 Haiti earthquake and the outpouring of sympathy that followed. Many were understandably moved by the constant media coverage of how one of the poorest countries in the world was especially vulnerable after such a natural disaster.[87] Compelled to try to alleviate such suffering, several adoption workers reported that they had a groundswell of contact from people interested in adopting from Haiti.

Jennifer, whose job entails answering the intake calls at an adoption agency, can attest to how a natural disaster often catalyzes interest in adoption. She juxtaposes those callers with clients who tend to come to adoption from infertility, describing how few of these callers ever go on to pursue adoption:

> The other time we will see an uptick in information calls will be after a natural disaster, like with Haiti. For about two weeks we were quite busy with phone calls where we weren't necessarily talking about our programs as educating the public. Because there was a larger percentage of people than usual who hadn't necessarily thought about adoption or weren't drawn to adoption in terms of infertility calling. So there is a whole different air that you have when talking with people like that too. . . . A handful of those people would go on to inquiring in greater detail. Most were moved by the urgency of the moment.

Looking back on this phenomenon, Nora conjectures, "People saw kids in Haiti, and they want to adopt from Haiti. But those parents won't necessarily take an American foster kid. The same black face, the same desperate need, but it is the American way to go out and save the world."

Tracy also spoke of how the emotional humanitarian urge creates dissonance between Black children overseas and native-born Black children at home. I asked her why she thought people were so interested in adopting from Haiti, and she responded, "It is more along the lines of 'We are saving one of those children in Haiti.' It looks better. Adoptive parents perceive it as

'It looks better because we saved a child,' rather than having a child who is born here who is African American."

She goes on to tell a story about how she received many interested calls from her roster of existing clients. To clarify, these prospective parents had deliberately decided not to pursue the adoption of African American children and were currently waiting to be chosen by expectant women placing White children. However, as Tracy details, many of these waiting families saw a clear difference between a Haitian child and an American Black child. She recalls:

> We had several parents who were in our Caucasian group who called us and said, "How can we adopt from Haiti? How can we get one of those children from Haiti?" I say, "Okay, but you're not in our African American/biracial book." And they are like, "We know." And I say, "Can you explain the difference to me?" They're like, "They're Haitian." That was a hard pill for us to swallow as social workers, but they were clearly able to see in their heads that this child is of Haitian descent, and *they are not Black.*

Given that many adoptive parents had the notion that their African-born children were "not Black," or at least a different type of Black, several social workers I interviewed mentioned their concern that some White parents were purposely trying to distance themselves from the African American community. Nicole describes how families adopting from Ethiopia would come to her and say, "'There is no Ethiopian adoptive community in my neighborhood.' And I would say, 'Well, what about domestic adoption and families who have adopted transracially [native-born Black children]?' And for so many families, they were like, 'Wow, it never really occurred to me.'" Rather than try to make connections with African Americans, or even White parents with African American children, these adoption professionals emphasize how White parents of foreign-born Black children prioritize their child's ethnic identity, rather than a racial one.

Later in the conversation Nicole describes the potential drawbacks of this emphasis on culture instead of race, stating, "One thing that wasn't talked about among the families but was often talked about among the staff was that a lot of these families are really committed to connecting to the Ethiopian community but not connecting to the African American or Black community." She continues, "A lot of parents were clinging so tightly to this Ethiopian identity. That is really big in the Ethiopian adoptive community, going out for Ethiopian food, using Amharic words. . . . I think there is this whole place of wanting your child to be part of not the African American community but of the African or Ethiopian community."

As several scholars have pointed out before, the act of engaging with a child's cultural origins by going out for ethnic food and peppering one's vocabulary with key phrases learned at culture camp has become the normative strategy for transnational adoptive parents.[88] Jacobson coins this strategy as "culture keeping," writing, "For international-adoptive parents, culture keeping can be hugely enjoyable and personally rewarding. Learning about a new culture, purchasing and consuming new ethnic goods and foods, and participating in new holiday traditions can be pleasurable experiences."[89] She continues that culture keeping "provides a comfortable avenue for mothers" that can "fulfill the ethnic expectation they place on their children based on racial difference, yet the cultural practices themselves are loose enough that they can easily be slipped on or off."[90] This comfortable approach to engaging with an exotic culture stands in stark contrast to the perceived risks and pitfalls associated with the appropriation and performance of African American culture such that White parents may feel like they have less license to slip on or off elements of domestic Black culture.

Yet for foreign-born Black children, the practice of culture keeping seems to be more accessible since White parents can follow the well-worn model of going out for Ethiopian food and attending culture camps, activities that allow parents to remain firmly in control of the narrative of racial difference. Lindsay describes how the White parents she works with distinguish their children, stating, "Somehow if you take a Black Caribbean child or a Black child from another country, somehow it is more exotic, so they are not African American; they are just African or Caribbean. Somehow that doesn't come with as much baggage in this person's mind."

While White parents navigating the adoption marketplace may choose to apply these finely graded distinctions, it does not necessarily mean that the outside world will abide by the same logic. Parents may think they are getting a pass by adopting an honorary White child, or they may try to mitigate racial stigma by adopting a biracial or a foreign-born Black child, but race remains a master status no matter how much some people may want to wish away its power. Because so many prospective adoptive parents come to adoption with a color-blind frame of reference, adoption practitioners have their work cut out for them. Nicole details how she tries to prepare her clients for the road ahead: "I would say [to prospective parents] that nobody is going to look at them and say, 'Look at this sweet Ethiopian child.' I was like, 'Your kid is Black and will be recognized and treated as such in the United States.'"

Despite some social workers' best efforts to adequately prepare future transracial adoptive parents that their children will grow up to become persons of color, many acknowledged that they often fell short. Erin explains that many of her clients just want to adopt a baby and are not thinking about the future. She laments, "I don't know how much this resonates with families. Because it is almost like tunnel vision. They just want a family; they just want to adopt a baby and they maybe can't get to that level of thinking."

Presumably, it is the responsibility of the adoption social worker to move prospective adoptive parents out of their tunnel vision toward a more nuanced level of thinking about the role of race in society. Yet as this chapter shows, many of the policies and practices employed by adoption providers do not just reflect the racial hierarchy; they also perpetuate it. This replication of the color line partially stems from the consumer model of private adoption. As Briggs argues, would-be parents intentionally seek out private adoption precisely because "they become more like consumers, seeking a child and then paying a fee."[91] Cognizant of their role, agencies and employees may be hesitant to set the bar higher and require additional time and money from applicants. Some workers were clearly worried about turning away potential customers or losing families to competitors. Nicole describes how supervisors at her previous agency discouraged her from mandating more rigorous training, rationalizing, "We really need these families."

In the following chapter, I show how there are several missed opportunities for thoughtful and engaged dialogue regarding transracial adoptive parenting. I argue that the silence surrounding the responsibilities and implications of transracial adoption gets perceived as an implicit endorsement of color blindness. By diminishing and in some cases obliterating any discussion of racial difference, adoption workers send the message that race should not matter. Ironically, this color-evasive attitude starkly contradicts what I call the color-explicit descriptions that some practitioners use to describe available children. These mixed messages perpetuate a consumer approach to transracial adoption that ultimately undermines adoption workers' goal of serving the best interests of children.

# 5

## Selling Transracial Adoption

*Social Workers' Ideals and Market Concessions*

In this chapter I return to the broader inquiry of how transracial adoption is sold to prospective clients and argue that social workers utilize a strategy of color-evasiveness, opting to minimize discussions of race so as not to dissuade potential customers. First, I examine social workers' characterizations of how their clients perceive transracial adoption. While many adoption professionals adamantly state that preparing White parents to adopt across race is of utmost importance, I detail how the fear of losing business to competitors leads some providers to minimize its significance. Even when adoption providers *do* try to engage in conversations about race, these discussions are hindered by adoption workers' own reticence to discuss race and racial inequality in terms of power and privilege. Paradoxically, despite the desire to use a color-blind approach, adoption workers employ color-explicit descriptions of children's phenotypes with a startling level of specificity that goes so far as to even detail children's skin shade. I discuss the implications of these strategies, detailing how a down market leads some providers to loosen their standards around transracial adoption.

Readers familiar with adoption policy may wonder if the "Multiethnic Placement" provisions of the Improving America's Schools Act of 1994 (PL 103-382), also known as the Multiethnic Placement Act, and the Interethnic Adoption Provisions of 1996 (MEPA-IEP) were factors in social workers' hesitancy to discuss race. At first glance, this conclusion seems logical, considering that MEPA-IEP makes it illegal to take into account a child's race, color, or national origin when making an adoptive placement from foster

care.[1] As Ruth McRoy and colleagues note, "The assumption behind the legislation was that African American children were lingering in the foster care
system despite the many approved waiting white families who stood ready
to adopt them. The goal was clearly to make it easier for white families to
adopt children of color in foster care and to penalize states that failed to
ensure this outcome."[2]

Yet as Patricia Jennings argues, the tenets of the Multiethnic Placement
Act are based on "faulty assumptions" that posit White middle-class parents
as queuing up to adopt Black children from foster care. As I have argued
throughout the book, most parents pursue private adoption precisely because
they want to avoid adopting children from the public child welfare system.
Jennings asserts that it was not so-called "reverse discrimination" that pre-
vented Black foster children from finding permanent adoptive families, but
instead it was White parents' "racial and ethnic preferences" that funneled
applicants away from foster care and toward private adoption.[3] Similarly,
Laura Briggs astutely notes that MEPA-IEP served as a "red herring," stress-
ing that there is little evidence that the legislation was even necessary, considering that most foster care agencies did not have formal race-matching
policies before the laws made them illegal.[4] MEPA-IEP was more ideological
than functional because, according to Briggs, "it seems to capture all of the
things we worry about—vulnerable children, drugs, questions of law and
race, irresponsible parenting, the danger of losing one's own children."[5]

It is important to emphasize that MEPA-IEP only applies to foster care
placements, not private adoptions. State foster care agencies that do not abide
by these provisions risk losing federal funds, but since private adoption is not
government-funded, these domestic and intercountry adoption agencies are
not subject to the same jurisdictions. Briggs confirms this point, stating,
"Private agencies, unless for some reason they receive public funds, are unaf-
fected by MEPA-IEP and were always far less likely to have race matching
policies."[6] If anything, in private adoption it is almost the opposite—
transracial adoption is often encouraged, especially if it can serve as an expedient market option.

As this chapter details, a tension emerges as adoption providers navigate
their responsibilities as social workers and as financial stewards of their organization. These actors face the dual roles of simultaneously anticipating
applicants' consumer mind-sets while also following their own obligations
as child welfare professionals by modeling how to talk about race and
adoption. Despite their stated goal of wanting to prepare White parents to
adopt across race, few adoption providers are willing to engage in potentially
off-putting conversations about the commitment transracial adoption
entails. Although there has been a surge of research about the complexities
associated with growing up in transracial adoptive families highlighting
the importance of racial socialization practices,[7] adoption providers are

reluctant to enter into these discussions, especially at the early stages of the application process.

During my interview with Patricia, I asked her why her agency chooses not to discuss issues related to transracial adoption from the get-go, doubtful but curious as to whether it had anything to do with MEPA. Notably, she had never even heard of the legislation, confirming my suspicion that the law seemed to have little relevance in the private adoption sector. In response to my question, she responds, "I think at the info meeting, you are just trying to get information out about your agency and what makes your agency sort of special or unique, or why someone would want to work with your agency." Patricia discusses how her agency does not want to scare off potential clients at this critical juncture. She does try to "give them a little general information about adoption," but overall, she asserts, the "primary goal at an information meeting [is] let me tell you about who we are and what we do." Since the top priority is to sell one's agency, she conjectures, "[that] might be why most people don't bring it up." Patricia is all too aware that this information might be off-putting, since "transracial adoption is still a pretty hot topic and it can still get a little heated."

Given that most adoption providers are reluctant to broach more controversial issues, I was curious as to whether social workers thought their clients were even considering the long-term ramifications associated with raising children of color. Erin asserts that when initiating a transracial adoption, most families she works with do not have a clear grasp of the commitment they're making. I asked her, "When families are coming in, how much are they thinking about becoming a transracial family and all the things that it entails?" Her response is telling because she pauses and stumbles, trying to formulate her thoughts before she admits, "During the home study we start bringing up that transracial piece, but my sense is that most families don't really think about that at all prior to deciding to adopt from another country."

Sylvia, a counselor with a long history of working with prospective adoptive parents, deftly summarizes how availability tends to be the driving factor in parents' decision-making process: "They go abroad, and they find out that these are the countries that are sending." She traces the expansion and contraction of the supply chain, detailing how people think to themselves, "Oh boy, a lot of these cute little Chinese girls are coming over. I see one here and one there. I could see myself with a cute little Chinese girl, and I hear that I can get one quickly." Once this pipeline stops, hopeful parents regroup, wondering, "Where are the options? Which countries as sending?" Sylvia then lists a roster of countries that once had thriving programs, recounting, "When Columbia was sending, so many people were adopting from Columbia. When Korea was sending, so many people were adopting from Korea. And then Honduras, and then Guatemala."

Attributing this global migration to the vagaries of the market supply, she asserts, "It shifts, not because people are—it is what is available. It is, where are the kids coming from? It is, what's available at the time?" These were the forces that propelled Ethiopia's growing popularity. Sylvia affirms, "A lot of people are adopting from Ethiopia because you can. . . . I think it is just availability that drives them; that's what I think." Later in the interview, she touches on her clients' mind-set when adopting across race, declaring, "People don't necessarily adopt across racial lines because they have thought through all of the complexities of the issues and worked it through. No, they want a kid, and they find that you can get a kid over here. . . . People will adopt kids from African American backgrounds and not give it a thought." Despite her blunt characterization of how availability drives the market, Sylvia remains empathetic to her clients' predicament, stating, "It is so overwhelming that people just—people have very idealistic, very, very unrealistic, idealistic, ideals of what it is like to have—why parents adopt a minority child."

As argued in Chapter 3, the desire for the youngest and healthiest baby available was a significant factor in driving the surge in transracial, and often, transnational, adoptions. Kiera reiterates how her clients' preference for babies tends to trump all other considerations, attesting, "Most of the time they come to us because they want a baby. They don't see anything because they are so fixated on the baby." Similarly, Beth expressed doubts as to whether White parents adopting Black children had considered the serious challenges they would encounter. She characterizes the situation this way: "I think they are coming from [the idea that] this is a cute baby. This is another country where you can get a baby." With this in mind, I ask her whether she thinks parents are prepared to adopt across race, and she responds, "I don't think they are. I don't know. I don't think they're well prepared."

With her training as a counseling psychologist, Sylvia offers some clinical insight as to why so few parents are able to think forward past getting the baby. She states that ideally adoption should be in the best interest of the child, but prospective adoptive parents do not always share this ethos. Sylvia summarizes, "A lot of people who are adopting [think], 'Why do I have to go through all these hoops? I'm doing the kid a favor.'" While she hopes this parent-centric mentality "changes later on when it is a real person," and parents "stop looking at the person as an object, and [the child] becomes a real subject," it is difficult for parents to break out of this mind-set. Sylvia explains, "A lot of people feel that the kid is beholden to them, that they are sort of doing them a favor." Even though several experts on adoptive families have warned parents about promoting this damaging narrative, Sylvia acknowledges, "The stuff that you don't want to see happens. . . . And some of that changes later on, and some of it doesn't, in my experience."

She details how occasionally she comes across "people who are very thoughtful and very reflective, and they do all of that nice stuff that you read about in the books; in my experience, that is not a lot of people you come across." Sylvia says, "I do my very best to help people think this through, and I am pretty challenging." Sometimes she gets a lot of pushback from clients, describing how "people get very angry at me because I draw their attention to the fact that they are talking about a human being and it is not all about them." Despite her cynical interpretation, she is quick to emphasize, "People love their kids; don't get me wrong."

Yet Sylvia knows that love is not enough to adequately prepare transracial adoptive families for the road ahead. When asked, "If you could change the way that adoption is done, what would you want to see different?" she passionately discusses the need for more education: "I think that anyone who knows anything about adoption would want families who adopt to become better educated." Wishing that adoptive parents would find role models for their children and "would work hard to have their kids be similar to other kids racially, ethnically," she asserts that these efforts should be "a bare minimum." Despite her advice, Sylvia discloses that few heed her suggestions, "because it is hard, and people want to live their lives." She gives a litany of competing priorities that usurp parents' energies, noting, "There is so much going on, and homework, and grandma [*trails off*]." These immediate aspects of parenting often take precedence, especially for White parents who may feel like it is too hard to travel out of one's comfort zone to seek out same-race friends and role models for their child. Since this blasé attitude toward racial difference often prevails, Sylvia concludes, "I would like people to be more educated and to think through what this [transracial adoption] means for the child."

Throughout my interviews, several adoption professionals espoused similar views that White adoptive parents needed better education to be prepared to adopt transracially. As social workers, they saw this as an integral aspect of their roles. For example, I interviewed Michele, an agency worker who went back to school to get her MSW with the sole purpose of building a career in adoption. She explains, "My focus from day one was to work in this field." Michele is clearly passionate about her job. She describes her role in her agency: "I am a senior social worker, and I was doing home studies and postplacement work with families and also doing marketing around adoption information meetings for people who are just thinking about it, kind of testing the waters. And I love that part of it, as well as the educational part of it."

Like Sylvia, Michele wishes that her clients would be willing to think more about what transracial adoption means for the child. With the adoption clock ticking, many prospective clients want to jump right ahead to the application phase to expedite the process. Michele continues, "Sometimes there are people who are focused on what is going to be the quickest program, and I sort of struggle with that, since that is not really the question. It may seem like, 'What can we do now to hurry this up and become parents?' . . . So part of my role is also educating them."

Even though social workers hold the belief that education is important, this ideology is tempered by the notion that prospective adoptive parents should not be pushed too far on these issues. For example, Jennifer, a social worker whose job entails talking with prospective applicants who reach out to her agency, describes the "tender territory" that she traverses, especially for prospective parents "who have quite literally left the fertility clinic and have been given the advice that they need to look into adoption as a means of building their family." Knowing that prospective clients are reeling, she is especially cautious and only introduces issues associated with transracial adoption "as the topic arises." Jennifer discloses that compared with her colleagues, "I will have a tendency to go a bit further with this, in terms of families, [telling them], 'Here are some resources.'" She attempts to grasp a teachable moment, relating, "If I have a family who mentions that they are color blind, I will very often take them down the road [of] 'But you are not going to be living in a color-blind society.'" She wants the early phase of the application process to help clients "understand the issues that you will be facing as a mixed-race family. And we will start using that terminology in the [intake] phone call in terms of being a mixed-race family." Yet she is wary about pushing too hard, continuing, "I don't want to say that it is a topic we avoid because it certainly is not, but it is sort of woven in there subtly rather than, 'Here, you have to read these before you decide to move forward with Ethiopia.'"

Although Jennifer hopes to educate potential clients, she tends to give prospective parents the benefit of the doubt, even if they say something racist. She describes how "some people are real upfront, . . . in what would be perceived by most ears as a racist comment." Surprisingly, these racist comments are not necessarily deal breakers, and rather than turn down potential applicants, Jennifer tries to turn the exchange into a teachable moment. "Our [social work] worldview is quite well informed about racial issues and inequities and so on," and given this knowledge, she reasons, "our job is to at least speak to what bias looks like." She sees this gentle approach as part of her agency's mission "to help families understand, at every step along the way." Because these racist comments happen at the intake stage, she expects that through the course of the training and home study process, these things can be corrected. Jennifer continues, "Families are going to integrate and adapt and absorb the education that we provide them" but admits that not all parents come around: "How's this for a cliché: you can lead a horse to water [*trails off*]."

According to Jennifer's metaphor, she tries to lead prospective applicants to the "water," or a place where future transracial adoptive parents will have an opportunity to think critically about race and privilege in American society. However, going back to Patricia's words, the temperature of the water cannot get too heated because the goal of the initial stages of the adoption process is to recruit future customers, so keeping White applicants comfortable is a priority. As Kristi Brian has noted in her research on Korean adoption, some social workers are wary of inviting adult Korean adoptees to speak to prospective parents because some are "just so negative" about their experiences. She describes this desire to shield "adopters from the harsh realities that some adoptees have experienced" as a missed opportunity that may ultimately hinder adoptive parents' development.[8] Thus, to reframe transracial and transnational adoption as a promising pathway to parenthood, adoption facilitators act as gatekeepers, only allowing those who "expressed their views appropriately" to enter into the conversation.[9] In my interview with Penelope, she echoes this sentiment, describing her colleagues' aversion to inviting adult adoptees to speak at trainings because "if you use some adult voices of adoptees, some of that can be scary."

## Color-Evasiveness: Minimizing Race and Maximizing Applicants' Comfort

When transracial adoption *does* get mentioned at the preadopt stage, it is often done with a soft touch that positions parents as consumers and prioritizes their needs. Just as the notion of fit gets euphemistically employed to cover a range of demographics about a child's profile, adoption social workers describe transracial adoption in terms of White parents' levels of comfort. For example, I attended a conference for prospective adoptive parents. A social worker with a long history of writing home studies for transracial adoptive families presented a session called "Deciding on the Type of Adoption That Works for *You*." Employing a strategy of emotion work, the presenter gave her audience permission to take on a consumer mentality, reminding them, "Adoption is a lifelong decision, so you want to choose the one that works for you." Similarly, during another conference session, "Making the Race, Age, Cost Comparison," the social worker framed the winnowing process in terms of clients' comfort, advising them to consider "With what program do you feel comfortable?"

With this consumer-focused mind-set, adoption workers communicate mixed messages about the relevance of racial difference. For example, at the Baby Talk information session, the presenter mentioned, "I think it is really, really important just to be very prepared to adopt a child that is going to be out of your ethnicity. If they are Hispanic, or African American, or Asian, or whatever they are, it is important just to be really prepared for that." Yet the message changed when she showed audience members a chart listing an inventory of countries that "we get kids out of most often." She instructed parents to downplay race and instead prioritize other criteria such as eligibility requirements, estimated waiting times, and their willingness to travel. She advised, "So if you're not really big on travel, maybe Russia is not for you. Maybe South Korea is. It is one trip, usually a week or so. Sometimes it is a lot easier. So it really depends on you and what you are looking for, the kind of kid, you know, depending on what kind of country you want to go to." In other words, the underlying message is that the decision to adopt across race should depend on parents' tolerance for overseas travel and what they think will be easier in terms of getting a child.

Cornerstone Adoptions, a large placement agency that offered an array of international programs, also advised parents to weigh these market factors. They were even more explicit in their advice, ranking the factors to consider in descending order. But before articulating this list, the speaker made sure to voice the caveat that prospective parents should think carefully about the implications of transracial adoption. She advised potential clients, "This is a good time to start assessing your comfort level and your extended family's comfort level with the openness of becoming an interracial, transracial family." Her message took on a serious tone as she stated, "There are inherent challenges to the child, parents, extended family members, and siblings, and these cannot be taken lightly."

Once these warnings were communicated, she shifted her tone to a more consumer-oriented approach as she launched into a list of factors prospective parents should consider when choosing a program. She detailed how Cornerstone advises prioritizing the following in descending order: (1) eligibility requirements, (2) age and gender, (3) length of wait, (4) care of children, (5) interracial families, (6) cultural affinity, and (7) travel requirements. The fact that race is listed well after other market variables like length of wait provides a powerful point of contrast to the speaker's previous statement that race "cannot be taken lightly."

One thing that was interesting about Cornerstone was the speaker's tendency to shy away from using the word "race," shifting it to a discussion of culture. The speaker informed prospective parents that they do not require any previous exposure or knowledge about a country to adopt from it, framing this cultural capital as something nice to have but not a requirement. She asserted, "If there are parts of the world where you have ancestors from, or you were born there, or you speak the language, or you've traveled there ... and you can claim some of that culture, that is really just a nice thing to do, if you have that opportunity."

Cornerstone was not alone in downplaying race by relegating it to the near bottom of the list of considerations. I attended an information meeting at Kid Connection, another large placement agency. Although Kid Connection ordered its list somewhat differently, the overall message is the same— only this time, any mention of race is obliterated because the subject gets framed in terms of ethnicity and culture. The agency lists its priorities as (1) age of the child, (2) gender of the child, (3) health of the child, (4) siblings, (5) ethnicity of the child, (6) travel or escort wait times, and (7) fee and budget. Having listed these factors, the Kid Connection representative went down the list, asking her audience to consider, "Would it make sense for you to adopt siblings?" and "How much traveling can you do? Some programs require more travel than others." When she got to transracial adoption, the speaker framed ethnicity—leaving out race entirely—as something that may or may not matter: "Does the ethnicity of the child matter to you? And would you be willing to incorporate elements of their cultural heritage into your family's rituals and traditions?" Through this linguistic strategy, she implies that the racial difference can be effectively dealt with by occasionally incorporating cultural elements.

There was one important outlier among the sessions I observed. At an information meeting on adoption from Ethiopia, the speaker articulated a powerful message about the importance of engaging in discussions of race. Whereas other adoption agency representatives avoided bringing up race, lest the conversation become too heated, this social worker prioritized the benefits of this teachable moment over the risk of alienating potential customers. She advised her audience, "I also think that talking about race and ethnicity is an important piece. The reason why I bring this up is that oftentimes I feel that families feel that love is enough. If any of you are married or have experienced longer-term relationships, you know that love is not enough. You have to really work together as partners, and you have to make sacrifices, and you oftentimes have to put a lot of energy into those relationships." She was frank that, depending on their age at adoption, their future sons and daughters will have complex and varied identities as Africans and Americans: "Your child will come home very literally African American but may not identify as African American. We have definitely seen some older kids come home and say that they are not Black; they are brown. We have also seen kids come home and very much identify with African American culture, much more so than they seem to identify with their Ethiopian heritage."

While she stated that it is important to "kind of take their child's lead" when navigating issues of race and identity, in a marked departure from other agency representatives, the facilitator brought race to the forefront. She acknowledged that the conversations can be difficult for White parents, but she compelled them to fight through their discomfort for the sake of their children:

> I think that it is really important to talk about race, ethnicity, adoption, heritage. Those types of topics should be discussed early, and it is really not a good idea to wait for your child to talk to you about it. I often equate these types of conversations to sex. I don't know how

many of us would be approaching our parents to say can you please have this conversation with us. Most of these types of things you don't want to talk about, or there is never enough time in the day to bring these things up. And so I think that if you can start these conversations when the child is a baby or early coming home in your family . . . you are showing them that this is a topic that you are comfortable with.

In contrast to this more head-on acknowledgement of racial difference, among most of the information sessions I observed presenters eschewed mentioning race altogether. For example, the speaker at Family Union downplayed the role of race and did not even mention it as a consideration. The presenter informed her audience, "The first step that I suggest for them to do is take a look at the country requirements. And for most people, once they review those requirements, they realize there are some countries that they are not eligible to adopt from. This helps narrow down the list." After this step, she advised, "it is important to think about the profile of the child you are willing to adopt." Among these decisions, she listed several options, directing her audience to think about, "What are your hopes regarding gender, age, health situation? Are you hoping to adopt a baby as young as possible? Are you really thinking about a young school-age child? Do you have all boys and want to adopt a girl? Do you have all girls and want to adopt a boy? Are you open to a correctable medical condition? All of those things will impact the country you choose to adopt from." It is important to highlight that this presenter was willing to blatantly discuss the role of market variables like gender, age, and health in parents' calculations. With this in mind, the paucity of race from the discussion is even more noticeable.

## Conflating Race and Culture

Race may be largely absent when adoption social workers sell transracial adoption to prospective parents, but discussions of birth culture—especially for intercountry adoptions—are far more prevalent. Describing findings from her research, Brian asserts, "Children are frequently classified according to their birth country for transnational adoption and according to their "race" in domestic adoption, further configuring transnational adoptees as somewhat outside of the racial hierarchy."[10] She continues that adoption facilitators tend to uphold this oversimplified view of race and culture, often characterizing any attempt to include discussions of difference as a virtuous effort. Brian notes, "This embrace of 'difference' happens precisely on adopters' own terms, in limited doses, and from a comfortable distance away from adoptees' own birth communities."[11] Likewise, in her study examining how White mothers embark on "culture keeping" activities with their

Chinese-born daughters, Jacobson argues that the tendency to play up culture and downplay race originates with adoption providers. She states, "Culture is marketed and celebrated as one of the joys and obligations of international adoptive parenting. It is part of the way all international adoptive programs are packaged, made appealing, and sold to adoptive parents."[12]

In line with this strategy, the presenter at Family Union swathed her discussion of racial difference in a comfortable conversation about cultural affinity. She told her audience, "Some families come to us, and they already have a connection with the birth culture of the country they are adopting from. They may share that cultural heritage, or they may have a strong tie to that culture through their church or community or family. Other families are excited about making a connection to their child's birth culture and are seeking out those resources in their community as they start an adoption process."

Adherence to the notion that participation in fun cultural activities was a sufficient strategy to effectively address racial difference was evident at the preadoption panels. For example, at one conference session on transracial adoption, the organizer invited a few transracial adoptive mothers to talk about how they work to develop their children's ethnic and racial identities. The panelists spoke of "getting culturally reflective books and dolls" and "belonging to a Listserve" of similar adoptive families. I saw a similar trend at another conference sponsored by Family Orchard during its session titled "Multicultural Families," a label that effectively rebranded race, moving it to the more comfortable territory of culture. The session organizers invited Gail,[13] a White single mother raising a Chinese daughter, to participate in the panel and share her experiences. Endorsing the culture-keeping model, Gail details that she wanted to adopt from China because "I was going to be enriched to have another culture to dialogue with."

This phrase is worth unpacking. Dialogue usually means conversation, a two-way exchange. But that does not seem to be what is happening here. The use of the word "dialogue" is notable considering that the woman did not speak Mandarin, so it was impossible for her to enter into an actual dialogue with someone from China unless he or she spoke English. Second, the mother confidently stated that she is enriched by making connections with Chinese culture but then disclosed that her daughter is the only Asian in her school, so it is doubtful that her family has the opportunity to make connections with other Asian Americans. But according to the culture-keeping model promoted by adoption agencies, neither language fluency nor relationships with Chinese Americans are necessary to "dialogue with a culture," because culture is positioned as something attainable via consuming ethnic food or art and is divorced from actual people.

As Jacobson argues, there are drawbacks to this "primordial view of ethnicity," noting that for transracial adoptive parents, culture keeping is not only the "best way to address race for families, but, in essence, the *only* way many know how to do so."[14] While the mothers Jacobson interviewed report a strong affinity for China and its people, these sentiments rarely translated into "actual friendships or deep meaningful day-to-day relationships with Chinese people here in the United States."[15] As prior research has shown,[16] these transracial adoptive parents tended to raise their children in what Jacobson calls "relative social segregation," detailing that "few of the families had Asian friends and . . . although they desired intimate relationships with Chinese ethnics, most experienced a deep awkwardness in their attempts to connect."[17]

It is important to emphasize that adoption social workers implicitly give adoptive parents permission to conflate race and culture with the way that they talk about transracial adoption. In my interview with Michele, she describes how she broaches transracial adoption to her clients: "Most of the families we see are Caucasian families, and they are interested in adopting, many times, a child of another race. And it is really important that those families not see that they are adopting an Asian child, a Black child, a Hispanic child, but that they become a multicultural family." Her choice of words is interesting because she begins by mentioning the race of the child (e.g., Hispanic, Asian, or Black) but promotes the idea that White parents should not "see" the race of their children. Once advocating that seeing race should not be the priority, she pivots to a discussion of culture, reframing transracial adoption as becoming a multicultural family.

In *We Are All Multiculturalists Now*, the sociologist Nathan Glazer traces the origins and ideology behind the term "multiculturalism," explaining that the word is relatively new, having only made it into the Oxford English Dictionary in 1989.[18] Glazer details how the word was initially used in educational circles as a buzzword meant to describe curriculum that includes perspectives of racial and ethnic minorities in the United States. He writes, "Many terms have thus arisen to encompass the reality that groups of different origin all form part of the . . . common culture and society. Multiculturalism is just the latest in this sequence of terms describing how American society, particularly American education, should respond to its diversity."[19] Glazer shows how, since its inception, the word connotes the embodiment of neoliberal American ideals, arguing that the term "becomes the new image of a better America, without prejudice and discrimination."[20] With this interpretation, it is no wonder that the phrase "multicultural family" has gained so much traction among adoption professionals to describe a quixotic view of transracial adoption. As Kazuyo Kubo argues, "The normative perspectives of multiculturalism—embracing differences—provide a convenient and helpful ethos for adoption agencies in promoting transnational adoption to prospective parents."[21]

This tactic generated the creation of "culture camps," programs designed to introduce transnationally adopted children and their families to the culture of a specific country. Although the content and the mission of the camps can vary, as Lori Delale-O'Connor finds in her research, "culture is limited to experiences with food, clothing, songs, dance, and games that are easily taught and are age appropriate."[22] Drawing from her observations at Hands Around the Globe culture camp, she recounts how the program divides children into subcamps, with a focus on China, Korea, or a homogenized "Latin America" curriculum. She depicts how activities are based on "safe or acceptable aspects of children's birth cultures."[23] One of the signature events involves having children make the flag of the country of their birth, and at the camp finale children participate in the "Parade of Flags." This ceremony is the very personification of multiculturalism because it is limited to a symbolic view of diversity, promoting "a view of the adoptee's birth culture that allows children and families to 'put on' their culture and take it off within the space of camp."[24]

Nowadays, there is the general consensus that these camps can be helpful tools for families, but they are not sufficient resources for transracially adopted children.[25] I spoke with Nicole about this issue. She describes the conversations she would have with prospective adoptive parents about her expectations, detailing that she would like to see families go beyond surface explorations of culture. "We would always talk about that [with clients]," she states. "As much as you're asking your child to come into your White social circle and style, you should be putting yourself in situations where you are in the minority." This is a useful party line, but it is often unrealistic for families living in rural areas where there are few, if any, opportunities for parents to put themselves in settings where they are the racial minority and their children of color are among the majority. Nicole acknowledges, "I feel like we would say this, and talk about this, but a lot but our clients were in Tennessee. I mean, going to culture camp might be as good as it was going to get for them."

Whereas Nicole articulates that she wants families to go beyond the culture camp model, in contrast Michele implicitly endorses this strategy, equating becoming a multicultural family with cultural tourism. She states, "I do say [that] it is not that you've adopted a child from China; it is that your family becomes a multiracial, multicultural family, and what do you need to do to support that?" In answering her rhetorical question, Michele veers away from discussions on race and focuses on a consumer-friendly view of culture. According to her definition, "supporting" a multiracial family does not necessarily entail finding one's child same-race role models, preparing him to encounter racial discrimination, or teaching her the language spoken in the country where she was born. Instead, Michele reframes becoming a multiracial family as a consumptive process that can be achieved by eating ethnic food. Switching to a discussion of Korean adoption, she states, "There are some people who don't like Korean food, and it will be really hard to support a culture if there are aspects of it that you hate." However, she softens her position, stating that not liking Korean food is not necessarily a deal breaker, emphasizing that the most important thing is that White parents are comfortable: "I am not saying that you can't adopt from Korea [if you don't like Korean food], but you need to find elements that you are comfortable to embrace."

Despite her tendency to conflate culture and race and to equate proactive transracial adoptive parenting with liking Korean food, it is important to underscore that Michele perceives herself as an expert who is well equipped to guide prospective parents through these discussions. She states, "I think that there are many families that just think [*pauses and chuckles*]—not as much now—I am laughing because I am thinking, 'Not when I get through with them,'—but families who think that race isn't important." She explains that a lot of her clients start out thinking, "I don't see color, and I am very open," detailing that her job "is really to help them see how inaccurate that statement is." This can be an uphill battle with families, since "race is a very tough issue to talk about with people, and you have to be willing to go there." Michele attests that these conversations remain some of her biggest challenges, recalling, "I would say that the most difficult experiences I have with clients is about race, but I think they are necessary."

As Michele asserts, a willingness to "go there" and engage in difficult conversations about race is an integral component of education for transracial adoptive parents. The role of the social worker is a key component in communicating this information and modeling how to engage with complex and potentially volatile subjects. These trainings are especially important considering my argument that for most White parents, transracial adoption is a market calculation and at this stage in the adoption process few have seriously considered the responsibility this commitment entails. However, as I argue in the following section, adoption social workers may not be fully prepared to lead these discussions because of their own reluctance to talk about race.

## Social Workers' Discomfort Talking about Race

Since placing non-White children in White homes is a core component of adoption workers' duties, one would expect that trained adoption social workers would command a high level of sophistication regarding these matters. Yet, as I learned from talking with adoption social workers, few receive any clinical training on adoption in graduate school, and most insights come from on-the-job learning.[26] With this lack of formal instruction, it is not surprising that some of the practitioners were incredibly uncomfortable broaching the subject of transracial adoption. Instead of addressing the topic with confidence and fluency, they exhibited what Eduardo Bonilla-Silva would call rhetorical incoherence, or the "digressions, long pauses, repetitions, and self corrections," that characterize the ways in which White interlocutors discuss race.[27] Bonilla-Silva argues that bouts of rhetorical incoherence are "the result of talking about race in a world that insists race does not matter."[28]

I witnessed this phenomenon at an information meeting offered by Forever Family. During the question-and-answer session, a man raised his hand and asked the social worker about transracial adoption, inquiring about the agency's thoughts on placing children outside of their ethnic or racial group. Considering that the majority of Forever Family's adoptions are transracial, one would think that she would be able to articulate her reasoning as to why her agency stands by these placements. However, the presenter seemed to be caught off guard and uncomfortable with the question, because she stuttered throughout her response. Although she was poised and articulate throughout the rest of the presentation, she morphed into a different speaker as she struggled to get the words out. Her answer was hard to hear because her voice got so quiet. Her body language changed, she mumbled her response, and she shrugged her shoulders, saying in short and disjointed sentences, "There are a lot of different schools of thought on this. [*Pauses.*] It can be controversial. [*Pauses.*] Some people don't agree [*trails off*]. But obviously [*mumbling*] we don't share that opinion." She stuttered a bit, starting a new sentence multiple times without finishing her thought, and then quickly said, "Luckily we live in [a city], and it is a diverse community."

While this woman's response was the most extreme, in my other conversations I witnessed similar discomfort. For example, Abigail describes how she often struggles with language around race. I asked her, "How much is race on the radar when they are starting to think about adopting from Ethiopia?" Even though she is describing her clients' discomfort, her own uncertainty talking about race is evident. She answers, "This is like the million-dollar question. We do a lot of talking about it amongst our staff. I think that a lot of families—I do wonder what a lot of families [*pauses*] bring to this process in their conceptions with race. I think that for the most part people minimize it, but they may just be minimizing it to us. They may not want us to see how anxious they are about parenting transracially, especially a child of African descent."

The fact that Abigail chooses to characterize Ethiopian children as of "African descent" deserves further explication. The word "descent" evokes ancestry, or something that occurred in the past that is no longer relevant today. Abigail details how her clients avoid labeling their children as Black and prefer to describe them as Ethiopian. However, it is not only clients who

struggle with these terms but also the social workers themselves. She remarks, "Just getting the language around it: African American or Black. I
know we struggle with it here, and families have to get comfortable with
that. I don't think that a lot of them are sure what words they are going to
say. They are very comfortable with Ethiopian."

While adoptive parents may be "comfortable" with the term Ethiopian,
it does not change the fact that their children are Black, and they will have
to live in the United States as Black Americans. Many social workers recognized that no matter how much adoptive parents might prefer to play up
their children's Ethiopian roots, as Olivia puts it, "The bottom line is, here in
the United States, your child is not Ethiopian; they're Black." Yet she concedes that some families may not see it this way, stating, "If families are not
thinking about it, they absolutely should be thinking about it."

Granted, we cannot assume that White adoption social workers find it
difficult to talk about race just from a few jumbled responses. But we do not
have to. I was fortunate to interview two social workers who shared their
frustrations regarding their colleagues' blasé treatment of race and privilege.
The first was with Penelope, a social worker who was also in the process of
completing a transracial adoption, so she had been primed to think about
race, family, and social work practice. During the interview, she describes
the training she went through as a prospective adoptive parent: "We had a
really bad facilitator. We had a very poor group experience." They had
watched a well-known documentary featuring the voices of adult transracial
adoptees and the challenges they faced. Penelope compliments the film, stating, "It is a very good documentary to watch." She notes that the poor group
experience stemmed from bad planning on the part of the facilitator, who
did not leave time for discussion. Penelope details, "We watched it. At the
end, people had been there four hours and were ready to go home. But we
were like, 'Wait a minute. We don't have time to talk about it?' So much of it
hinges on the quality of the facilitator."

Taking advantage of her insider perspective, I ask Penelope, "Would you
say there is a big range of adoption social workers' understanding of race and
ethnicity among themselves?" Her answer is telling:

> My hunch is you definitely have people, especially Whites, who are
> talking about transracial issues who haven't fully explored their own
> White privilege. Our facilitator danced around questions and
> wouldn't answer them. And we are a room full of White people. You
> have a White person in a room full of White people who is really
> uncomfortable talking about race.

My exchange with Penelope underscores the value of my backstage
methodology that highlights the insights gleaned from interviews with

adoption workers. During our conversation, she is unrelenting in her criticism of some White adoption social workers, stating, "I have always thought that they [social workers] missed the mark. I have never heard anyone mention the phrase 'White privilege,' and I always thought that is where it should start. . . . So I feel like they missed the mark by at least not having a definition and discussion about White privilege."

Of course, Penelope is not saying that all social workers act this way. There may be some adoption workers who are highly aware of these issues. However, Brian's research indicates that these conversations rarely occur, and if they happen at all, the content tends to remain limited and surface level.[29] The implications of this, coupled with the fact that Penelope's training consisted of "a White person in a room full of White people who is really uncomfortable talking about race," are troubling. It is even more worrisome to hear that from an institutional perspective, there is little impetus to engage in these admittedly difficult conversations. Penelope laments that the ethos among agency directors is, "We just don't have time to do it all," suggesting that while many will say that race is an important consideration, making room for these conversations is not an actual priority.

Nicole inadvertently explains how White privilege can get normalized in transracial adoption, recalling how her agency once invited some guest speakers who challenged Nicole and her colleague's practice of placing children of color in predominately White communities. She recalls:

> I remember we had these [White] mothers come in to talk with us, who had children from Guatemala. They traveled to Guatemala every summer, and their children had this fierce Guatemalan identity. And they talked with us about how to spot racism. And they were like, "You shouldn't place children with parents who live in all-White areas." And we place kids in rural Maine and Vermont. I remember the director of international programs raising her hand and saying, "Someone has to integrate schools." It is a lot of pressure to put on these kids to be the diversity in this area. For these areas, this may be the only way to get more diverse.

Nicole's response highlights some important threads worth following. First, notice how she defends her decision to place non-White children in rural states that are over 95 percent White.[30] Second, her use of the word "fierce" to describe these Guatemalan children's identity is telling. The term connotes something aggressive and threatening. Here I am reminded of Sara Dorow's analysis of White social workers, profiled in the Introduction of this book. The women Dorow interviews derided parents who "become totally Asian" and did "too much" with culture and hence lost "respect for their own backgrounds."[31] Similar to their assessment, in Nicole's phrasing, there is an implicit judgment hinting that these mothers' annual travel to Guatemala was too much, since it spawned a "fierce Guatemalan identity." With this rhetorical maneuver, there is less impetus for Nicole and her colleagues to take seriously the rebuke that adoption providers should not place non-White children in rural areas where they are likely to be racially isolated. Notably, it was Nicole's supervisor, the director of international programs, who offered the strongest rebuttal. She raised her hand and argued, "Someone has to integrate schools." Her rejoinder implicitly positions the adoption agency as pioneers taking the first needed step toward racial integration. Granted, a lone racial minority child raised by White parents in a White community may technically be integration, but at the expense of the child, who has to bear the brunt of it. Nicole concedes that it is "a lot of pressure" for these children, but she suggests that their isolation may be for the greater good, since, for these areas, it "may be the only way to get more diverse."

In my interview with Olivia, she offers further evidence supporting the argument that many White social workers do not recognize how White privilege pervades private adoption. She discusses attending a conference held by a national organization supporting intercountry adoptions. Despite the fact that the majority of transnational placements are also transracial, Olivia notes, "There were very few workshops on race. I attended two, and they were fantastic." Olivia laments that these workshops were not better attended and relates how among those who did attend, "there were all these discussions. There were all these adoption professionals in the audience, and afterwards there was a lot of discussion how this is something that people are still not comfortable talking about, including adoption professionals." The fact that private adoption is overwhelmingly facilitated by White social workers who are uncomfortable talking about race hit home during the lunch session since Olivia got to compare the small minority of workers who attended the race-specific conversations compared to the full body of conference attendees. Olivia continues, "It was on my mind, and at this luncheon I looked around to my coworker and said, 'Do you realize that you are one of three people of color in this entire room of three hundred people?'" Although Olivia knew that White women are disproportionately represented among intercountry adoption social workers, the visual brought the racial imbalance in stark relief. She states, "We are in an international adoption conference, and there are a lot of transracial and transcultural [adoptions], and that just sort of blew my mind. And there were some heated discussion on how people just want to glaze over it, minimize it."

Ironically, even though adoption social workers were hesitant to proactively engage in discussions about racial privilege and racial difference, several had no qualms about invoking highly explicit racialized descriptions of the children they placed. In the following section I describe this phenomenon, paying particular attention to how notions of race, color, and beauty played into these accounts.

## Color-Explicit Depictions

In her essay analyzing photographs of waiting children, sociologist Lisa Cartwright astutely notes that the circulation of images depicting heart-wrenching pictures of children available for adoption provides a telling glimpse into the adoption marketplace. She writes, "These images functioned initially as lures, drawing prospective clients into the adoption market, helping them to imagine 'their' child or themselves as parents of children 'like these.'"[32] While it can be beneficial for prospective adoptive parents yearning for a child to identify with one in need, Cartwright warns that these portraits increase the "potential for racial and esthetic discrimination,"[33] as some waiting children are bypassed in favor of more attractive children. In my interview with Nora, she describes how this bias routinely affects adoptive placements, especially when parents have the opportunity to select their son or daughter from a photo roster of available children. Nora states, "People want to adopt a pretty child," because they have "the assumption that if the outside is good, the inside is good. That is a bias. There is social bias all over the place."

Adoption providers play into these biases by providing explicit racial descriptions of the children they place. Whether these descriptions are meant to "lure" parents in or serve as a caveat emptor, the use of specific racial descriptions sharply contrasts with the race-evasive discourse characterizing the rest of the information meetings. The use of color-explicit warnings was especially prevalent when the typical phenotype of children placed might not align with parents' expectations. For example, despite the fact that there are over fifty ethnic groups living in mainland China,[34] because the children placed from China are perceived as uniformly East Asian, adoption providers never offer any specific racial descriptions of Chinese children. The presenter at Baby Talk reinforced this point, stating with certainty, "Obviously, with Asian countries your child is going to look a little more Asian." This matter-of-fact depiction contrasted with the caveats she offered when adopting from Russia. Aware that some parents were considering Russia because it provided a source of White children, she warns prospective parents that Russia "is a huge country which goes all the way to Europe. Depending on what part of Russia he's from, he might look very Caucasian—you know, blond hair, blue-eyed. Or he might look very Asian, you know, when you get more into Siberia and part of the country. I have kids who come home from Russia who look very Asian. So it really depends."

Perhaps wanting to drive home this point further, later in Baby Talk's presentation the speaker reiterated her cautionary message about children from the former Soviet Bloc. She advised, "If you want a Caucasian child, there are very few. I shouldn't say very few, but there aren't as many countries that have Caucasian children. The former Soviet countries do, depending. Like I said, Russian children can look very Asian. Kazakhstan can look very Asian. All those countries can look [*trails off*]—they look a little bit darker than you would assume. If you think you're going to Russia to get a blond, blue-eyed child, that is not always the case."

Representatives from Baby Talk were not alone in warning parents that some children might not fulfill prospective applicants' preferences for White children. At the information session given by Coordinated Care, the social worker introduced the Kazakhstan program, providing a similar warning about the children's racial composition, describing them as "an exotic-looking people." Likewise at Coastal Adoptions, the presenter introduced the Bulgaria program by informing audience members, "Most [children] have an olive complexion, brown eyes, and brown hair." Later, when she got to the program in Peru, she also warned parents about the children's skin color, emphasizing that some can be dark-skinned, stating, "Children are of mixed Spanish and Incan heritage. Beautiful children. Skin tone ranges from fair to dark."

Taken together, these comments deserve further analysis. What does it mean when social workers tasked with modeling child-centered approaches to transracial adoption rely on such explicit descriptions? To play devil's advocate, as described in the previous chapters, social workers believe that achieving the best interest of children means allowing parents to be picky consumers who need to be armed with the knowledge of what their child could look like in order to make informed decisions. Abiding by this reasoning, such racial descriptions are necessary. Although I can understand how fighting against a "see no color" mentality is useful, I would counter that this hyperawareness about pigmentation and phenotype is for the benefit of the parents, not the children. It is important to take into account how the racial hierarchy gets embedded in these descriptions, such that the darker the child, the more embellished the description. As argued in Chapter 4, adoption providers incentivize White parents to choose children that are lower on the racial hierarchy by applying what I call a "dark-skinned discount." In intercountry adoption, the fees are not as fungible. So instead, many providers, perhaps unconsciously, take the time to assure their White clients that dark-skinned children can still be considered valuable because of their beauty.

When discussing White Russian children, the social worker did not feel compelled to comment on the children's attractiveness. Perhaps the description "Caucasian, blond hair, blue-eyed" is enough to evoke beauty, so no further assurances were needed. But with Kazakhstan, since the children do not align with the dominant definition of what it means to be pretty, the speaker gave an additional description, highlighting the children's "exotic" appearance. Notably, the darker the children, the more the presenter felt compelled to emphasize their extrinsic worth. Peruvian children, with their Spanish and Incan heritage, were labeled "beautiful." But the strongest endorsements are reserved for Ethiopian children, who have the darkest hues among the spectrum of children placed. For example, at Synergy Adoption, the presenter introduced her agency's Ethiopian program, spontaneously exclaiming, "The children are fabulous and beautiful." Similarly, at Kid Connection's information session, the presenter worked to assure potential customers that "for Ethiopians, I can tell you for every child I have seen, these kids have some kind of light that just shines." Her choice of words is significant. Although these children have dark skin, she alludes that there is "lightness" about them. Put another way, the extent that compliments are doled out is inversely proportional to the children's racial status: White Slavic children are described as blond-haired and blue-eyed without explicit mention of their beauty, Kazakh children are racially different enough that they get the Orientalist label "exotic," Peruvian children whose skin tone can range from fair to dark are just "beautiful," and the darkest children are "fabulous and beautiful."

It is important to underscore that the same social workers that employ explicit racial descriptions of children's phenotypes are also responsible for training prospective adoptive parents to adopt transracially. While as social workers, they may hope to impart a strong educational curriculum that equips parents to think about race and privilege in a nuanced way, by approaching transracial adoption as a market calculation and downplaying the role of race (except when highlighting children's features), I show how these social workers undermine their capacity to do so. The overarching message they put forth becomes one that underscores parents' roles as customers and consumers while minimizing the significance of race.

## Market Concessions

In a down market, when retaining every paying client is paramount to business survival, the focus on appeasing the parent customer can be even more pronounced. Beth describes how sometimes she has to make concessions that may not fully align with her ideals. She laments that private adoption has become "adoptive parent driven," and some clients approach it thinking, "I paid you, so when do I get my child?" Although she and like-minded colleagues try to fight against this attitude that children are paid-for goods to be delivered, some competitors do not follow suit. Since "there is an agency for every family who wants a situation," Beth describes how consumers can search around for a provider that requires the bare minimum. With this in mind, Beth wonders whether it is better for her agency to take on these clients, knowing she can provide them with opportunities for education, or reject them outright. If she does turn down their application, she is fully aware that, "if I say no, I know that they are going to go down the road to another agency to get their child."

In this section, I detail three ways in which adoption professionals concede to market demands. First I describe how some social workers allow clients to be even pickier in identifying the profiles of their preferred children, essentially creating a gendered racial color line. Second, I outline how providers relax their standards regarding parent education by permitting applicants to do their trainings online despite their deep misgivings about the pedagogical benefits of this medium. Third, I show how social workers are reluctant to turn away potential clients, even if they foresee that these parents will not necessarily be good transracial adoptive parents.

As argued in Chapter 4, adoption agencies' policies are reformulating a new racial divide that positions monoracial native-born African Americans on one side of the divide, and everyone else on the other. Ceding to this delineation, practitioners often allow White parents to pursue adopting biracial Black children while excluding monoracial Black children. As if this color line was not specific enough, some go a step further by enabling prospective parents to pinpoint a willingness to adopt Black girls but not Black boys. For example, at the session "Is Transracial Adoption Right for You?" the social worker acquiesced to the racial hierarchy, telling her audience, "You may feel okay with a Hispanic child but not a Black child." She assured listeners that this "is an okay choice" because "you have to pick the child who is going to work for you." After endorsing the notion that transracial adoption is a customer-focused negotiation, she went a step further, giving parents permission to winnow their search even more by assuring them, "Some parents say they cannot parent an African American boy."

This presenter was not the only one to articulate a gendered color line. During my interview with Alyssa, she describes how she has a White client "who is only open to African American girls but not boys." She notes, "Most of our birth moms don't get prenatal care," meaning that the sex of the baby is unknown. Given her client's unwillingness to adopt Black boys, "[these birth mothers] can't be shown [in the mix of profiles presented to the client]." I was somewhat taken aback by this allowance because at the information session at her agency, I was told that it does not fulfill gender preferences. Yet when gender and race intersect, perhaps the organization loosens its policies, conceding to White parents who only want to raise African American daughters but not sons.

In my conversation with Sylvia, she explains how her clients are often opposed to adopting darker-skinned males, bluntly stating, "Any Latino or African American male is scary." She acknowledges that these gendered racial stereotypes are complex, citing the disproportionate representation of

Hispanic and Black men in the criminal justice system: "If you look at who's in prisons and things like that, it is complicated." In contrast to a young brown or Black boy who will grow into a brown or Black man, Sylvia surmises that girls are "much less threatening." The desire for girls is especially pronounced among White prospective adoptive fathers, since, "males are much more interested in having a little girl if they are going to go there [and adopt]. It is much less threatening or strange to adopt a little girl. They think they are cute. Different aspects of objectification, like the child is a pet. I think it is a lot less threatening than having a male enter the home."

Similarly, Danielle details how many of her clients draw the line at adopting African boys. "I think that people are more uncomfortable with Black men. So I think that there are people—and we get this in the [Ethiopia] program as well—who say that they would be comfortable raising a Black girl but wouldn't be comfortable raising a Black boy. And that's racism, and images of Black men in our culture—so that's very concerning to me. I feel like, who are those Black girls going to marry?"

She goes on to tell a story about when she answered the intake lines at her agency and the phone call she fielded:

> I had one couple. I turned them down. It was actually on an intake phone call, so it wasn't like I had to turn them *down* down. I just had to say, "This isn't for you." The woman said, "I really want to adopt from Africa, but my husband is afraid that if we adopt from Africa, it will give our other children the message that is okay to marry a Black person." And I said, "You know what, he's right. It will give them that message, and if that's not the message you want to give, you shouldn't adopt."

As previous social science research has shown, although the number of interracial marriages has increased,[35] the prospect of White-Black intermarriage remains the most controversial pairing.[36] Although it is presumptuous to assume that transracially adopted Black girls eventually will want to romantically partner with Black men, I think that Danielle's question speaks to a larger issue about belonging. If parents make the trade-off that a Black girl is a palatable market calculus but a Black boy is not, what is the ultimate message to Black daughters about their race and self-worth? I was reminded by Kathryn Sweeney's research on White transracial adoptive parents' racial attitudes and her assessment that "adoptive parents may not understand the experiences of people of color and those that do adopt across racial lines are not prepared to assist their multiracial or Latino or Hispanic child to navigate life as a person of color."[37] She raises the concern that parents are left to negotiate transracial adoption "with little guidance" from adoption workers, suggesting that these workers could do more to prepare parents.[38] However,

Sweeney suggests that White adoption social workers may lack a critical understanding of race, finding that "agency workers may benefit from a better understanding of the experiences of various groups."[39]

Yet as Brian uncovers via her conversations with social workers facilitating Korean adoption, few adoption professionals are equipped to adequately educate parents. These potential shortcomings are especially disconcerting because, according to Brian, "adoption social workers have an immensely vital role to play in ensuring that adopters are prepared to do the hard work of parenting children who will be confronting multiple forms of marginalization."[40] But instead of tackling these issues, adoption facilitators treat parents like consumers and hence do not want to push them into uncomfortable territory. She cautions that this tactic has ramifications for adopted children because "when facilitators merely encourage adoptive parents to bring an easy color-blindness or cultural openness to the adoption process, they fail to alert white adoptive parents to the prejudice and racial isolation virtually all transracial/transnational adoptees confront at some point in their lives."[41]

As child welfare advocates, many of the adoption workers I interviewed were insistent that their training and curriculum were sufficient to adequately prepare transracial adoptive parents. Jennifer explains how her organization asks participants to formulate a "transcultural parenting plan," describing it as

actually forcing families to sit down and write down a worksheet, so it launches a process of conversation with the social workers and so on. They can, in turn, leap into additional books and videos that expand beyond what we've talked about with them. That's pretty hard for families. . . . Now we've got them in these classes, and that's kind of, *boom*, there it is. The video that we use and the conversation that we have is launched from young adults that have been adopted internationally, and some of what they have to say is quite candid and difficult to hear. So right off the bat, we are talking with families right from the start.

While Jennifer frames the education process as bringing up race "right from the start," I wonder if by this juncture it is already too late to reach some of these families. Applicants already have been sold on the idea that their needs as consumers are central to the adoption process and that transracial adoption is a valid and even savvy market calculation. With this foundation, it could be difficult for social workers to break applicants out of this customer mind-set.

Heather describes the limit of these trainings. Although she qualifies it by saying, "Some people really use the home study process as a learning process," she acknowledges that there are some clients "who are just going to hear what they want to hear." Despite Heather's reservations, these families are still allowed to adopt because "there's not a lot that we can do about that, if they are not saying things that alarm us that they will be an inappropriate family for a child. So what we can do is just hope that there will be some recollection of that later when they will need it."

Even Michele, the social worker who confidently declared that her clients would have a good understanding of race and privilege when she "got through with them," concedes, "I think that people aren't always ready [to talk about race]. What is important is to point out multiple opportunities for people to learn. People aren't always totally ready. The aspect of race or culture or identity [is one] that they have not come across." She admits, "I know that people aren't 100 percent with us while we are doing the educating, but my goal is really to plant a seed to think about these things. And my hope is that in the future, they will remember this."

Nicole laments that when working with preadoptive families, she expects very little to actually sink in, no matter what she does. She insists, "Sometimes I feel like the best we can do, when we are working with families pre-adoption—I can require a million hours of training and for them to read all of these books, but 90 percent of the time it is not going to seep in until they are dealing with it. So sometimes I think that my goal is more for families to be aware of what the resources are and to know where to turn and to know what to be mindful of."

The stakes are even higher for families who live in remote geographic locations where they do not have access to in-person adoption trainings. Here the influence of the market is especially important to understand. As placement agencies grew their operations and expanded their geographic reach, they were compelled to network with more regional affiliates that oversaw the education and home study process. To efficiently process these applicants, many large agencies relaxed their standards requiring applicants to take part in face-to-face trainings and instead permitted clients to take their trainings online. As a social worker, Gretchen is critical of this interface because "it is hard to know how much is being absorbed and how effective and impactful it is. And where do they go when they have a question?" She also notes that the online model allows parents to eschew potentially uncomfortable topics, like race, and take other trainings instead. "And that is kind of my biggest pet peeve," she states, "that families don't come in with a cohesive understanding and training. They are all over the map in terms of their understanding. They may choose to do infant CPR instead of race or ethnicity."

Similarly, Penelope expresses concerns about the pedagogical implications of online trainings, describing how "people can click, click, click, rush through and not pay much attention and just get to the end to get their certificate to show that they've done it." In contrast, if they were in an in-person group, "people might be more engaged. There is a level of challenge that is not there [online]." Michele also articulates her reservations about online trainings, stating, "I would not replace the work that is done in the group experience with an online training." However, with the market downturn, agencies have fewer resources. She realistically surmises, "But due to budget cuts, there are many agencies that do that," even if it means, "online you are in a bubble."

While these trade-offs may compromise the best interests of children, in a time of crisis when the threat of losing paying customers is the main concern, once competitors started accepting these credentials, others had to follow suit or risk losing business. Nora describes this capitulation, noting, "We are in a different world now. There is a great deal to be said for clustering people and letting them ask questions. There is a lot to be said. It works. It would be wonderful to get people in a room together. To laugh, talk, to have a cup of coffee. But people have no time. It is two working parents; they are glad to sit at the computer and do the training. Does it sink in? Probably no. You would hope."

It is disconcerting to think that some of the applicants who live in the most racially segregated rural areas are the least likely to access in-person education before adopting transracially. Angela, an adoption social worker, details how her agency expanded, and now "we work with families all over the country, though in some of the truly rural areas of the country." With these geographic barriers, applicants have limited options outside of online trainings. With this in mind, Angela describes how "we often help families piece together sort of the best of the online options, which we are willing to accept as a requirement." Likewise, Fiona's client roster mostly consists of White families living in remote areas adopting Black children. She shares, "All of my families are all Caucasian, and they all live in very rural White towns. Very rural, like rural, rural, rural, and these children are going to stand out." Following up, I asked her about offering only online trainings to these vulnerable families, and she responds that she wishes these families had access to in-person trainings, but they are not available: "We would like to have them. I have been really trying to get—I look all the time to . . . find trainings to send families to. But it is hard to get people to come together for me to do it."

Of course, the irony is that the more adoption providers rely on adoptive parent education to serve far-flung clients, the less leverage they have to compel these very customers to participate. Providers faced competition from other agencies with less stringent requirements that would accept online trainings. This interface was easier to access and potentially more cost-effective. Moreover, it enabled applicants to skip lengthy and potentially uncomfortable in-person discussions that would challenge White parents to recognize how race and privilege manifests itself. Even though social workers harbored reservations that applicants could just "click, click, click" through these surface-level presentations and not really absorb the material, adoption providers still accepted these certifications and moved applicants through the paper process.

The goal of this project is not to judge the content of online adoption trainings or assail a specific agency's practice but to show how, at the aggregate level, adoption social workers sell the idea of transracial adoption. As my findings indicate, race gets repeatedly downplayed and when it *is* discussed, race gets conflated with culture. Penelope's assessment that social workers "missed the mark" by not grounding their work in a framework of White privilege is an important critique. Olivia confirms this appraisal, describing how among the three hundred White attendees at an adoption advocacy conference there was a palpable desire to glaze over discussions. The overarching message is that frank conversations about race, privilege, and adoption are peripheral, such that when colleagues do try to initiate further dialogue, they are told, "We just don't have time to do it all." What does it mean when race gets pushed to the margins in transracial adoption? What are the implications for adoptive families? I tackle this question in the Conclusion, bringing together my arguments about race, kinship, and the marketplace.

# Conclusion

*The Consequences of Selling Transracial Adoption and the Implications for Adoptive Families*

This book shines a spotlight on the pathway toward transracial adoptive parenthood and the ways in which market constraints shape how adoption providers sell their services to prospective customers. During this bureaucratized exchange, the fiscal realities of running a small business often conflict with workers' espoused ideology that adoption should be a practice purely grounded in child welfare. Over the course of my research, the landscape of the adoption marketplace continued to evolve, especially as potential clients looked to other forms of family building such as assisted reproductive technologies and surrogacy. Although adoption workers would like to solely focus on finding parents for children, faced with greater financial pressures they must also convince customers that they can find children for parents. To do so, adoption facilitators rely on a form of emotion work that subtly (and not so subtly) urges clients to see themselves as consumers and winnow the pool of children to find the child who will best "fit" their family.

Of note, I have purposely avoided the subject of what happens after the adoptions are completed. This question, although important, is outside the scope of the project. Yet prior research indicates that transracial adoptees face unique challenges and may struggle at times to make sense of their upbringing. In her study featuring the voices of adult Black transracial adoptees, Sandra Patton shares her interview with Kristin, a Black woman raised by White parents. Kristin describes the disconnect she feels between her Black appearance and her White racial socialization, stating, "I would probably say I'm White with very, very dark skin."[1] Later in the interview she adds, "I feel like I have been conditioned White, and I am White in a Black body."[2] Patton's work is not the only study to report a mismatch between the way that transracial adoptees look versus how they feel. Kim Park Nelson's ethnographic research on adult Korean adoptees uncovers similar themes, such that among her respondents many "experienced a great desire to be White."[3] She cites an interview with John, who recalls how "growing up, I didn't wan[t to] be Korean; I wanted to be more Caucasian because [that is] what this society values as beautiful."[4] These findings indicate that there are consequences to selling transracial adoption as an expedient market option because this promotional strategy can leave White parents unprepared to navigate the racial issues which will inevitably arise.

I do want to stress my firm belief that most White adoptive parents are doing the best that they can with the resources that they have. Recall Sylvia's assessment of her decades-long work with adoptive parents as she adamantly states, "Parents love their children; don't get me wrong." The goal of this book is not to question this indisputable fact. Indeed, as someone who grew up in a transracial adoptive family, I can testify to the irrevocable bond that adoptive families can form. But as Gretchen insightfully points out, love is necessary but not sufficient when raising children of another race. Thus, the goal of the conclusion is to pose the question, so what? Why does it matter that private adoption operates as a marketplace where parents are positioned as consumers and children are advertised as the products? If parents are directed to think about transracial adoption as a market calculation that allows them to maximize getting a healthy baby or toddler, what are the implications when these children grow up? What are the missed opportunities and barriers as social workers attempt to prepare White parents to adopt transracially?

Overall, I follow two main points of inquiry. First, I examine how private adoption workers sell transracial adoption to prospective clients who often come to adoption only after facing significant barriers to biological reproduction. While infertile heterogamous married couples have long been a mainstay of private adoption, their customer base has expanded to serve homogamous couples and single parents. These applicants are often looking to emulate the as-if-begotten model of biological reproduction by adopting the most racially similar, healthiest, and youngest child available. However, as regulations tighten making it harder for those who fall outside of the traditional mold to adopt from abroad, these would-be parents are often relegated to the second tier of the marketplace. Adoption professionals are faced with the challenge of breaking the news to these prospective adopters that they do not qualify for certain programs and thus part of the adoption workers' role is to funnel disadvantaged applicants into transracial adoption—a pathway where they are more likely to be successful.

My second research question analyzes how transracial adoption in the private sphere is shaped by racial hierarchies such that Asian and Hispanic children are seen as preferable to Black children. Yet, there is a crucial exception to this color line, such that biracial Black and foreign-born Black children are distinguished from monoracial native-born Black children. Adoption providers underscore these differentiations in two key ways. First, some allow White parents to limit their transracial adoptions to biracial Black children as opposed to monoracial Black children. Second, they play up supposed differences between foreign-born and native-born Black children by subtly positioning foreign-born Black children as higher status.

My findings suggest that because of this consumer orientation toward finding children for parents, adoption social workers may be selling transracial adoption to those who do not fully understand the implications of raising children of color. Of course, it may be that White parents will grow into their roles. According to Danielle, one of the phenomenal things about transracial adoption is that it catalyzes White parents to reevaluate their racial boundaries in the pursuit of parenthood. She attests that the desire to love and raise a child can supersede racial differences, stating, "People's drive to be parents is stronger than anything. It is stronger than racism. It is stronger than their fears. People have such a strong desire to love a child that it trumps [all]."

She describes how this shortage can actually be a good thing in terms of overcoming racism: "In a world where they [White parents] can choose, they are going to choose the fairer kid, and that's about racism. But in a world where they can't, they are going to get over it." This was certainly the case in the early years of international adoption, when Asian children were perceived as forever foreigners,[5] but the availability of healthy young infants in closed adoptions outweighed these concerns.[6] Danielle references this calculus: "I think, if you look at the beginning at international adoption too, people got over wanting a child that looked like them too and adopted an Asian child. And I do think that the parents are forever changed by that."

Notably, Danielle sees this change as an optimistic harbinger, arguing that the experience of becoming a transracial adoptive family irrevocably alters parents' conceptions of race. Despite this evolution, she admits that some White parents maintain their racist worldviews. She continues, "You or I might interview them and still think, 'Oh my God, they are so racist, and they have kids of color, and blah blah blah.' But they are in a very different place than if they didn't have their children." She closes on an optimistic note, describing how these parents "do learn and grow."

Parenthood, whether biological or adoptive, provides a life-changing opportunity for growth and self-reflection. Thus I have no doubt that Danielle is correct in her assessment that transracial adoptive parents "do learn and grow" from their experiences. However, what does it mean to expect transracially adopted children to be the source of parents' racial education? At whose expense are these teachable moments originating? It is important to juxtapose this positive interpretation with Danielle's admission that if some transracial adoptive parents were interviewed, one might rightfully conclude, "Oh my God, they are so racist." Danielle seems to dismiss the significance of this admission ("blah blah blah"), which is worrisome, since the goal of transracial adoption is supposed to prioritize the needs of children. But as this book shows, at the selection stage, the private marketplace is inherently structured to favor the wants of paying clients.

One thing that surprised me about my research was the fact that adoption social workers had little latitude to turn down prospective clients. Instead, many saw it as a given that even applicants who were considered below par would eventually be approved. Describing this perfunctory process, Nicole concedes that she hardly ever turns down clients, even if she harbors doubts that they are adequately prepared to parent across race. She attests, "I never feel like I can turn down families because their lifestyle wasn't diverse enough or they don't live in a diverse enough area." She echoes the sentiment that the home study serves as a rubber stamp of approval, stating, "My role there—it wasn't my job to turn down people." Likewise, Lindsay confirms that she writes positive home studies for applicants who might be considered marginal, noting, "Would I want these people to be my parents? Not necessarily, but you can't use that as your guide."

Heather also expressed a hesitancy to reject applicants, much preferring for prospective clients to come to the realization on their own. Part of this motivation may be clinical, as social workers try to shield vulnerable parents who have come to adoption after significant losses. But the preference also protects the provider's image, since getting a reputation of being difficult to work with could be bad for business. As Heather puts it, "I think that our goal generally if we feel that adoption is not right for a family, we help them try to come to that themselves. It would be preferential for all involved to kind of screen themselves out of the process. And better for the family to control that decision rather than be denied. It is not good for everybody."

Recall from Chapter 5 Danielle's story regarding how she dealt with a caller who wanted to know if adopting an African child would signal to her White children that it was acceptable to marry a Black person. In telling the story, Danielle differentiates between dissuading a caller at the intake stage versus "turning them *down* down." As the interview progressed, she went on to describe that she has only blatantly turned away a few people in the course of her career, stating, "I can count on one hand the amount of people I have said no to in fifteen years. I have said that 'I am sorry, but I am not going to be able to write a positive home study for you no matter how much you want it.'" However, she juxtaposes this small number with a larger group of people she has proactively dissuaded from applying, essentially turning them down by not encouraging them to continue. She relates, "But I am sure there is probably a couple dozen people who I have counseled out [by conveying the message], 'You need to go to couples' counseling. It doesn't sound like he is on board with this plan. You can come back after this. Is this is really right for you?' Getting people to take a break, getting people to really think about it."

But in a down market, when there is a limited supply of adoptable children, and every paying customer matters, it is getting harder to counsel people out or move them toward what are seen as easier placements. Danielle recounts the new dilemma she faces when deciding whether to approve applicants for adoptions that they are not ready for or turn them down altogether. She elaborates, "If you know they can only adopt from Ethiopia— otherwise they are not going to be parents—then saying no to them is very, very hard." Danielle describes how in the past she would funnel parents into what she saw as an easier placement. "We used to be able to counsel that family younger, [telling them,] 'Why don't we look at China? That would be a good option for you. [You would adopt] one at a time, under one [year old]." In retelling her story, notice how Danielle depicts China's program as a good trade-off between age and race, emphasizing the benefit of getting an infant ("under one") with a seemingly innocuous transracial placement. But with this option no longer available, often applicants now qualify to adopt only from Ethiopia, a country with less-stringent eligibility requirements. Danielle continues, "But now I get couples who only qualify for a child over four or five. For those people, ten years ago I would have counseled those people down to a baby." But in this market downturn, she faces a new ethical quandary, stating, "I either have to approve them for, or accept a home study from another agency approving them for, a four-year-old child from Africa, or I have to turn them down and say we don't have any options for you. So it is tough."

Danielle emphasizes that in general, her preference is not to outright reject these applicants, even if they are not prepared to transracially adopt a school-age Black child who has grown up in a different country speaking a different language. Instead, she and her colleagues take this strategy: "I think that most of what we do is try to push people more through education. You know, try to really ask people to do extra education, to really work [pauses], to really try to consider to whether they would move, whether they would go to church in another place. Getting them to really try to consider what it will be like for their child, to get to know families who do understand race. So by and large, as a social worker we have always tried to counsel people out but not refuse them."

Daniele's statement raises an important issue regarding the goal of adoption. By their own admission, several social workers disclosed that they harbored doubts about the readiness of some of these families, acknowledging that they would "not necessarily" want them to be their parents. Although Danielle hopes to push her less-prepared clients through education, she has little leverage to compel disinterested clients from heeding her advice. Whereas those adopting internationally—especially via a country that has signed the Hague treaty on intercountry adoption—have to complete ten hours of education and training,[7] for private domestic adoption only thirteen states require *any* education and training to adopt.[8]

Several of the social workers I interviewed lamented that some domestic adoption providers did little to offer training for future parents. Wanting to rectify these deficiencies, they often went above and beyond their paid duties to augment the mediocre curriculum. For example, Nicole subcontracts for an agency that provided only a cursory level of training. She describes it as "ridiculous, like two to four hours." Wanting her families to be prepared to be adoptive parents, she recounts how she would "mandate additional training" to try to fill in some of these knowledge gaps. Likewise, Penelope describes a similar strategy. She shares her frustration that the applicants she works with have not been taught even the most rudimentary skills, such as protecting the details of their child's privacy regarding his or her adoption story. She angrily describes how, "when people get to me for the home study, by the time they've supposedly gone through the training, they haven't heard, 'You're the guardian of your child's story; give your child control.' They don't know about life books. We talk a little bit about basic open adoption stuff. *They kind of don't know anything*, which is kind of scary. So in the basic home study process, although I am not being paid to provide training and education, I feel like I am doing a lot of that anyway."

As a private adoption attorney, Christine has witnessed firsthand the gaps in the home study process. She describes how occasionally she works with applicants that she knows will make subpar adoptive parents. Despite their shortcomings, these would-be parents are still able to find a social worker willing to approve the home study. Christine is blunt in her critique of the process, detailing that among her clients she has seen "lots of horrible, disgusting marriages of men and women," elaborating that these couples have gone on to adopt children. Since her role is to advise clients, she admits that the approval process is out of her control, stating, "I have, in my practice, made a conscious decision that it is not up to me. The court has to approve them. They have to have an approved home study, and the court has to approve them."

I followed up with Christine, asking her if she wonders who approved the home studies for these questionable families. In her response, she gives an honest, even brutal, characterization of the fallibility of the procedure, stating, "You know, that's why the home study is sort of baloney." She notes that it is easy for prospective adoptive parents to impart a good impression, since "when you sit with a caseworker for a couple of hours, you can have the best marriage in the world." This polished image is easy to maintain when creating a profile meant to market oneself to expectant women. Through this medium, clients can selectively emphasize and embellish their biographies. Noting this tendency for clients to exaggerate their circumstances, Christine cynically continues, "And the profiles, that's what is hysterical. Everyone is awesome. Everyone is totally awesome. I have the best husband in the whole world." These depictions can be outright disingenuous, as Christine describes how she had had clients who represent themselves as happily married despite the fact that, "in the middle of an adoption, she is like, 'He doesn't want to be married to me anymore.' And I looked at their profile, and it's glowing."

Following a best interest of the child model, one would assume that if an adoption worker felt that a prospective adoptive parent was going to be a mediocre transracial adoptive parent, than that parent would be turned down. Instead, what I more often heard was that facilitators tend to acquiesce, often hindered by loose state regulations that make it difficult to justify denying these applicants. Thus, these marginal parents were moved onto the next stage of the process, and all that social workers could do was hope that some of the information would imprint. Olivia describes this capitulation, rhetorically asking and answering, "Do I think every one of the parents I work with totally get it and are going to be fabulous transracial families? No, I don't."

The stakes for preparing White parents to adopt non-White children are even higher given that the population of children available for adoption is changing, as the supply shifts away from White and Asian children toward Black and Hispanic children. This is not to say that Asian Americans do not face racial discrimination.[9] But in a society where violence against black and brown bodies is carried out with frightening regularity,[10] there is particular cause for concern about the future safety of these children. If White parents are encouraged to adopt Black (and to a lesser extent, Hispanic) children because these children can be obtained in a shorter time frame and for a cheaper price, the White parents making this transracial adoption calculus may not be thinking ahead to what happens when these children grow into adult persons of color.

I spoke with Patricia about the potential drawbacks of this mind-set and she responds:

> People look at babies and think, 'Oh, I can raise any baby. But your baby turns two and five and ten, and thirteen, and eighteen. I think that people want to be parents, and they think baby, and they forget that they are babies [*makes a pinching sign with her fingers*] for this long. They are babies for this long, and then you have to send them out in this world. And how do you do this when you have no understanding of what their experience is like when you walk through life? Yes, we have a human experience, but you have to be realistic too.

As Patricia insightfully states, some of these children are raised by White parents who "have no understanding of what their experience is like," and they then grow up and are sent "out into this world." The fallibility of this color-blind approach is brought into stark relief by the events that a Black man and his White adoptive mother describe during a joint interview as part of the NPR StoryCorps program. The son describes how "we never talked about race growing up," while his mother states, "I thought that love would conquer all, and skin color really didn't matter."[11] The notion that we have achieved a postracial society was shattered for this family during a traffic stop when, at nineteen years old, the son was pulled over for a minor traffic violation and then brutally beaten by three police officers.[12] In a later interview, the mother describes how she regrets not doing more to prepare her son for the possibility of these encounters, stating, "Had I prepared [him] properly, he would have suffered less."[13] One has to wonder whether the adoption professionals involved with the placement adequately communicated the gravity of the commitment that transracial adoption entails.

It is troubling that, during the early phases of the adoption process, several opportunities that could help prospective parents are missed. These occur at every stage as social workers repeatedly describe how they have little leverage to compel clients to do more. Instead, applicants are passed through the pipeline, and adoption professionals hope for the best. Irene, a private adoption attorney, details how she often works with parents who quixotically endorse a color-blind perspective when pursuing transracial adoption. "We definitely have families where race is not a factor at all." In her follow-up, she states, "And we just hope that they have really thought it through and [thought about] the issues that they will be confronting." Notice how Irene's statement frames the potential implications in terms of whether the parents made a well-informed consumer choice in selecting the right child for themselves, rather than emphasizing the needs of the child.

From the intake stage forward, a consumer attitude, coupled with a "hope for the best" approach, prevails. Recall from Chapter 5 how Jennifer opts not to turn away a caller who makes a racist comment, with the justification that these misconceptions can be addressed once applicants sign on. "My hope would be that everything that I had said to a family is in fact complemented and considerably expanded on."

However, there is little impetus for uninterested adoptive parents to more deeply engage in discussions about uncomfortable issues, even when these subjects are raised during preadoption education. Penelope describes how she wishes she could compel her clients to undergo more training. While the Hague convention mandates ten hours of training, according to Penelope, this only "scratches the surface." She states, "As a social worker I thought, there is so much information out there, and the ten hours required by the Hague, it is not enough. It is just scratching the surface. It is hopeful that people will continue to do their own reading and learning, but I bet they don't in general once they get that kid home."

Those living in rural areas where their child may represent the sole racial diversity in a homogeneous White community potentially need the greatest additional support. Yet paradoxically, precisely because of their isolation, these future parents are allowed to take online classes to fulfill their training. Even though social workers articulate their concerns that these families are "in a bubble" and could simultaneously be "watching *American Idol*," these providers bow to logistical constraints and the threat of competition from agencies that will accept online training.

Michele acknowledges the inherent limitations of her agency's educational curriculum, admitting, "I know that people aren't 100 percent with us while we are doing the educating, but my goal is really to plant a seed to think about these things." Whereas Michele tries to remain optimistic about the trajectory of these families, stating, "And my hope is that in the future they will remember this," Nora is more cynical. She describes these limitations of the education process, bluntly concluding, "Does it sink in? Probably no. You would hope." Olivia sums up the compromises social workers have to make when approving some parents, detailing how she hopes for the best, even if evidence suggests that there are few reasons to be hopeful. She states, "And being hopeful that parents are going to get it—that's the reality." Yet Olivia is all too aware that her hope may be unfounded, since, in her experience, she has found that "people can be very uncomfortable with race." Considering that many of her clients come to adoption only after exhausting all options for biological parenthood, she laments that some of her past clients "can be very uncomfortable with the whole adoption piece too."

Given the fact that adoption can be seen as "still not quite as good as having your own child,"[14] it is vital that adoptive parents get the training that they need. But in reality, the bar seems to be getting *lower* for prospective families, not higher. For example, I was on the e-mail list of one agency that routinely advertised to potential clients that its application process was the most accommodating, since "no mileage fees or classroom attendance is needed for your adoption home study." Another boasted to its recipients that all of its training can be completed online "from the comfort of their home." While this consumer-friendly approach prioritizing customer convenience may be good for business, it is less clear whether this approach makes sense for child welfare.

Abigail describes how the threat of losing clients led her agency to soften its once-rigorous training requirements. Cognizant that "we lose a ton of families because of our gender policy, and our home study process takes way more time and is way more invasive than other agencies," she states that "we've started to flex a lot of our guidelines." She elaborates,

"They're no longer policies. They are all guidelines. Like fertility work—it is now a guideline that you be done with it. Gender, it used to be a policy. Now it is like, 'Well, if you've adopted a child of one gender, you can request one of another gender.' We can put in preferences, but we can't put in requests."

With the focus on applicants' preferences, there is little leverage to compel prospective parents to do more to prepare themselves. In my interview with Heather, she describes how race, like age, health, and gender, is "just one of several things on the table." She acknowledges that race is often one of the things that parents are flexible about but stresses that her agency assumes that if parents opt for transracial adoption, they will change their lives to accommodate raising a child of color. Heather avows that there is "this expectation that they are going to adjust their lives accordingly in order to parent a child from whatever race or ethnicity they are adopting from."

It seems that we can and should do better—beyond just articulating the expectation that parents will "adjust their lives accordingly." One way to do this is to raise the bar higher. For example, it has long been considered best practice to encourage transracial adoptive parents to seek out same-race role models for their children.[15] While social workers often espouse this advice, adoption providers frame it as nice to have, rather than as an essential element of transracial adoptive parenting. In terms of policy changes, adoption providers could mandate that one of the required letters of recommendation furnished by applicants has be written by a friend or family member who is the same race as their future son or daughter. If prospective parents do not have anyone in their immediate circle willing to write on their behalf, it signals that these applicants may not yet have the resources in place to adopt transracially.

But this type of policy change will likely never happen. First, it goes against MEPA-IEP's ordinance that prohibits taking race into account in the placement process. But as others have argued, MEPA's color-blind approach is inherently flawed.[16] Since race will inevitably play a significant role in the lives of transracial adoptive families, it is shortsighted not to allow it to play a role in the matching process. Second, unless adoption practitioners enact universal standards, these types of policy initiatives will never get off the ground because customers can seek out providers that do not adhere to the same strict rules. With these barriers, it is impossible to institute significant change, and adoption providers are left to hope for the best.

Although some providers would like to institute greater oversight and training, in some cases adoption agencies are organizing *against* changes that could potentially strengthen adoptive families. In September 2016 the U.S. Department of State (the government body in charge of regulating intercountry adoptions) published a document detailing suggested changes regarding accrediting adoption agencies working in overseas adoption and new rules for training prospective parents.[17] The proposed changes included mandating that adoption agencies obtain country-specific authorization (CSA), thus increasing oversight when placement agencies decide to branch into an emerging market—for example, expanding from Ethiopia to Ghana.[18] Another suggested change would increase the number of hours of mandatory training from ten to twenty, either by requiring applicants to take part in their home state's preexisting public training for foster care adoptive parents or by having private agencies develop their own curricula.[19] Considering that several workers I spoke with lamented that the current regulation delineating ten hours of training could only scratch the surface of what they wanted to cover, raising the bar to require more preparation could have been a step in the right direction.

But despite the U.S. Department of State's assertion that these new rules would institute "stronger preparations of prospective adoptive parents for successful intercountry adoption, greater transparency as to adoption fees in both the United States and abroad, and the potential for improving practices in certain countries of origin through CSA,"[20] these proposed regulations generated a passionate campaign led by adoption agencies that painted these safeguards as an "anti-adoption agenda." A coalition of adoption representatives banded together to argue that the additional step of obtaining country-specific authorization would "restrict the number of agencies working in foreign countries," perhaps making it harder for agencies to generate revenue by continually opening up programs. Moreover, they contended that the rules requiring additional training and fee disclosures would be difficult to put into practice and that implementing this level of supervision would "put the nail in the coffin" of international adoption.[21] Perhaps in response to the outcry among adoption providers, in April 2017 the Department of State withdrew its proposal.[22]

Although I strongly support requiring comprehensive training for prospective adoptive parents, critics of my analysis could retort that biological parents do not need to jump through any hoops outside of sexual reproduction to become parents, so why should adoptive parents be held to a higher standard? Certainly, there are biological parents who would benefit from training and education. Kiera describes this seeming double standard, stating, "Sometimes I tell [adoptive] families that I wish that biological parents had to do this. Adoptive parenting is like thinking forward. We ask people to imagine what it is like for the child when they become teenagers just to help to make it real." Similarly, Nora responds, "Let me do devil's advocate: you don't have to do training to give birth. You should."

In response to this rejoinder, I would counter that it is a mistake to compare adoptive parenting to biological parenting. This is the weakness of the as-if-begotten model. Adoptive parenting is inherently different (not inferior, just different) from biological parenting because the child being placed was somebody else's child first. The birth mother relinquished her son or daughter to adoption, probably hoping that he or she could have a proverbial "better life." Given the sacrifice made by the placing mother, it does not seem too much to ask transracial adoptive parents to do slightly more to prepare for the road ahead.

This obligation is especially important in the case of transracial adoption, as it may not have been the first choice of the birth mothers placing their children. Patricia describes how women of color making adoption plans tend to have fewer family profiles to choose from, making it more likely that these women will have to settle for families that might not have been their first choice. She states:

> And so that's where the pain is for me, that they don't have the choice. If a woman of color decides that a non-Black or a non-Hispanic family is the family for her child, I think that is wonderful, and it's absolutely her choice to do that. But I think what happens is that they have an absence of choice because they are so limited in what is available. So they end up with families who, even though they may like, would not have been their first choice for their child.

Patricia's response underscores how birth mothers' feelings are often overlooked when adoption workers sell transracial adoption. For White prospective adoptive parents to have an array of choices when pursuing adoption, these options often come at the expense of less-privileged women. As Patricia poignantly states, "They have an absence of choice." These women's perspectives are often silenced because they trouble the win-win consumer narrative of choice that encapsulates private adoption. But just as generations of adult adoptees have grown up and are beginning to research and write about their experiences,[23] in the future we are likely to see new waves of birth mothers (and to a lesser extent, fathers) speak out about their concerns and open new directions for research.[24]

The increasing focus on first mothers' experiences is just one of the ways in which private adoption is changing. When I was collecting research for this book, the field was facing a time of crisis as the number of adoptions declined and the balance of placements shifted away from intercountry toward private domestic placements. Data from the Child Welfare Information Gateway indicate that the number of total adoptions fell between 2008 and 2012, from almost 140,000 adoptions per year to 120,000.[25]

Since the number of foster care adoptions remained relatively stable,[26] the decline most likely originated in the private sector as the number of international placements dwindled. But the weakening numbers may also signal that overall interest in adoption is diminishing as would-be parents either seek out fertility treatments or surrogacy, or perhaps forego parenthood altogether in favor of being child-free.[27]

Just as the prior decade witnessed a vast evolution in the scope of private adoption, the following years are likely to generate other changes and challenges. For example, there has been a resurgence of interest in intercountry adoption led by evangelical Christians wanting to alleviate the global orphan crisis, especially in Africa.[28] Many of the children placed in these families tend to be in grade school and older, suggesting that they will have very different transracial adoption experiences than the cohorts of infants and toddlers who came before them. For adoption professionals, the practice of placing older children who are bound to face greater acculturation barriers raises new issues about how to adequately prepare adoptive families. Although some may applaud these plucky parents for taking on harder-to-place kids, news reports that a subset of these children are being "rehomed"—passed on to new adoptive families without any legal or clinical oversight—are very worrisome.[29]

As adoption practitioners and policy makers grapple with this new world of adoption, it will be all the more important to contextualize these placements within the market framework. It may be that the marketplace will become even more segmented, with foster care still perceived as an inferior pathway that places troubled children. International adoption will likely become more of a "boutique" industry, catering to parents willing to pay tens of thousands of dollars to adopt older children who have not been through the U.S. foster care system. Absent another blockbuster intercountry program with a large supply of babies, private domestic adoption will likely be the sole remaining outlet for healthy infants.

Regardless of the market sector, a subset of these adoptions will be transracial placements. Thus, adoption providers will still be faced with selling transracial adoption to prospective parents. For some of these applicants, transracial adoption will be their first choice, but for many, the decision to adopt across race will likely result from a complex evaluation of their market options. As this book shows, this market mentality makes it difficult for adoption workers to adequately prepare White parents adopting across race, and several of the women I interviewed harbor doubts that parents are adequately prepared for the road ahead. Yet in a down market, it will be even harder for adoption providers. With the diminishing supply of high-demand children, workers will face an uphill battle selling transracial adoption, let alone educating parents. These market concessions are poised to have significant implications for children's well-being, because, in an unequal racial society, these minority children and their White parents will likely need continued support and resources to strengthen their families.

# Notes

## INTRODUCTION

1. All names of adoption providers and adoption agencies are pseudonyms.
2. William Feigelman and Arnold Silverman (1983) were among the first to use this term.
3. Dorow 2006, chap. 1.
4. Zelizer 1994.
5. The name of the country has been changed to protect anonymity of the adoption agency.
6. Selman 2009, 594.
7. For examples of past research, see Blackstone et al. 2008, Hogbacka 2008, and Goodwin 2010.
8. Pertman 2008, 8.
9. Chittister 2015.
10. Colaco 2014.
11. Modell 1994, 2.
12. Modell 1994, 2.
13. See also Dan Savage's memoir, *The Kid* (1999), which chronicles his journey to adopt. Notably, each section (fertilization, gestation, birth, afterbirth) is likened to pregnancy.
14. Zelizer 1994, 23.
15. Zelizer 1994, 195.
16. Radin and Sunder 2005, 8.
17. For examples, see Donner 1997, Quiroz 2007, Fedders 2010, and Krawiec 2010.
18. "Six Words" 2013.
19. "Six Words" 2013.
20. For a list of adoption-related blogs, see https://creatingafamily.org/adoption/adoption-blogs.

21. Quiroz 2007, 41.
22. Pavao 2005.
23. Zelizer 2010, 267.
24. Zelizer 2010, 267.
25. Spar 2006, 160.
26. Spar 2006, 161.
27. Williams and Zelizer 2005, 368.
28. Healy 2006, 117.
29. Healy 2006, 42.
30. Williams and Zelizer 2005, 372.
31. Statistics Sweden, n.d. In addition, there were 313 adoptions by one parent, but it is likely that many of these are second-parent adoptions. See Roden 2017.
32. Rothman 2006, 17.
33. For a discussion of adoption in Sweden and how the shortage of Swedish-born babies was related to the rising popularity of transnational adoption, particularly from Korea, see Yngvesson 2010.
34. Selman 2009.
35. Solinger 2002.
36. Solinger 2002, 7.
37. Rothman 2006, 58.
38. Briggs 2012, 18 (emphasis in original).
39. Briggs 2012, 7.
40. Unless otherwise stated, all the women I quote are adoption providers I interviewed for this book.
41. Gordon 1964.
42. Qian and Lichter 2001.
43. See Hughes 1945; Waters 1990.
44. Alba and Nee 2005.
45. Ignatiev 1995.
46. Ignatiev 1995, 89.
47. Roediger 2006.
48. See Alba and Nee 2005; Gonsoulin and Fu 2010.
49. Lee 2015.
50. Greico et al. 2012.
51. Portes and Rivas 2011.
52. See Haller et al. 2011; Zhou 1997.
53. See Alba and Nee 1997; Zhou and Lee 2007.
54. See Bratter 2007; Fu 2007.
55. Bonilla-Silva 2004, 2.
56. Yancey 2003, 15.
57. Yancey 2003, 15.
58. Gans 2005, 19.
59. Warren and Twine 1997.
60. See U.S. Census Bureau 2016.
61. Qian and Lichter 2007, 33.
62. Passel, Wang, and Taylor 2010.
63. See Kalmijn 1998; Schwartz 2013.
64. Dalmage 2000, 70.
65. Kubo 2010, 281.

66. Rothman 2006, 107.

67. Rothman 2006, 107.

68. Dorow 2006a, 357.

69. Ishizawa et al. 2006, 1218.

70. Raleigh 2012.

71. Quiroz 2007, 7. For more on racial projects, see Omi and Winant 1994, 55.

72. Quiroz 2007, 7.

73. Quiroz 2007, 3.

74. Raleigh 2002.

75. Sweeney 2013, 53.

76. Hutson 2012.

77. Jennings 2006, 578.

78. Goffman 1959, 35.

79. For a similar discussion, see Kubo 2010.

80. Brian 2012.

81. Brian 2012, 28.

82. Dorow 2006b, 91.

83. Dorow 2006b, 87.

84. Dorow 2006b, 88.

85. Dorow 2006b, 88.

86. Dorow 2006b, 88.

87. Dorow 2006b, 85.

88. Dorow 2006b, 89.

89. Dorow 2006b, 89.

90. Dorow 2006b, 89.

91. Dorow 2006b, 69.

92. Quiroz 2007.

93. Quiroz 2007, 79.

94. Jennings 2006.

95. Carter-Black 2002, 363.

96. Bailey 2009.

97. U.S. Department of State 2006.

98. Bailey 2009, 181.

99. Kirton 1999.

100. Lee, Crolley-Simic, and Vonk 2013.

101. Ishizawa and Kubo 2014.

102. Ishizawa and Kubo 2014.

103. Choy 2013.

104. For discussions of dynamics in insider-outsider research, see Humphrey 2013 and Taylor 2011.

105. Hodkinson 2005, 136.

106. Goffman 1959, 126.

107. Wilson 1987, 91.

108. Harknett and McLanahan 2004.

109. Landes and Posner 1978.

110. Landes and Posner 1978, 327.

111. Cohen 1987.

112. Bachrach, London, and Maza 1991, 705.

113. Jones 2009.

114. Almeling 2011.
115. Almeling 2011, 59.
116. Haberman 2014.
117. Jacobson 2016.
118. Markens 2007.
119. Twine 2015.
120. Pande 2014.
121. Jacobson 2016.
122. Rudrappa 2015.
123. Berend 2012.
124. Child Welfare Information Gateway 2013b.
125. Fessler 2007.
126. Henney et al. 2007.
127. Appadurai 2005, 36.
128. Yngvesson 2002, 229.
129. Dorow 2006b, 138.
130. Mauss 1954.
131. U.S. Department of State 2015a.
132. DeNavas-Walt and Proctor 2014, 5.
133. I would almost expect the percentage to be higher. It may be that some of these parents were not reporting the sticker price of the fees paid but the incurred net cost after taking into account the generous adoption tax credit available during the time. This credit lowered families' tax burdens by about $13,000, which could have made some of the domestic adoptions cost-free.
134. Vandivere, Malm, and Radel 2009.
135. Children's Bureau 2016.
136. Ishizawa and Kubo 2014.
137. Vandivere, Malm, and Radel 2009.
138. Children's Bureau 2016.
139. Blackstone et al. 2008.
140. Argys and Duncan 2013.
141. Blackstone et al. 2008.
142. Zhang and Lee 2011, 94.
143. For a similar result, see Gailey 2010, 88.
144. Roberts 2002.
145. Brooks, James, and Barth 2002.
146. Pertman 2011, 226.
147. Katz and Doyle 2013.

## CHAPTER 1

1. Berebitsky 2000, 5.
2. Berebitsky 2000, 135.
3. Berebitsky 2000, 130.
4. Donner 1997.
5. Berebitsky 2000, 5.
6. Herman 2008, 122.
7. Herman 2008, 125.
8. Herman 2008, 155.

9. Balcom 2011, 31–32.

10. Balcom 2011, 71.

11. Berebitsky 2000, 150.

12. Berebitsky 2000, 150.

13. Berebitsky 2000, 150.

14. Herman 2008, 153.

15. Herman 2008, 144.

16. Herman 2008, 232.

17. Berebitsky 2000, 169.

18. Donner 1997, 487, 492.

19. See, e.g., Obama 2016.

20. Park Nelson 2016, 91.

21. Christian World Adoption 2013.

22. Bailey 2009.

23. U.S. Department of State 2015a.

24. U.S. Department of State 2015b.

25. Raleigh 2011, 247.

26. Moon 2015.

27. Davis 2011.

28. Harris Interactive 2002.

29. This program has since largely closed, and in total, Nepal only sent 478 children to the United States between 1999 and 2015. See U.S. Department of State 2015b.

30. U.S. Department of State 2015b.

31. Joyce 2013.

32. Dorow 2006b, 85.

33. See Smolin 2006; Tong 2010.

34. Balcom 2011.

35. Balcom 2011, 4.

36. Balcom 2011, 172.

37. World Bank 2016.

38. Bartholet 2010.


## CHAPTER 2

1. See Schneider 1968; Modell 1994.

2. Kreider and Lofquist 2014.

3. Bausch 2006; Vandivere, Malm, and Radel 2009.

4. In line with Cohen 2011, 48, I use "heterogamous" to describe a union between people of different sexes and "homogamous" to classify a union between two people of the same sex.

5. Smock and Greenland 2010.

6. Gailey 2010, 88.

7. The actual text is "[Name of the agency] delivers," but it has been changed to protect confidentiality.

8. Quiroz 2007, 62.

9. Quiroz 2007, 62.

10. Pertman 2000, 130.

11. For more on the toll of infertility treatment, see Greil, Slauson-Blevins, and McQuillan 2010.

12. Pertman 2000, 130.

13. Chandra et al. 2005.

14. Hochschild 2012.

15. Hochschild 2012, ix.

16. Hochschild 2012, 137.

17. Hochschild 2012, 137.

18. Jones 2008.

19. It is important to note that I did not sample forty separate adoption agencies. Some of the larger agencies offered multiple sessions specific to certain programs. For example, I attended Kid Connection's general information meeting (in person) and then sat in on a webinar about their African American program. To protect against having a disproportionate representation of one agency in my sample, I limited my exposure to two webinars (if offered) and one in-person information meeting.

20. U.S. Department of State 2017c.

21. U.S. Department of State, n.d.

22. Bailey 2009.

23. For the most recent version of the guide, see http://buildingyourfamily.com/digital-edition.

24. See U.S. Department of State 2017a.

25. In the few cases where I mention the name of a respondent's employer, I refer to respondents by new pseudonyms that are not described elsewhere in the text.

26. Glaser and Strauss 2017, 61.

27. Chandra et al. 1999.

28. Freundlich 2000, 43.

29. Raleigh 2016.

30. Although undoubtedly her agency serves an important role in connecting pregnant women with hopeful adoptive parents, it is unlikely that these children would languish in foster care, since relatively healthy infants with siblings are a rarity. A quick search of the AdoptUSKids website's photo listings (at http://www.adoptuskids.org/meet-the-children/search) showed that nationally, out of the 4,356 children legally free for adoption, only two were singletons under one year old. Both of these children had severe medical conditions that required significant care. Once legally free for adoption, relatively healthy infants are quickly adopted by eager parents.

31. Some states have more restrictive laws about attorney-led adoption that further limit parents' choices. See Child Welfare Information Gateway 2016b.

32. Briggs 2012, 112.

33. Briggs 2012, 112.

34. Herman 2008, 228.

35. Brian 2012, 25.

36. Dorow 2006b, 109.

37. Dorow 2006b, 109. For examples of agencies that offer preadoption medical reviews, see Dr. Jane Aronson's website, at http://www.orphandoctor.com, and the website of the Adoption Medicine Clinic at the University of Minnesota, at https://adoption.umn.edu/preadoption/preadoption-medical-reviews.

38. See Dorow 2006b, 108, for a similar interpretation.

39. Brian 2012, 25.

40. Since my fieldwork, the landscape of adoption continues to change. On December 28, 2012, President Vladimir Putin signed into law Federal Law No. 272-FZ.

This law went into effect on January 1, 2013. It bans the adoption of Russian children by U.S. citizens, bars adoption service providers from assisting U.S. citizens in adopting Russian children, and requires termination of the U.S.–Russia Adoption Agreement. See U.S. Department of State 2013.

41. Kreider and Cohen 2009; Judge 2003; Albers et al. 1997.

42. Child Welfare Information Gateway 2016b.

43. U.S. Department of State 2016a.

44. The name of the country has been changed to protect the anonymity of the adoption agency.

## CHAPTER 3

1. Jacobson 2008; Lee 2003; Patton 2000.

2. Raleigh 2012; Ishizawa et al. 2006.

3. Kim 2010, 76.

4. Oh 2015, 80.

5. Kim 2010, 27.

6. Oh 2015, 9.

7. Jennings 2006.

8. Krawiec 2010.

9. Bell 2014.

10. McQuillan et al. 2003.

11. National Center for Health Statistics 2016.

12. Goldberg 2012.

13. Children's Bureau 2016.

14. Ishizawa and Kubo 2014.

15. Vandivere, Malm, and Radel 2009.

16. "Infertility" 2017. For a more in-depth discussion, see Centers for Disease Control and Prevention 2017.

17. Ryan and Moras 2017.

18. Rothman 2006, 52.

19. Berebitsky 2000, 150.

20. Berebitsky 2000, 149.

21. Berebitsky 2000, 149.

22. Berebitsky 2000, 116, 102.

23. Chappell 2016.

24. Dorow 2006b.

25. Holt International, n.d., "Parent."

26. Some countries, such as Mexico, have loosened their restrictions and allow married homogamous couples to adopt from certain areas, such as Mexico City. See U.S. Department of State 2014.

27. Dorow 2006b, 82–83.

28. Dorow 2006b.

29. For more information on gay dads who adopt, see Goldberg 2012.

30. Bachrach, London, and Maza 1991.

31. Jones 2008; Chandra et al. 1999.

32. Melosh 2002, 277.

33. Vandivere, Malm, and Radel 2009.

34. Vandivere, Malm, and Radel 2009.
35. Child Welfare Information Gateway 2014.
36. Juffer and van IJzendoorn 2005; Judge 2003; Albers et al. 1997.
37. Netter and Magee 2010.
38. Crarry 2014.
39. The Russian law banning intercountry adoptions by Americans was supposedly in response to the tragic death of Dima Yakovlev, a Russian-born child accidentally
left in the car by his adoptive father. However, many foreign policy experts argue that
the adoption ban may have been in retaliation against the United States' passage of the
Magnitsky Act. See Taub 2017; Englund and Bahrampour 2012.
40. Reitman 2007.
41. Powell et al. 2010.
42. Raleigh 2012.
43. Bonilla-Silva 2004, 931.

## CHAPTER 4

1. Simon 2010, 21.
2. Bonilla-Silva and Dietrich 2011, 190.
3. Simon 2010, 81.
4. Pertman 2011, 5.
5. Pertman 2011, 5.
6. For recent work, see Aspinall and Song 2013 and Saperstein 2012; for classic
examples, see Waters 1990 and Hughes 1945.
7. Bonilla-Silva 2004, 931.
8. Lee and Bean 2012, 189.
9. Bobo 2015, xiii.
10. Melosh 2002, 200.
11. Melosh 2002, 61.
12. Briggs 2012, 64.
13. Briggs 2012, 59.
14. Briggs 2012, 61.
15. National Association of Black Social Workers 1972.
16. Briggs 2012, 56.
17. Melosh 2002, 175.
18. Park Nelson 2016; Oh 2015; McKee, forthcoming.
19. Oh 2015, 4, fig. 2.
20. Park Nelson 2016, 74.
21. Oh 2015, 127.
22. Tuan 2008, 1849.
23. Park Nelson 2016, 95–96.
24. See Park Nelson 2016; Oh 2015; Briggs 2012; Smith et al. 2011; Quiroz 2007;
Jennings 2006; Dorow 2006a.
25. Jennings 2006; Zhang and Lee 2011.
26. Sweeney 2013, 50.
27. Khanna and Killian 2015, 583.
28. Brian 2012.
29. Lee, Vonk, and Colley-Simic 2015; Kim 1999; Tuan 1999.
30. Dorow 2006b, 55.

31. Dorow 2006b, 80.
32. Brian 2012, 30.
33. Frankenberg 1993, 199.
34. Babtist 2014.
35. Zelizer 1985, 203.
36. Raleigh 2016.
37. Krawiec 2010.
38. Fedders 2010, 1688.
39. "Six Words" 2013.
40. Bonacich 1973.
41. Sociologists have also found a preference for multiracials among Internet daters. See, for example, Curington, Lin, and Lundquist 2015.
42. Ishizawa and Kubo 2014.
43. The program name has been changed to protect the anonymity of the agency.
44. Patillo-McCoy 1999.
45. Lacy 2007.
46. Hairston and Williams 1989.
47. Sandven and Resnick 1990.
48. Herman 2008, 238.
49. Herman 2008, 56.
50. Herman 2008, 199.
51. Kreider and Lofquist 2014.
52. Ishizawa and Kubo 2014.
53. Although race scholars often decry the term "Caucasian," I use the term because it is widely used in adoption parlance. For a discussion of the issue, see Dewan 2013.
54. "Six Words" 2013.
55. I do not cite the website here to protect the anonymity of the agency.
56. Citrin, Levy, and Van Houweling 2014; Khanna 2010; Roth 2005.
57. Lee and Bean 2012, 121.
58. Doyle and Kao 2007; Brunsma 2005.
59. Bonilla-Silva 2004, 2.
60. Sweeney 2013, 54.
61. Patton 2000; Samuels 2009.
62. Sweeney 2013, 54.
63. Hochschild and Weaver 2007.
64. See Hamilton and Goldsmith 2009; Keither and Herring 1991; Hughes and Hertel 1990.
65. Burton et al. 2010; Hunter 2007.
66. For different views, see Banks 2003 and Kennedy 2003.
67. For discussions of Black hetereogeneity and intersectionality, see De Walt 2011 and Moore 2011.
68. For a discussion of adoption as a racial project, see Quiroz 2006.
69. Jacobson 1998, 43.
70. Jacobson 1998, 42.
71. Jacobson 1998, 94.
72. Waters, Kasinitz, and Asad 2014, 380.
73. Waters 1999, 123.
74. U.S. Department of State 2015b.
75. Vandivere, Malm, and Radel 2009.

76. U.S. Department of State 2015a.
77. Holt International, n.d., "Adoption."
78. Yngvesson 2010, 43.
79. Dorow 2006b, 61.
80. Dorow 2006b, 61.
81. Ortiz and Briggs 2003, 46.
82. Ortiz and Briggs 2003, 40.
83. Ortiz and Briggs 2003, 53.
84. Ortiz and Briggs 2003, 53.
85. Jacobson 1998, 46.
86. Dorow 2006b, 50.
87. Hoffman 2012.
88. Louie 2012; Traver 2010.
89. Jacobson 2008, 5.
90. Jacobson 2008, 45.
91. Briggs 2012, 113.

## CHAPTER 5

1. For more information on the act, see Child Welfare Information Gateway. n.d.
2. McRoy et al. 2007, 50.
3. Jennings 2006, 578.
4. Briggs 2012, 120–121.
5. Briggs 2012, 118.
6. Briggs 2012, 119.
7. See, e.g., Roorda 2015; Docan-Morgan 2010a, 2010b; Lee 2003; Grotevant et al. 2001.
8. Brian 2012, 43; see also 48.
9. Brian 2012, 43.
10. Brian 2012, 25.
11. Brian 2012, 36.
12. Jacobson 2008, 81.
13. This is a pseudonym.
14. Jacobson 2008, 71, 75 (emphasis in original).
15. Jacobson 2008, 111.
16. See Kreider and Raleigh 2016; Docan-Morgan 2010a, 2010b.
17. Jacobson 2008, 138.
18. Glazer 1997.
19. Glazer 1997, 8.
20. Glazer 1997, 11.
21. Kubo 2014, 170.
22. Delale-O'Connor 2014, 161.
23. Delale-O'Connor 2014, 161.
24. Delale-O'Connor 2014, 167.
25. McGinnis et al. 2009.
26. See also Atkinson et al. 2013; McRoy 2006.
27. Bonilla-Silva 2009, 71.
28. Bonilla-Silva 2009, 71.
29. Brian 2012, 42.

30. U.S. Census Bureau 2016.
31. Dorow 2006, 89.
32. Cartwright 2003, 83.
33. Cartwright 2003, 83.
34. Hannum 2002.
35. Wang 2012.
36. Lee and Bean 2012, 93.
37. Sweeney 2013, 54.
38. Sweeney 2013, 53.
39. Sweeney 2013, 53.
40. Brian 2012, 40.
41. Brian 2012, 40.

## CONCLUSION

1. Patton 2000, 87.
2. Patton 2000, 89.
3. Park Nelson 2016, 133.
4. Park Nelson 2016, 133.
5. Tuan 1999.
6. Oh 2015.
7. Bailey 2009.
8. Child Welfare Information Gateway 2016a.
9. See Chou and Feagin 2008.
10. Fryer 2015.
11. "After a Traffic Stop" 2014.
12. Meyer 2011.
13. Valby 2015.
14. Fisher 2003, 352.
15. Lee, Vonk, and Colley-Simic 2015; Mohanty 2013; DeBerry, Scarr, and Weinberg 1996.
16. Jennings 2006; Briggs 2012.
17. U.S. Department of State 2016b.
18. U.S. Department of State 2016b, 32322.
19. U.S. Department of State 2016b, 62328.
20. U.S. Department of State 2016b, 62328.
21. Save Adoptions 2016.
22. See U.S. Department of State 2017b.
23. For examples of this writing, see Park Nelson 2016; Gibney 2015; Roorda 2015; Myers 2014; Raible 2012; Docan-Morgan 2010a, 2010b; Samuels 2009; and McKee, forthcoming.
24. For an example of new writing on first mothers, see Hosu Kim's (2016) work on Korean birth mothers.
25. Child Welfare Information Gateway 2016b.
26. Children's Bureau 2016.
27. Blackstone and Stewart 2012.
28. Perry 2014; Joyce 2013.
29. See Twohey 2013. See also J. Kim 2014 for a discussion of internationally adopted children with disabilities in out-of-home care.

# References

AdoptUSKids. n.d. "Photolisting." Available at http://www.adoptuskids.org/photolisting (accessed June 2, 2017).

"After a Traffic Stop, Teen Was 'Almost Another Dead Black Male.'" 2014. *National Public Radio*, August 15. Available at http://www.npr.org/2014/08/15/340419821/after-a-traffic-stop-teen-was-almost-another-dead-black-male.

Alba, Richard, and Victor Nee. 1997. "Rethinking Assimilation Theory for a New Era of Immigration." *International Migration Review* 31 (4): 826–874.

———. 2005. *Remaking the American Mainstream: Assimilation and Contemporary Immigration*. Cambridge, MA: Harvard University Press.

Albers, Lisa H., Dana E. Johnson, Margaret K. Hostetter, Sandra Iverson, and Laurie C. Miller. 1997. "Health of Children Adopted from the Former Soviet Union and Eastern Europe: Comparison with Preadoptive Medical Records." *Journal of the American Medical Association* 278 (11): 922–924.

Almeling, Rene. 2011. *Sex Cells: The Medical Market for Eggs and Sperm*. Berkeley: University of California Press.

Appadurai, Arjun. 2005. "Definitions: Commodity and Commodification." In *Rethinking Commodification: Cases and Readings in Law and Culture*, edited by Martha M. Ertman and Joan C. Williams, 34–44. New York: New York University Press.

Argys, Laura, and Brian Duncan. 2013. "Economic Incentives and Foster Child Adoption." *Demography* 50 (3): 933–954.

Aronson, Jane. 2009. "Assessment of Child's Medical History." *Orphan Doctor*, September 11. Available at http://www.orphandoctor.com/services/assessment.

Aspinall, Peter, and Miri Song. 2013. "Is Race a 'Salient . . .' or 'Dominant Identity' in the Early 21st Century: The Evidence of UK Survey Data on Respondents' Sense of Who They Are." *Social Science Research* 42:547–561.

Atkinson, Anne J., Patricia A. Gonet, Madelyn Freundlich, and Debbie B. Riley. 2013. "Adoption Competent Clinical Practice: Defining Its Meaning and Development." *Adoption Quarterly* 16 (3–4): 156–174.

Babtist, Edward. 2014. *The Half Has Never Been Told: Slavery and the Makings of American Capitalism*. New York: Basic Books.

Bachrach, Christine A., Kathryn A. London, and Penelope L. Maza. 1991. "On the Path to Adoption: Adoption Seeking in the United States, 1988." *Journal of Marriage and Family* 53 (3): 705–718.

Bailey, Jo Daugherty. 2009. "Expectations and Consequences of New International Adoption Policy in the U.S." *Journal of Sociology and Social Work* 36 (2): 169–184.

Balcom, Karen A. 2011. *The Traffic in Babies: Cross-border Adoption and Baby-Selling between the United States and Canada, 1930–1972*. Toronto: University of Toronto Press.

Banks, Richard R. 2003. "The Color of Desire: Fulfilling Adoptive Parents' Racial Practices through Discriminatory State Action." *Yale Law Journal* 107:875–964.

Bartholet, Elizabeth. 2010. "International Adoption: The Human Rights Position." *Global Policy* 1 (1): 91–100.

Bausch, Robert S. 2006. "Predicting Willingness to Adopt a Child: A Consideration of Demographic and Attitudinal Factors." *Sociological Perspectives* 49 (1): 47–65.

Bell, Ann. 2014. *Misconception: Social Class and Infertility in America*. New Brunswick, NJ: Rutgers University Press.

Berebitsky, Julie. 2000. *Like Our Very Own: Adoption and the Changing Culture of Motherhood, 1851–1950*. Lawrence: University of Kansas Press.

Berend, Zsuzsa. 2012. "The Romance of Surrogacy." *Sociological Forum* 27 (4): 913–936.

Blackstone, Amy, and Mahala Dyer Stewart. 2012. "Choosing to be Childfree: Research on the Decision Not to Parent." *Sociology Compass* 6 (9): 718–727.

Blackstone, Erwin A., Andrew J. Buck, Simon Hakim, and Uriel Spiegel. 2008. "Market Segmentation in Child Adoption." *International Review of Law and Economics* 28 (3): 220–225.

Bobo, Lawrence D. 2015. "Foreword: The Racial Double Homicide of Trayvon Martin." In *Deadly Injustice: Trayvon Martin, Race, and the Criminal Justice System*, edited by Devon Johnson, Patricia Y. Warren, and Amy Farrell, xi–xv. New York: New York University Press.

Bonacich, Edna. 1973. "A Theory of Middleman Minorities." *American Sociological Review* 38 (5): 583–594.

Bonilla-Silva, Eduardo. 2004. "From Bi-Racial to Tri-Racial: Towards a New System of Racial Stratification in the USA." *Ethnic and Racial Studies* 27 (6): 931–950.

———. 2009. *Racism without Racists: Colorblind Racism and the Persistence of Racial Inequality*. New York: Rowman and Littlefield.

Bonilla-Silva, Eduardo, and David Dietrich. 2011. "The Sweet Enchantment of Color-Blind Racism in Obamerica." *Annals of the American Academy of Political and Social Science* 634:190–206.

Bratter, Jennifer. 2007. "Will 'Multiracial' Survive to the Next Generation? The Racial Classification of Children of Multiracial Parents." *Social Forces* 86 (2): 821–849.

Brian, Kristi. 2012. *Reframing Transracial Adoption: Adopted Koreans, White Parents, and the Politics of Kinship*. Philadelphia: Temple University Press.

Briggs, Laura. 2012. *Somebody's Children: The Politics of Transracial and Transnational Adoption*. Durham, NC: Duke University Press.

Brooks, Devon, Sigrid James, and Richard P. Barth. 2002. "Preferred Characteristics of Children in Need of Adoption: Is There a Demand for Available Foster Children?" *Social Service Review* 76 (4): 575–602.

Brusma, David. 2005. "Interracial Families and the Racial Identification of Mixed-Race Children: Evidence from the Early Childhood Longitudinal Study." *Social Forces* 82 (2): 1131–1157.

Burton, Linda M., Eduardo Bonilla-Silva, Victor Ray, Rose Buckelew, and Elizabeth Hordge. 2010. "Critical Race Theories, Colorism, and the Decade's Research on Families of Color." *Journal of Marriage and Family* 72 (3): 450–459.

Carter-Black, Jan. 2002. "Transracial Adoption and Foster Care Placement: Worker Perception and Attitude." *Child Welfare* 81 (2): 337–370.

Cartwright, Lisa. 2003. "Photographs of 'Waiting Children': The Transnational Adoption Market." *Social Text* 21 (1): 83–109.

Centers for Disease Control and Prevention. 2017. "ART Success Rates." Available at http://www.cdc.gov/art/reports/index.html.

Chandra, Anjani, Joyce Abma, Penelope Maza, and Christine Bachrach. 1999. "Adoption, Adoption Seeking, and Relinquishment for Adoption in the United States." *Advance Data*, May 11, pp. 1–16.

Chandra, Anjani, Gladys M. Martinez, William D. Mosher, Joyce Abma, and Jo Jones. 2005. *Fertility, Family Planning, and Reproductive Health of U.S. Women: Data from the 2002 National Survey of Family Growth*. Hyattsville, MD: U.S. Department of Health and Human Services.

Chappell, Bill. 2016. "Judge Strikes Down Last Same-Sex Adoption Ban in the U.S." *National Public Radio*, April 1. Available at http://www.npr.org/sections/thetwo-way/2016/04/01/472667168/judge-strikes-down-last-same-sex-adoption-ban-in-the-u-s.

Child Welfare Information Gateway. n.d. "Multiethnic Placement Act of 1994." Available at https://www.childwelfare.gov/topics/systemwide/laws-policies/federal/search/?CWIGFunctionsaction=federallegislation:main.getFedLedgDetail&id=46.

———. 2013a. "Consent to Adoption." Available at https://www.childwelfare.gov/pubPDFs/consent.pdf.

———. 2013b. "Regulation of Private Domestic Adoption Expenses." Available at https://www.childwelfare.gov/pubPDFs/expenses.pdf.

———. 2014. "Postadoption Contract Agreements between Birth and Adoptive Families." Available at https://www.childwelfare.gov/pubPDFs/cooperative.pdf.

———. 2016a. "Home Study Requirements for Prospective Parents in Domestic Adoption." Available at https://www.childwelfare.gov/topics/systemwide/laws-policies/statutes/homestudyreqs-adoption.

———. 2016b. "Trends in U.S. Adoptions: 2008–2012." Available at https://www.childwelfare.gov/pubPDFs/adopted0812.pdf.

———. 2016c. "Who May Adopt, Be Adopted, or Place a Child for Adoption?" Available at https://www.childwelfare.gov/topics/systemwide/laws-policies/statutes/parties.

Children's Bureau. 2015. "The AFCARS Report: Preliminary FY 2014 Estimates as of July 2015." Available at https://www.acf.hhs.gov/sites/default/files/cb/afcarsreport22.pdf.

———. 2016. "The AFCARS Report: Preliminary FY 2015 Estimates as of June 2016." Available at https://www.acf.hhs.gov/cb/resource/afcars-report-23.

Chittister, Robyn. 2015. "3 Ways to Respond to Stupid Things People Say about Adoption." *Adoption.com*, October 8. Available at http://adoption.com/3-ways-to-respond-to-stupid-things-people-say-about-adoption.

Chou, Rosalind S., and Joe R. Feagin. 2008. *The Myth of the Model Minority: Asian Americans Facing Racism*. Boulder, CO: Paradigm.

Choy, Catherine Cenzia. 2013. *Global Families: A History of Asian International Adoption in America*. New York: New York University Press.

Christian World Adoption. 2013. "CWA Closing Letter on Website." Available at http://poundpuplegacy.org/node/59339.

Citrin, Jack, Morris Levy, and Robert P. Van Houweling. 2014. "Americans Fill Out President Obama's Census Form: What Is His Race?" *Social Science Quarterly* 95 (4): 1121–1136.

Cohen, Jane Maslow. 1987. "Posnerism, Pluralism, Pessimism." *Boston University Law Review* 67:105–175.

Cohen, Philip. 2011. "Homogamy Unmodified." *Journal of Family Theory and Review* 3 (1): 47–51.

Colaco, Maria. 2014. "11 Things Never to Say to an Adoptive Parent." *Huffington Post*, November 13. Available at http://www.huffingtonpost.com/maria-colaco/11-things-never-to-say-to-an-adoptive-parent_b_6134422.html.

Crary, David. 2014. "Russia Adoption Ban: One Year Later." *Christian Science Monitor*, January 18. Available at http://www.csmonitor.com/The-Culture/2014/0118/Russian-adoption-ban-One-year-later.

Creating a Family. 2015. "Best Adoption Blogs." Available at https://creatingafamily.org/adoption/adoption-blogs.

Dalmage, Heather M. 2000. *Tripping on the Color Line: Black-White Multiracial Families in a Racially Divided World*. New Brunswick, NJ: Rutgers University Press.

Davis, Mary Ann. 2011. "Intercountry Adoption Flows from Africa to the U.S.: A Fifth Wave of Intercountry Adoptions?" *International Migration Review* 45 (4): 784–811.

DeBerry, Kimberly, Sandra Scarr, and Richard Weinberg. 1996. "Family Racial Socialization and Ecological Competence: Longitudinal Assessments of African-American Transracial Adoptees." *Child Development* 67 (5): 2375–2399.

Delale-O'Connor, Lori. 2014. "Safely 'Other': The Role of Culture Camps in the Construction of Racial Identity for Adopted Children," in *Race in Transnational and Transracial Adoption*, edited by Vilna Bashi Treitler, 155–168. New York: Palgrave Macmillan.

DeNavas-Walt, Carmen, and Bernadette D. Proctor. 2015. *Income and Poverty in the United States: 2014*. Washington, DC: U.S. Government Printing Office.

De Walt, Patrick S. 2011. "In Search of an Authentic African American and/or Black Identity: Perspectives of First Generation U.S.-born Africans Attending a Predominantly White Institution." *Journal of Black Studies* 42 (3): 479–503.

Dewan, Shaila. 2013. "Has 'Caucasian' Lost Its Meaning?" *New York Times*, July 6. Available at http://www.nytimes.com/2013/07/07/sunday-review/has-caucasian-lost-its-meaning.html.

Docan-Morgan, Sara. 2010a. "Korean Adoptees' Retrospective Reports of Intrusive Interactions: Exploring Boundary Management in Adoptive Families." *Journal of Family Communication* 10 (3): 137–157.

———. 2010b. "'They Don't Know What It's Like to Be in My Shoes': Topic Avoidance about Race in Transracially Adoptive Families." *Journal of Personal Relationships* 28 (3): 137–157.

Donner, Danielle Saba. 1997. "The Emerging Adoption Market: Child Welfare Agencies, Private Middleman, and 'Consumer' Remedies." *University of Louisville Journal of Family Law* 35 (3): 473–535.

Dorow, Sara. 2006a. "Racialized Choices: Chinese Adoption and the 'White Noise' of Blackness." *Critical Sociology* 32 (2–3): 357–379.

———. 2006b. *Transnational Adoption: A Cultural Economy of Race, Gender, and Kinship*. New York: New York University Press.

Doyle, Jamie Mihoko, and Grace Kao. 2007. "Are Racial Identities of Multiracials Stable? Changing Self-Identification among Single and Multiple Race Individuals." *Social Psychology Quarterly* 70 (4): 405–423.

Englund, Will, and Tara Bahrampour. 2012. "Russia's Ban on U.S. Adoptions Devastates American Families." *Washington Post*, December 28. Available at https://www.washingtonpost.com/world/europe/russia-set-to-ban-us-adoptions/2012/12/27/fd49c542-504f-11e2-8b49-64675006147f_story.html.

Fedders, Barbara. 2010. "Race and Market Values in Domestic Infant Adoption." *North Carolina Law Review* 88:1687–1714.

Feigelman, William, and Arnold Silverman. 1983. *Chosen Children: New Patterns of Adoptive Relationships*. New York: Praeger.

Fessler, Ann. 2007. *The Girls Who Went Away: The Hidden History of Women Who Surrendered Children for Adoption in the Decades before Roe v. Wade*. New York: Penguin Books.

Fisher, Allen P. 2003. "Still 'Not Quite as Good as Having Your Own'? Toward a Sociology of Adoption." *Annual Review of Sociology* 29:335–361.

Frankenberg, Ruth. 1993. *White Women, Race Matters: The Social Construction of Whiteness*. Minneapolis: University of Minnesota Press.

Freundlich, Madelyn. 2000. *Adoption and Ethics: The Market Forces in Adoption*. Washington, DC: Child Welfare League of America Press.

Fryer, Roland G., Jr. 2016. "An Empirical Analysis of Racial Differences in Police Use of Force." National Bureau of Economic Research Working Paper 22399. Available at http://www.nber.org/papers/w22399.pdf.

Fu, Vincent Kang. 2007. "How Many Melting Pots? Intermarriage, Pan Ethnicity, and the Black/Non-Black Divide in the United States." *Journal of Comparative Family Studies* 38 (2): 215–232.

Gailey, Christine Ward. 2010. *Blue Ribbon Babies and Labors of Love: Race Class, and Gender in U.S. Adoption Practice*. Austin: University of Texas Press.

Gans, Herbert J. 2005. "Race as Class." *Contexts* 4 (4): 17–21.

Gibney, Shannon. 2015. *See No Color*. Minneapolis, MN: Carolrhoda Lab.

Glaser, Barney G., and Anselm L. Strauss. 2017. *The Discovery of Grounded Theory: Strategies for Qualitative Research*. Abingdon, UK: Routledge.

Glazer, Nathan. 1997. *We Are All Multiculturalists Now*. Cambridge, MA: Harvard University Press.

Goffman, Erving. 1959. *The Presentation of Self in Everyday Life*. New York: Random House.

Goldberg, Abbie E. 2012. *Gay Dads: Transitions to Adoptive Parenthood*. New York: New York University Press.

Gonsoulin, Margaret, and Xuanning Fu. 2010. "Intergenerational Assimilation by Marriage: Hispanic and Asian Immigrants." *Marriage and Family Review* 46 (4): 257–277.

Goodwin, Michelle, ed. 2010. *Baby Markets: Money and the New Politics of Creating Families*. Cambridge: Cambridge University Press.

Gordon, Milton. 1964. *Assimilation in American Life: The Role of Race, Religion, and National Origin*. New York: Oxford University Press.

Greico, Elizabeth, Yesenia D. Acosta, G. Patricia de la Cruz, Christine Gambino, Thomas Gryn, Luke J. Larsen, Edward N. Trevelyan, and Nathan P. Walters. 2012. "The Foreign Born Population in the United States: 2010." *American Community Survey Reports*, May. Available at https://www.census.gov/prod/2012pubs/acs-19.pdf.

Greil, Arthur, Kathleen Slauson-Blevins, and Julia McQuillan. "The Experience of Infertility: A Review of the Recent Literature." *Sociology of Health and Illness* 32 (1): 140–162.

Grotevant, Harold, Gretchen Miller Wrobel, Manfred H. van Dulmen, and Ruth G. McRoy. 2001. "The Emergence of Psychosocial Engagement in Adopted Adolescents: The Family as Context over Time." *Journal of Adolescent Research* 16 (5): 469–490.

Haberman, Clyde. 2014. "Baby M and the Question of Surrogate Motherhood." *New York Times*, March 23. Available at https://www.nytimes.com/2014/03/24/us/baby-m-and-the-question-of-surrogate-motherhood.html.

Hairston, Creasie F., and Vicki G. Williams. 1989. "Black Adoptive Parents: How They View Agency Adoption Practices." *Social Casework* 70 (9): 534–538.

Haller, William, Alejandro Portes, and Scott M. Lynch. 2011. "Dreams Fulfilled, Dreams Shattered: Determinants of Segmented Assimilation in the Second Generation." *Social Forces* 89 (3): 733–762.

Hamilton, Darrick, Arthur H. Goldsmith, and William Darity Jr. 2009. "Shedding 'Light' on Marriage: The Influence of Skin Shade on Marriage for Black Females." *Journal of Economic Behavior and Organization* 72 (1): 30–50.

Hannum, Emily. 2002. "Educational Stratification by Ethnicity in China: Enrollment and Attainment in the Early Reform Years." *Demography* 39 (1): 95–117.

Harknett, Kristen, and Sara McLanahan. 2004. "Racial and Ethnic Differences in Marriage after the Birth of a Child." *American Sociological Review* 69 (6): 790–811.

Harris Interactive. 2002. "National Adoption Attitudes Survey." Available at http://www.adoptioninstitute.org/wp-content/uploads/2013/12/Adoption_Attitudes_Survey.pdf.

Healy, Kieran. 2006. *Last Best Gifts: Altruism and the Market for Human Blood and Organs*. Chicago: University of Chicago Press.

Henney, Susan M., Susan Ayers-Lopez, Ruth G. McRoy, and Harold D. Grotevant. 2007. "Evolution and Resolution: Birthmothers' Experience of Grief and Loss at Different Levels of Adoption Openness." *Journal of Social and Personal Relationships* 24 (6): 875–889.

Herman, Ellen. 2008. *Kinship by Design: A History of Adoption in the Modern United States*. Chicago: University of Chicago Press.

Hochschild, Arlie Russell. 2012. *The Managed Heart: Commercialization of Human Feeling*. Berkeley: University of California Press.

Hochschild, Jennifer L., and Vesla Weaver. 2007. "The Skin Color Paradox and the American Racial Order." *Social Forces* 86 (2): 643–670.

Hodkinson, Paul. 2005. "'Insider Research' in the Study of Youth Cultures." *Journal of Youth Studies* 8 (2): 131–149.

Hoffman, Diane M. 2012. "Saving Children, Saving Haiti? Child Vulnerability and Narratives of the Nation." *Childhood* 19 (2): 155–168.

Hogbacka, Ritta. 2008. "The Quest for a Child of One's Own: Parents, Markets, and Transnational Adoption." *Journal of Comparative Family Studies* 39 (3): 311–330.

Holt International. n.d. "Adoption Fees: China." Available at http://www.holtinternational.org/adoption/fees.php.

———. n.d. "Parent Eligibility: China." Available at http://www.holtinternational.org/adoption/criteria.php.

Hughes, Everett C. 1945. "Dilemmas and Contradictions of Status." *American Journal of Sociology* 50 (5): 353–359.

Hughes, Michael, and Bradley R. Hertel. 1990. "The Significance of Color Remains: A Study of Life Chances, Mate Selection, and Ethnic Consciousness among Black Americans." *Social Forces* 68 (4): 1105–1120.

Humphrey, Caroline. 2013. "Dilemmas in Doing Insider Research in Professional Education." *Qualitative Social Work* 12 (5): 572–586.

Hunter, Margaret. 2007. "The Persistent Problem of Colorism: Skin Tone, Status, and Inequality." *Sociology Compass* 1 (1): 237–254.

Hutson, Michael. 2012. "Adoption, Destiny and Magical Thinking." *New York Times*, August 15. Available at http://parenting.blogs.nytimes.com/2012/08/15/adoption-destiny-and-magical-thinking.

Ignatiev, Noel. 1995. *How the Irish Became White*. New York: Routledge.

"Infertility and In Vitro Fertilization." 2017. *WebMD*. Available at https://www.webmd.com/infertility-and-reproduction/guide/in-vitro-fertilization.

Ishizawa, Hiromi, Catherine T. Kenney, Kazuyo Kubo, and Gillian Stevens. 2006. "Constructing Interracial Families through Intercountry Adoption." *Social Science Quarterly* 87 (5): 1207–1224.

Ishizawa, Hiromi, and Kazuyo Kubo. 2014. "Factors Affecting Adoption Decisions: Child and Parental Characteristics." *Journal of Family Issues* 35 (5): 627–653.

Jacobson, Heather. 2008. *Culture Keeping: White Mothers, International Adoption, and the Negotiation of Family Difference*. Nashville, TN: Vanderbilt University Press.

———. 2016. *Labor of Love: Gestational Surrogacy and the Work of Making Babies*. New Brunswick, NJ: Rutgers University Press.

Jacobson, Matthew Frye. 1998. *Whiteness of a Different Color: European Immigrants and the Alchemy of Race*. Cambridge, MA: Harvard University Press.

Jennings, Patricia K. 2006. "The Trouble with the Multiethnic Placement Act: An Empirical Look at Transracial Adoption." *Sociological Perspectives* 49 (4): 559–581.

Jones, Jo. 2008. *Adoption Experiences of Women and Men and Demand for Children to Adopt by Women 18–44 Years of Age in the United States, 2002*. Washington, DC: National Center for Health Statistics.

———. 2009. "Who Adopts? Characteristics of Women and Men Who Have Adopted Children." *NCHS Data Brief*, no. 12. Available at https://www.cdc.gov/nchs/data/databriefs/db12.pdf.

Joyce, Kathryn. 2013. *The Child Catchers: Rescue, Trafficking and the New Gospel of Adoption*. New York: Public Affairs.

Judge, Sharon. 2003. "Developmental Recovery and Deficit in Children Adopted From Eastern European Orphanages." *Child Psychiatry and Human Development* 34 (1): 49–62.

Juffer, Femmie, and Marinus H. van IJzendoorn. 2005. "Behavioral Problems and Mental Health Referrals of International Adoptees: A Meta-analysis." *Journal of the American Medical Association* 293 (20): 2501–2515.

*Juno*. 2007. Directed by Jason Reitman. Century City, CA: Fox Searchlight. DVD.

Kalmijn, Matthijs. 1998. "Intermarriage and Homogamy: Causes, Patterns, Trends." *Annual Review of Sociology* 24 (1): 395–421.

Katz, Jennifer, and Emily K. Doyle. 2013. "Black and White Thinking? Understanding Negative Responses to Transracial Adoptive Families." *Adoption Quarterly* 16 (1): 62–80.

Keith, Verna, and Cedric Herring. 1991. "Skin Tone Stratification in the Black Community." *American Journal of Sociology* 97 (3): 760–778.

Kennedy, Randall. 2003. *Interracial Intimacies: Sex, Marriage, Identity and Adoption.* New York: Pantheon Books.

Khanna, Nikki. 2010. "'If You're Half Black, You're Just Black': Reflected Appraisals and the Persistence of the One-Drop Rule." *Sociological Quarterly* 51 (1): 96–121.

Khanna, Nikki, and Caitlin Killian. 2015. "'We Didn't Even Think about Adopting Domestically': The Role of Race and Other Factors in Shaping Parents' Decisions to Adopt Abroad." *Sociological Perspectives* 58 (4): 570–594.

Kim, Claire J. 1999. "The Racial Triangulation of Asian Americans." *Politics and Society* 27 (1): 105–138.

Kim, Eleana. 2010. *Adopted Territory: Transnational Korean Adoption and the Politics of Belonging.* Durham, NC: Duke University Press.

Kim, Hosu. 2016. *Birth Mothers and Transnational Adoption Practice in South Korea.* New York: Palgrave Macmillan.

Kim, JaeRan. 2014. "Internationally Adopted Children with Disabilities in Out-of-Home Care: Emerging Research on Adoptive Parent Perspectives." *The Roundtable* 27(2):12–14. Available at http://spaulding.org//wp-content/themes/twentyfifteen -child-sfc/archive%20pdf/V27N2-2014.pdf.

Kirton, Derek. 1999. "Perspectives on 'Race' and Adoption: The Views of Student Social Workers." *British Journal of Social Work* 29:779–796.

Krawiec, Kimberly. 2010. "Price and Pretense in the Baby Market." In *Baby Markets: Money and the New Politics of Creating Families*, edited by Michele Bratcher Goodwin, 41–55. Cambridge: Cambridge University Press.

Kreider, Rose M., and Philip Cohen. 2009. "Disability among Internationally Adopted Children in the United States." *Pediatrics* 124:1311–1318.

Kreider, Rose M., and Daphne Lofquist. 2014. "Adopted Children and Stepchildren: 2010." Available at https://www.census.gov/prod/2014pubs/p20-572.pdf.

Kreider, Rose M., and Elizabeth Raleigh. 2016. "Residential Racial Diversity: Are Transracial Adoptive Families More like Multiracial or White Families?" *Social Science Quarterly* 97 (5): 1189–1207.

Kubo, Kazuyo. 2010. "Desirable Difference: The Shadow of Racial Stereotypes in Creating Transracial Families through Transnational Adoption." *Sociology Compass* 4 (4): 263–282.

———. 2014. "Producing Multiculturalism: Family Formation through Transnational Adoption." In *Race in Transnational and Transracial Adoption*, edited by Vilna Bashi Treitler, 169–189. New York: Palgrave Macmillan.

Lacy, Karyn. 2007. *Blue Chip Black: Race, Class, and Status in the New Black Middle Class.* Berkeley: University of California Press.

Landes, Elizabeth, and Richard Posner. 1978. "The Economics of Baby Shortage." *Journal of Legal Studies* 7:323–348.

Lee, Erika. 2015. *The Making of Asian America: A History.* New York: Simon and Schuster.

Lee, Jaegoo, Josie Crolley-Simic, and M. Elizabeth Vonk. 2013. "MSW Students' Attitudes toward Transracial Adoption." *Journal of Social Work Education* 49 (1): 122–135.

Lee, Jaegoo, Elizabeth M. Vonk, and Josie Colley-Simic. 2015. "A Model of Factors Related to Cultural and Racial Socialization Practices among International Transracial Adoptive Parents." *Families in Society* 96 (2): 141–147.

Lee, Jennifer, and Frank Bean. 2012. *The Diversity Paradox: Immigration and the Color Line in Twenty-First Century America.* New York: Russell Sage Foundation.

Lee, Richard M. 2003. "The Transracial Adoption Paradox." *Counseling Psychologist* 31 (6): 711–744.

Lewis, Oscar. 1966. "The Culture of Poverty." *Scientific American* 215 (4): 3–10.

Louie, Andrea. 2009. "'Pandas, Lions, and Dragons, Oh My!' How White Adoptive Parents Construct Chineseness." *Journal of Asian American Studies* 12 (3): 285–320.

Markens, Susan. 2007. *Surrogate Motherhood and the Politics of Reproduction*. Berkeley: University of California Press.

Mauss, Marcel. 1954. *The Gift: The Form and Reason for Exchange in Archaic Societies*. New York: Cohen and West.

McGinnis, Hollee, Susan Smith, Scott Ryan, and Jeanne Howard. 2009. *Beyond Culture Camp: Promoting Healthy Identity Formation in Adoption*. New York: Evan B. Donaldson Adoption Institute.

McKee, Kimberly. Forthcoming. *Legacies of Gratitude: Logics of the Korean Transnational Adoption Industrial Complex*. Champaign: University of Illinois Press.

McQuillan, Julia, Arthur L. Greil, Lynn K. White, and Mary Casey Jacob. 2003. "Frustrated Fertility: Infertility and Psychological Distress among Women." *Journal of Marriage and the Family* 65 (4): 1007–1018.

McRoy, Ruth. 2006. "Social Work Perspectives on Adoption." In *The Praeger Handbook of Adoption*, edited by Kathy S. Stolley and Vern L. Bullough, 549–554. Westport, CT: Praeger.

McRoy, Ruth, Maryanne Mica, Madelyn Freundlich, and Joe Kroll. 2007. "Making MEPA-IEP Work: Tools for Professionals." *Child Welfare* 86 (2): 49–66.

Melosh, Barbara. 2002. *Strangers and Kin: The American Way of Adoption*. Cambridge, MA: Harvard University Press.

Meyer, Jeremy P. 2011. "Man Beaten by Denver Officers Awarded $795,000 by City Council." *Denver Post*, May 2. Available at http://www.denverpost.com/2011/05/02/man-beaten-by-denver-officers-awarded-795000-by-city-council.

Modell, Judith. 1994. *Kinship with Strangers*. Berkeley: University of California Press.

Mohanty, Jayashree. 2013. "Ethnic and Racial Socialization and Self-Esteem of Asian adoptees: The Mediating Role of Multiple Identities." *Journal of Adolescence* 36 (1): 161–70.

Mohanty, Jayashree, and Christina Newhill. 2006. "Adjustment of International Adoptees: Implications for Practice and Future Research Agenda." *Children and Youth Services Review* 28 (4): 384–395.

Moon, Katharine H. S. 2015. "The Past and Future of International Adoption." Brookings, June 29. Available at http://www.brookings.edu/research/opinions/2015/06/29-south-korea-international-adoption.

Moore, Mignon. 2011. *Invisible Families: Gay Identities, Relationships, and Motherhood among Black Women*. Berkeley: University of California Press.

Moynihan, Daniel P. 1965. *The Negro Family: The Case for National Action*. Washington, DC: U.S. Department of Labor. Available at https://www.dol.gov/oasam/programs/history/webid-meynihan.htm.

Myers, Kit E. 2014. "'Real' Families: The Violence of Love in New Media Adoption Discourse." *Critical Discourse Studies* 11 (2): 175–193.

National Association of Black Social Workers. 1972. "Position Statement on Trans-racial Adoptions." Available at http://c.ymcdn.com/sites/nabsw.org/resource/collection/E1582D77-E4CD-4104-996A-D42D08F9CA7D/NABSW_Trans-Racial_Adoption_1972_Position_(b).pdf.

National Center for Health Statistics. 2016. "Infertility." Available at http://www.cdc .gov/nchs/fastats/infertility.htm.

Netter, Sarah, and Zoe Magee. 2010. "Tennessee Mother Ships Adopted Son Back to Moscow Alone." *ABC News*, April 9. Available at http://abcnews.go.com/WN/anger -mom-adopted-boy-back-russia/story?id=10331728.

Obama, Barack. 2016. "Presidential Proclamation—National Adoption Month, 2016." Available at https://obamawhitehouse.archives.gov/the-press-office/2016/10/27/ presidential-proclamation-national-adoption-month-2016.

Oh, Arissa. 2015. *To Save the Children of Korea: The Cold War Origins of International Adoption*. Palo Alto, CA: Stanford University Press.

Omi, Michael, and Howard Winant. 1994. *Racial Formation in the United States: From the 1960s to the 1990s*. New York: Routledge.

Ortiz, Anna T., and Laura Briggs. 2003. "The Culture of Poverty, Crack Babies, and Welfare Cheats: The Making of the 'Healthy White Baby Crisis.'" *Social Text* 21 (3): 39–57.

Pande, Amrita. 2014. *Wombs in Labor: Transnational Commercial Surrogacy in India*. New York: Columbia University Press.

Park Nelson, Kim. 2016. *Invisible Asians: Korean American Adoptees, Asian American Experiences, and Racial Exceptionalism*. New Brunswick, NJ: Rutgers University Press.

Patillo-McCoy, Mary. 1999. *Black Picket Fences: Privilege and Peril among the Black Middle Class*. Chicago: University of Chicago Press.

Patton, Sandra. 2000. *Birthmarks: Transracial Adoption in Contemporary America*. New York: New York University Press.

Pavao, Joyce Maguire. 2005. *The Family of Adoption*. Rev. ed. Boston: Beacon Press.

Perry, Samuel L. 2014. "Conservative Christians and Support for Transracial Adoption as an Alternative to Abortion." *Social Science Quarterly* 95 (2): 380–392.

Pertman, Adam. 2000. *Adoption Nation: How the Adoption Revolution Is Transforming America*. New York: Basic Books.

———. 2011. *Adoption Nation: How the Adoption Revolution Is Transforming Our Families—and America*. Cambridge: Harvard Common Press.

Portes, Alejandro, and Alejandro Rivas. 2011. "The Adaptation of Migrant Children." *Future of Children* 21 (1): 219–246.

Powell, Brian, Catherine Blozendahl, Claudia Geist, and Lala Carr Steelman. 2010. *Counted Out: Same-Sex Relations and Americans' Definitions of Family*. New York: Russell Sage Foundation.

Qian, Zhenchao, and Daniel T. Lichter. 2001. "Measuring Marital Assimilation: Inter-marriage among Natives and Immigrants." *Social Science Research* 30 (2): 289–312.

———. 2007. "Social Boundaries and Marital Assimilation: Interpreting Trends in Racial and Ethnic Intermarriage." *American Sociological Review* 72 (1): 68–94.

Quiroz, Pamela Anne. 2007. *Adoption in a Color-Blind Society*. New York: Rowman and Littlefield.

Radin, Margaret Jane, and Madhavi Sunder. 2005. "Introduction: The Subject and the Object of Commodification." In *Rethinking Commodification: Cases and Readings in Law and Culture*, edited by Martha M. Ertman and Joan C. Williams, 8–33. New York: New York University Press.

Raible, John. 2012. "New Directions in Critical Transracial and Transnational Adoption Research." *Journal of Social Distress and the Homeless* 21 (3–4): 111–121.

Raleigh, Elizabeth. 2002. "Going Home: An Oral History of Korean Adoptees Returning to Korea." Paper presented at meeting of the Royal Asiatic Society, Seoul, South Korea, May 8.

———. 2011. "The Adoption Marketplace: Transracial Assortative Adoption and the Black/Non-Black Divide." Ph.D. diss., University of Pennsylvania.

———. 2012. "Are Same-Sex and Single Adoptive Parents More Likely to Adopt Transracially? A National Analysis of Race, Family Structure, and the Adoption Marketplace." *Sociological Perspectives* 55 (3): 449–471.

———. 2016. "An Assortative Adoption Marketplace: Foster Care, Domestic, and Transnational Adoptions." *Sociology Compass* 10 (6): 506–517.

Raleigh, Elizabeth, and Barbara Katz Rothman. 2014. "Disability Is the New Black: The Rise of the Cleft Lip and Palate Program in Transracial International Adoption." In *Race in Transnational and Transracial Adoption*, edited by Vilna Treitler, 33–48. New York: Palgrave McMillan.

Roberts, Dorothy. 2002. *Shattered Bonds: The Color of Child Welfare*. New York: Basic Books.

Roden, Lee. 2017. "Why Some Parents in Sweden Are Having to Adopt Their Own Kids." *The Local*, April 11. Available at https://www.thelocal.se/20170411/why-some-parents-in-sweden-are-having-to-adopt-their-own-kids.

Roediger, David. 2006. *Working toward Whiteness: How America's Immigrants Became White; The Strange Journey from Ellis Island to the Suburbs*. New York: Basic Books.

Roorda, Rhonda M. 2015. *In Their Voices: Black Americans on Transracial Adoption*. New York: Columbia University Press.

Roth, Wendy D. 2005. "The End of the One-Drop Rule? Labeling of Multiracial Children in Black Intermarriages." *Sociological Forum* 20 (1): 35–67.

Rothman, Barbara Katz. 2006. *Weaving a Family: Untangling Race and Adoption*. Boston: Beacon Press.

Rudrappa, Sharmila. 2015. *Discounted Life: The Price of Global Surrogacy in India*. New York: New York University Press.

Ryan, Maura, and Amanda Moras. 2017. "Race Matters in Lesbian Donor Insemination: Whiteness and Heteronormativity as Co-constituted Narratives." *Ethnic and Racial Studies* 40 (4): 579–596.

Samuels, Gina M. 2009. "'Being Raised by White People': Navigating Racial Difference among Adopted Multiracial Adults." *Journal of Marriage and Family* 71 (1): 80–94.

Sandven, Kari, and Michael D. Resnick. 1990. "Informal Adoption among Black Adolescent Mothers." *American Journal of Orthopsychiatry* 60 (2): 210–224.

Saperstein, Aliya. 2012. "Capturing Complexity in the United States: Which Aspects of Race Matter and When?" *Ethnic and Racial Studies* 35 (8): 1484–1502.

Savage, Dan. 1999. *The Kid: What Happened after My Boyfriend and I Decided to Go Get Pregnant*. New York: Penguin.

Save Adoptions. 2016. "Important Adoption Announcement." *International Adoption Net*, October 3. Available at http://www.internationaladoptionnet.org/blog/2016/october/important-adoption-announcement.aspx.

Schneider, David M. 1968. *American Kinship: A Cultural Account*. Chicago: University of Chicago Press.

Selman, Peter. 2009. "The Rise and Fall of Intercountry Adoption in the 21st Century." *International Social Work* 52 (5): 575–594.

Simon, Scott. 2010. *Baby, We Were Meant for Each Other: In Praise of Adoption*. New York: Random House.

"Six Words: 'Black Babies Cost Less to Adopt.'" 2013. *NPR*, June 27. Available at http://www.npr.org/2013/06/27/195967886/six-words-Black-babies-cost-less-to-adopt.

Smith, Darron T., Cardell K. Jacobson, Brenda G. Juarez, and Joe R. Feagin. 2011. *White Parents, Black Children: Experiencing Transracial Adoption*. New York: Rowman and Littlefield.

Smock, Pamela, and Fiona Rose Greenland. 2010. "Diversity in Pathways to Parenthood: Patterns, Implications, and Emerging Research Directions." *Journal of Marriage and Family* 72:576–593.

Smolin, David M. 2006. "Child Laundering: How the Intercountry Adoption System Legitimizes and Incentivizes the Practices of Buying, Trafficking, Kidnapping, and Stealing Children." *Wayne Law Review* 52 (1): 113–200.

Solinger, Rickie. 2002. *Beggars and Choosers: How the Politics of Choice Shapes Adoption, Abortion, and Welfare in the United States*. New York: Hill and Wang.

Spar, Debora L. 2006. *The Baby Business: How Money, Science, and Politics Drive the Commerce of Conception*. Cambridge, MA: Harvard Business School Press.

Statistics Sweden. n.d. "Number of Adoptions of Children and Young Persons Ages 0–17, Number by Sex, Type of Adoption and Year." Available at http://www.statistikdatabasen.scb.se/pxweb/en/ssd/START__LE__LE0102__LE0102I/LE0102T27/table/tableViewLayout1/?rxid=675f8e8e-349a-4a6c-ac10-b6173ea7859b (accessed August 8, 2017).

*The Struggle for Identity: Issues in Transracial Adoption*. 2007. Directed by Deborah C. Hoard. Ithaca, NY: PhotoSynthesis Productions. DVD.

Sweeney, Kathryn A. 2013. "Race-Conscious Adoption Choices, Multiraciality, and Color-Blind Racial Ideology." *Family Relations* 62 (1): 42–57.

Taub, Amanda. 2017. "When the Kremlin Says 'Adoptions,' It Means 'Sanctions.'" *New York Times*, July 10. Available at https://www.nytimes.com/2017/07/10/world/americas/kremlin-adoptions-sanctions-russia.html.

Taylor, Jodie. 2011. "The Intimate Insider: Negotiating the Ethics of Friendship When Doing Insider Research." *Qualitative Research* 11 (1): 3–22.

Taylor, Paul, Jeffrey S. Passel, Wendy Wang, Jocelyn Kiley, Gabriel Velasco, and Daniel Dockterman. 2010. "Marrying Out: One-in-Seven New U.S. Marriages Is Interracial or Interethnic." Available at http://www.pewsocialtrends.org/files/2010/10/755-marrying-out.pdf.

Tong, Scott. 2010. "The Dark Side of Chinese Adoptions." *Marketplace*, May 5. Available at http://www.marketplace.org/2010/05/05/life/dark-side-chinese-adoptions.

Traver, Amy. 2010. "Adopting China: American China Adoptive Parents' Development of Transnational Ties to China." *International Journal of Sociology of the Family* 36 (2): 93–115.

Tuan, Mia. 1999. *Forever Foreigners or Honorary Whites? The Asian Ethnic Experience Today*. New Brunswick, NJ: Rutgers University Press.

———. 2008. "Domestic and International Transracial Adoption: A Synopsis of the Literature." *Sociology Compass* 2 (6): 1848–1859.

Twine, France Winddance. 2015. *Outsourcing the Womb: Race, Class, and Gestational Surrogacy in a Global Market*. New York: Routledge.

Twohey, Megan. 2013. "The Child Exchange: Inside America's Underground Market for Adopted Children." *Reuters*, September 9–11. Available at http://www.reuters.com/investigates/adoption/#article/part1.

U.S. Census Bureau. 2016. "QuickFacts: United States." Available at https://www.census.gov/quickfacts/table/PST045215/00.

U.S. Department of State. n.d. "Convention Countries." Available at http://travel.state
.gov/content/adoptionsabroad/en/hague-convention/convention-countries.html.
———. 2006. "The Hague Convention on Intercountry Adoption: A Guide for Prospective Parents." Available at http://travel.state.gov/content/dam/aa/pdfs/PAP_
Guide_1.pdf.
———. 2013. "Alert: Russian Supreme Court Letter on Implementation of Federal Law
No. 272-FZ." Available at http://travel.state.gov/content/adoptionsabroad/en/coun
try-information/alerts-and-notices/russia-10.html.
———. 2014. "Mexico." Available at https://travel.state.gov/content/adoptionsabroad/en/
country-information/learn-about-a-country/mexico.html.
———. 2015a. "FY 2014 Annual Report on Intercountry Adoption." Available at http://
travel.state.gov/content/dam/aa/pdfs/fy2014_annual_report.pdf.
———. 2015b. "Statistics." Available at http://travel.state.gov/content/adoptionsabroad/
en/about-us/statistics.html.
———. 2016a. "Intercountry Adoption: China." Available at https://travel.state.gov/
content/adoptionsabroad/en/country-information/learn-about-a-country/china
.html.
———. 2016b. "Intercountry Adoptions: Proposed Rule." *Federal Register* 81 (174):
62322–62343. Available at http://federalregister.gov/a/2016-20968.pdf.
———. 2017a. "Agencies Denied or Subject to Adverse Action." Available at https://
travel.state.gov/content/adoptionsabroad/en/hague-convention/agency-accredita
tion/agencies-denied-accreditation.html.
———. 2017b. "Intercountry Adoptions." *Federal Register* 82:16322. Available at https://
www.federalregister.gov/documents/2017/04/04/2017-06558/intercountry-adop
tions.
———. 2017c. "Understanding the Hague Convention." Available at http://travel.state
.gov/content/adoptionsabroad/en/hague-convention/understanding-the-hague
-convention.html.
Valby, Karen. 2015. "5 Things One Mom Wishes She'd Been Told Before Adopting Her
Black Son." *Time*, February 17. Available at http://time.com/3707193/5-things-one
-mom-wishes-shed-been-told-before-adopting-her-black-son.
Vandivere, Sharon, Karin Malm, and Lauren Radel. 2009. *Adoption USA: A Chartbook
Based on the 2007 National Survey of Adoptive Parents*. Washington, DC: U.S. De-
partment of Health and Human Services.
Wang, Wendy. 2012. "The Rise of Intermarriage." Pew Research Center, February 16.
Available at http://www.pewsocialtrends.org/2012/02/16/the-rise-of-intermarriage.
Warren, Jonathan W., and France Winddance Twine. 1997. "White Americans, the New
Minority? Non-Blacks and the Ever-Expanding Boundaries of Whiteness." *Journal
of Black Studies* 28 (2): 200–218.
Waters, Mary C. 1990. *Ethnic Options: Choosing Identities in America*. Berkeley: Uni-
versity of California Press.
———. 1999. *Black Identities: West Indian Immigrant Dreams and American Realities*.
Cambridge, MA: Harvard University Press.
Waters, Mary C., Philip Kasinitz, and Asad L. Asad. 2014. "Immigrants and African
Americans." *Annual Review of Sociology* 40:369–390.
Williams, Joan C., and Viviana Zelizer. 2005. "To Commodify or Not to Commodify:
That Is *Not* the Question." In *Rethinking Commodification: Cases and Readings in
Law and Culture*, edited by Martha M. Ertman and Joan C. Williams, 362–382. New
York: New York University Press.

Wilson, William Julius. 1987. *The Truly Disadvantaged: The Inner City, the Underclass, and Public Policy.* Chicago: University of Chicago Press.

World Bank. 2016. "Ethiopia: Economic Overview." Available at http://www.worldbank .org/en/country/ethiopia/overview.

Yancey, George. 2003. *Who Is White? Asians, Latinos, and the New Black/Nonblack Divide.* New York: Lynne Rienner.

Yngvesson, Barbara. 2002. "Placing the 'Gift Child' in Transnational Adoption." In "Nonbiological Parenting," edited by Susan M. Sterett, special issue, *Law and Society Review* 36 (2): 227–256.

———. 2010. *Belonging in an Adopted World: Race, Identity, and Transracial Adoption.* Chicago: University of Chicago Press.

Zelizer, Viviana. 1994. *Pricing the Priceless Child: The Changing Social Value of Children.* Princeton, NJ: Princeton University Press.

———. 2010. "Risky Exchanges." In *Baby Markets: Money and the New Politics of Creating Families,* edited by Michelle Goodwin, 267–277. Cambridge: Cambridge University Press.

Zhang, Yuanting, and Gary R. Lee. 2011. "Intercountry versus Transracial Adoption: Analysis of Adoptive Parents' Motivations and Preferences in Adoption." *Journal of Family Issues* 32 (1): 75–98.

Zhou, Min. 1997. "Segmented Assimilation: Issues, Controversies, and Recent Research on the New Second Generation." *International Migration Review* 31 (4): 975–1008.

Zhou, Min, and Jennifer Lee. 2007. "Becoming Ethnic or Becoming American? Reflecting on the Divergent Pathways of Social Mobility and Assimilation among the New Second Generation." *Dubois Review* 4 (1): 189–205.

# Index

abortion, 10, 30, 60, 111

adoption: downturn in (*see* down market); duration of process (*see* wait time); as an industry (*see* market metaphor); motivations for, 95–102, 111, 128, 191; professionalization of, 39–41, 81, 101–102; stigma of, 6, 127, 129, 161; transracial (*see* transracial adoption); types of, 38, 71 (*see also* foster care adoption; independent attorney-led adoption; international adoption; private domestic adoption). *See also* two-tiered adoption system

adoption agencies: advertising and marketing for, 3, 64–74 (*see also* marketing); competition among, 54–55, 70, 163, 188; economics of, 1–15, 19, 30–33, 44–58, 62–63, 74–75, 183–190 (*see also* down market); faith-based, 112; fees for services of (*see* fees); as full-service model, 80; and Hague Accreditation, 69; opposition to regulation of, 199–200; racial hierarchies and, 133–162; recruiting of birth mothers by, 114–115; success rates of, 72–73, 98–99, 114; turning down of prospective parents by, 74–75, 184–185, 193–196. *See also* international adoption; private domestic adoption

adoption conferences, 19–20, 65–66, 69. *See also* marketing

*Adoption Nation* (Pertman), 66, 129

adoption workers: as adoptive parents, 72; commitment of, to child welfare, 4, 55–58, 74–77 (*see also* child welfare); emotional labor of (*see* emotion work by adoption workers); on language of supply and demand, 30–32, 51; on market framework, 3, 6–7, 30–32, 36–38, 48–49, 51, 62–63 (*see also* market metaphor); research on, 7–8, 38–41; stress and, 50; training for, 42–43. *See also* backstage approach; frontstage approach; information sessions; marketing

adoptive parents. *See* parents, prospective

AdoptUSKids website, 208n30

advertising: by adoption agencies, 3, 64–74; soliciting expectant mothers, 80–83, 114

African adoption programs, 5, 52, 135, 151–162, 158, 202. *See also* Ethiopia adoption program

African Americans: as adoptive parents, 140–142, 144; as against transracial adoption, 130–132; marriage rates of, 23; as pathologized, 156–157; violence against, 196–197. *See also* Black children; Black–non-Black divide age of children, 23, 28–29, 86; age-race-health comparisons, 33, 93, 122–127; older children, 103, 202 (*see also* waiting child adoptions); wait times and, 113

age of prospective adoptive parents, 82, 99, 102

alcohol and drug use, 68, 83, 124, 157–158. *See also* health profiles of children

Almeling, Rene, 24

altruism, 8–10; children with illnesses and, 54; international adoption and, 17, 95; private adoption as, 77–78; of surrogates, 24–25

American Association of Indian Affairs, 131

American Community Survey (2005), 14

Appurdai, Arjun, 25

ART. *See* assisted reproduction technologies (ART)

Asad, Asad, 151

Asian adoption programs, 52, 153–154. *See also* China adoption program; Korean adoption program

Asian children: adoption fees for, 91–92, 138; color-explicit depictions of, 181–182; in foster care, 28; preferences for, 133–136; in racial hierarchy, 15, 95, 127, 133–136, 196; as racially flexible, 95, 134

Asian immigrants, 12–13, 134

as-if-begotten model, 6, 39–41, 102, 111, 191, 200–201, 203n13

assimilation, 12–13, 151

assisted reproduction technologies (ART), 23–25, 97–98, 190; emotional aspects of, 71–72; and parents as clients, 57. *See also* infertility

assortative adoption market, 96, 101–110

attorney-led adoption. *See* independent attorney-led adoption

available, use of term, 75. *See also* children, supply of

baby buying, 6, 25, 58–62, 78, 91, 140

Baby M, 24

backstage approach, 20–22, 33, 63, 66, 132, 178

Bailey, Jo, 19

Balcom, Karen, 39, 58–59

beauty, 181–183

belonging, 95

Berebitsky, Julie, 39–41, 102

Berend, Zsuzsa, 25

biological kinship: adoption as equated to, 6 (*see also* as-if-begotten model); as ideal, 22–23; training and, 200–201

biological reproduction, 68; barriers to, 23–25, 33, 64–66, 68, 99–100, 110, 191; parental rights, 85; replication of, 4, 6

biracial Black children, 5, 34, 133, 146–151, 184, 192

birth certificates: falsified, 59; new, 6

birth mothers: advertising for, 80–83, 114; change of heart by, 85, 115–117; and choosing of adoptive parents, 80, 114–115, 126–127, 150; counseling for, 116; grief of, 25; health of, 68, 83, 124, 126, 157–158 (*see also* health profiles of children); lack of choices for, 10–11, 42, 60, 127, 201; money and, 25, 91; non-traditional applicants and, 108; stigma against, 25, 111; supply of, 3, 30; terminology for, 6, 8; as turned down by prospective parents, 80–86

birth parents, contact with, 25, 68, 118–122. *See also* closed adoption; open adoption

Black children: biracial, 5, 34, 133, 146–151, 184, 192; first mothers' options for, 127; foreign-born, 5, 133, 135, 151–162 (*see also* Ethiopia adoption program); in foster care, 28 (*see also* foster care adoption); monoracial native-born, 5, 34, 130, 151, 184, 192; "one drop" rule, 138, 146–147; in racial hierarchy, 13–15, 18, 34, 125–127, 130, 136–147; racialized pricing for, 7, 18, 132, 136–148, 182; skin color of, 34, 146–151, 158; wait times for adopting, 112–113, 125. *See also* African Americans

Black identity, 171, 177–178

Black immigrants, status of, 151–152

black market, 9, 58–62, 136. *See also* baby buying

Black–non-Black divide, 13, 34, 133, 147–162, 184. *See also* color line

BMI (body mass index), 103

Bobo, Lawrence, 130

Bonilla-Silva, Eduardo, 13, 129, 133, 147, 177

boys, 117–118, 184–185

Brian, Kristi, 17, 87, 88, 134, 169, 172, 179, 186

bribes, 3, 59–60

Briggs, Laura, 11, 81, 131, 156–157, 162, 164
*Building Your Family: Infertility and Adoption Guide*, 69
Bulgaria, 51–52, 182

Cambodia, 45
Canada, 59
Caribbean, 151, 159–161
Carter-Black, Jan, 19
Cartwright, Lisa, 181
Caucasian: children's appearance as, 181–182; use of term, 211n53
celebrity adoptions, 158
Chad, 3
child commodification, 7–10, 23, 30–32, 33, 38, 166; adoption workers and, 55–58; analogy to slave trade, 136; marketing adoption and, 67, 77–79; money and, 39, 90–93
children: attractiveness of, 181–183; characteristics of, 68, 71, 78, 111, 156–158, 169; as clients, 2, 8–9, 55–58, 63 (*see also* child welfare); market value of, 2, 7, 23 (*see also* racialized pricing); with medical conditions (*see* health profiles of children); as priceless, 9, 78, 136
children, demand for, 29–32; foster care children, 23; by gender, 117–118; healthy infants, 56, 78, 107, 123, 166, 208n30; healthy White infants, 41, 96, 111–113, 127, 137; infants with medical conditions, 54–55, 78; minority children, 137, 139–140, 143–144
children, supply of, 29–32, 51, 165–166; competition for, 54–55; decrease in, 3–5, 21, 32–33, 41, 45–50, 78, 81–82, 87, 96, 111–113, 123, 138, 148, 202 (*see also* down market); demographics of, 46–47, 68, 75; domestic increase in, 43–44; emerging international markets, 50–54; by gender, 117–118; "unadoptable," 40, 102
child trafficking, 58–62. *See also* baby buying
child welfare, 2–4, 7–10, 30–32, 33, 38; adoption workers and, 55–58; customer service model and, 76–77, 196–202; in developing countries, 22–23; marketing adoption as, 67, 74–79, 190; racialized fees as, 139–140; racial preferences as, 149–150; turning down prospective parents as, 184–185, 193–196; waiting children and, 86–87

Child Welfare Information Gateway, 201
China adoption program, 10–11, 17–18, 21, 45; corruption in, 61; customer service focus of, 76; and donations to orphanages, 91–92; eligibility requirements of, 103; gift narrative of, 26; and girls, preference for, 156; and language of supply and demand, 31; and legal rights to children, 85; popularity of, 47, 165, 194; racial aspects of, 155; restrictions in, 46, 49–50, 154; and same-sex parents, 105; waiting children in, 54–55; wait times of, 113
China Center for Adoption Affairs (CCAA), 54–55
Chinese American adoptive parents, 113
Chinese children: culture and ethnicity of, 173–174; as perceived as East Asian, 181; in racial hierarchy, 15, 155. *See also* Asian children
Chinese Exclusion Act, 12
class privilege, 10–11
cleft lips and palates, 54–55
closed adoption, 68, 118–122, 153
Colombia, 165
color-blind approach, 5, 16, 129–130, 147, 161–163, 168, 174, 197, 199
color-evasiveness, 163–189
color-explicit depictions, 181–183. *See also* skin color
colorism, 148
color line: interracial marriage and, 12–14; transracial adoption and, 4–5, 14–15, 34, 130, 133–162, 184–186. *See also* racial hierarchies
consumers, parents as, 2, 40, 55–58, 65, 77–78, 190–192; autonomy of, 89, 149; color-evasiveness and, 169–172; and declining of referrals in international adoption, 86–90; and declining of situations in domestic adoption, 80–86; guilt of, 67, 78, 89; and independent attorney-led adoption, 80–84; race and, 149–151, 162, 181–189, 197
contraception, 10, 111
corruption, 9, 58–62, 136. *See also* baby buying
costs: children as priceless, 6, 9, 78, 136; unacceptableness of talking about, 6, 49, 90–93. *See also* as-if-begotten model; fees; market metaphor
country-specific authorization (CSA), 200

culture, 17–18, 160–161, 170–171; "culture
    keeping" activities, 172–176; race and,
    170–176, 189
culture camps, 175
customer service model, 5, 8–9, 33, 41, 57,
    63, 67; child welfare and, 76–77, 196–202.
    See also child commodification; consum-
    ers, parents as

Dalmage, Heather, 14
dark-skinned discount, 132, 136–147, 182.
    See also racialized pricing
declining referrals, 80–90, 126
Delale-O'Connor, Lori, 175
demand and supply: language of, 29–32, 51.
    See also children, demand for; children,
    supply of
Dietrich, David, 129
disrupted adoption, 115–116
diversity, 155, 175, 179–180, 187–188, 198
Dorow, Sara, 15, 17–18, 26, 55, 87, 105, 134,
    156, 159, 179
down market, 41–50, 183, 201–202; in
    international adoption, 4, 18–19, 21, 32,
    41–50, 56, 72, 123, 165, 202; transracial
    adoption and, 4–5, 183–189, 194
drug use, 68, 83, 124, 157–158
duration of adoption process. See wait time

Eastern Europe, 52, 89, 123–124
economy, U.S., 43–44
education and training: for adoption work-
    ers, 42–43; online, 187–189, 198; regula-
    tions on, 195, 197, 200; for White trans-
    racial adoptive parents, 17–18, 167–168,
    184–189, 193–202
egg donation, 24
eligibility of prospective parents: agencies
    turning down clients, 74–75, 184–185,
    193–196; heterogamous couples, 102–104;
    homogamous couples, 102–110, 127, 191,
    209n26; infertility and, 40, 112; interna-
    tional adoption requirements, 33, 46–47,
    49–50, 88, 94–96, 102–110, 127, 154, 194,
    209n26; single adoptive parents, 102–110,
    127, 191
emotion work by adoption workers, 64–74;
    and children as clients, 74–77; declin-
    ing referrals in international adoption,
    86–90; definition of emotional labor, 67;
    and fees and money issues, 90–93; find-

ing the right fit, 79–86, 88, 93, 169; and
    infertility, 97; and open adoption, 121;
    and parents as clients, 77–79, 190 (see
    also consumers, parents as); race and,
    139, 169–172
ethics, 6–8, 24–25, 59–60
Ethiopia adoption program: and birth
    mother choices, 42; and closed adop-
    tions, 153; decline in placements in,
    21, 45; and eligibility requirements for
    parents, 94–95, 103; and emphasis on
    culture, 160–161, 177–178; and pay-
    ments to government officials, 60; pop-
    ularity of, 33, 34, 46, 52–53, 122–123,
    151–161, 166, 194; and time to consider
    referrals, 88; wait times by gender in,
    118
Ethiopian children: color-explicit depic-
    tions of, 183; culture and, 160–161, 177–
    178; ethnic identity of, 160; exotification
    of, 158, 161
ethnic identity, 95, 160–161, 171–172,
    177–180
euphemisms, 11, 132; "finding the right fit,"
    79–86, 88, 93, 169; "waiting child," 54
exotification, 158, 161, 182–183
expectant women. See birth mothers

families: love and, 127, 129, 147, 167, 171,
    191; meaning of, 4–5, 32–35; mixed-race,
    168; multicultural, 174–176; ranked by
    structure, 2, 96, 101–110. See also as-if-
    begotten model; biological kinship; kin-
    ship; transracial adoption
Fedders, Barbara, 138
fees: ethics of, 6–7, 59–60; in foster care
    adoption, 26, 136, 206n133; in indepen-
    dent attorney-led adoption, 80–83, 114;
    in international adoption, 26, 45, 56,
    91–92, 136, 138, 152; in private domestic
    adoption, 2, 26, 49, 90–93, 98, 136–147;
    racialized pricing, 7, 18, 132, 136–148;
    uncertainty in, 114–115. See also costs;
    market metaphor
fertility barriers. See biological reproduc-
    tion: barriers to; infertility
fetal alcohol effect, 157. See also alcohol and
    drug use
first mothers, 6, 8. See also birth mothers
"fit" euphemism, 79–86, 88, 93, 169
food, ethnic, 160–161, 176

foreign-born Black children, 5, 133, 135, 151–162. *See also* Ethiopia adoption program

foster care adoption: age and race of children in, 23, 28–29; as alternative to international adoption, 37; biases against, 27–29, 38, 136, 156–158, 202; costs of, 26, 136, 206n133; motivation for, 100; and prospective parent demographics, 27, 56, 142; regulation of, 19, 163–164; trend toward, 32

foster care system: private adoption as alternative to, 43–44, 77; in Korea, 135–136

Frankenberg, Ruth, 135

Freundlich, Madelyn, 70

frontstage approach, 19–20, 33, 63, 67, 132

Gailey, Ward, 65

Gans, Herbert, 13

gay male couples, 99, 108–109. *See also* same-sex couples

gender: as market variable, 24, 117–118; race and, 184–185

Ghana, 152

gift exchange, 25–26

girls, 117–118, 184–185

Glazer, Nathan, 174

Goffman, Erving, 16, 20

Guatemala adoption program, 10; and children's identity, 179–180; closure of, 21, 46, 50, 61–62, 154; corruption in, 60, 61; popularity of, 47, 165; and same-sex prospective parents, 105

Hague Convention on Intercountry Adoption, 19, 43, 44, 46, 62; accredited agencies, 21, 69; black market and, 59–60; training mandate, 195, 197

Haiti, 159–160

health profiles of children, 39–40, 54–55, 78, 83–90, 122–127, 157–158; with special needs, 78, 86–87, 103

Healy, Kieran, 10

Herman, Ellen, 39–40, 141

heterogamous couples: and barriers to biological reproduction, 64, 97, 99 (*see also* infertility); and eligibility and access to adoption, 102–104; use of term, 207n4

Hispanic children: adoption fees for, 138–139; preferences for, 127, 133–136, 153–154

Hispanic immigrants, 12–13

Hochschild, Arlie, 67

Hodkinson, Paul, 20

home study, 97; education and training in, 186–187, 195–196; fees for, 139; for same-sex prospective parents, 105

homogamous couples. *See* same-sex couples

Honduras, 165

honorary White status, 133, 138–139, 161

humanitarianism: adoption agency programs and, 23, 58; international adoption as, 95, 159, 202

ICWA (Indian Child Welfare Act), 130–132

identity, racial and ethnic, 95, 160–161, 171–172, 177–180

immigrants: Asian and Hispanic, 12–13, 134; assimilation of, 12–13, 151, 158; Black, 151–152

Immigration Act (1965), 12

independent attorney-led adoption: advertising costs of, 80–83, 114; birth parent visitation and, 121; consumer power of parents in, 80–84; problems of, 72–73; single and same-sex parents and, 107–108; uncertainty in, 114–115

India, 51

Indian Child Welfare Act (ICWA), 130–132

infertility: eligibility for adoption and, 40, 112; emotional aspects of, 64, 66, 68, 71–72, 97–98, 100; as motivation for adoption, 24, 57, 96–102, 111, 128, 191; transracial adoption and, 168; treatments for, during adoption process, 81, 97, 100–101. *See also* assisted reproduction technologies (ART)

information sessions, 19–20, 66; emotional labor in (*see* emotion work by adoption workers); language used in, 67, 75; marketing transracial adoption at, 16–17, 33–35 (*see also* transracial adoption); on ranking priorities, 111–127. *See also* marketing

insider status, 20, 72

Interethnic Placement Act (IEP), 18–19, 163–165, 199

international adoption: adoption workers' ambivalence about, 37–38; certainty of, 113, 117; and closed adoptions, 118–119, 153; costs of (*see* fees); descriptions of, 1–3, 71; downturn in, 4, 18–19, 21, 32, 41–50, 56, 72, 123, 165, 202; education

international adoption (*continued*)
and training requirements of, 195, 200
(*see also* education and training); eligibility in (*see* eligibility of prospective parents); emerging markets, 50–54; humanitarianism and, 23, 58, 95, 159, 202; of
legal orphans, 48, 85, 91–92, 95, 117;
nontraditional families and, 104–106;
parents declining referrals in, 86–90; and
placement agencies, 48, 53; regulation of,
199–200; use of term, 132
interracial marriage, 12–14, 185
in vitro fertilization (IVF), 101
Irish immigrants, 12
Ishizawa, Hiromi, 15, 27, 100

Jacobson, Heather, 173–174
Jacobson, Matthew Frye, 151, 158
Jennings, Patricia, 16, 164
Jewish American parents, 59
Jolie, Angelina, 158
*Juno* (film), 125

Kasinitz, Philip, 151
Kazakhstan, 52, 94, 182–183
Kenya, 50
Khanna, Nikki, 132
*The Kid* (Savage), 203n13
Killian, Caitlin, 132
Kim, Eleana, 95
kinship, 4–5; curated, 39–41, 59, 102;
socially constructed, 64, 68. *See also* biological kinship
kinship marketplaces, 23–29
Kirton, Derek, 19
Korean adoption program, 15–17, 88; adult
adoptees of, 20, 169, 191; costs of, 152;
domestic adoption and, 46; eligibility
requirements of, 88, 103, 154; humanitarianism and, 95; popularity of, 47,
124, 131–132, 165; race and culture in,
134–136, 176
Korean children, 15. *See also* Asian children
Kubo, Kazuyo, 15, 27, 100, 174

Landes, Elizabeth, 23
Latin American adoption programs, 52,
153. *See also* Guatemala adoption program; Hispanic children
Latin American immigrants, 12–13

Lee, Gary, 28
lesbian couples, 99, 102. *See also* same-sex
couples
Lewis, Oscar, 156
LGBT adoption community. *See* same-sex
couples
Liberia, 152
Lichter, Daniel T., 14
love, family bonds and, 127, 129, 147, 167,
171, 191

Madonna, 158
Magnitsky Act, 210n39
marketing: and children as clients, 2, 8–9,
55–58, 63, 74–77 (*see also* child welfare);
color-evasiveness in, 163–189; and money
issues, 90–93; with pamphlets and websites, 65–66, 208n30; and parents as clients, 2, 8–9, 55–58, 63, 65, 77–79, 190 (*see
also* consumers, parents as); and racialized policies, 132–162. *See also* adoption
conferences; information sessions
market metaphor, 1–15, 22; adoption
worker attitudes toward (*see* adoption
workers); black market adoptions, 58–62;
down market, 41–50 (*see also* down market); emerging markets, 50–54; ethics of,
8–10; historical context of, 38–41; language used in, 29–32, 75, 78–79 (*see also*
children, demand for; children, supply
of); two clients in, 55–58 (*see also* child
commodification; child welfare). *See also*
backstage approach; consumers, parents
as; customer service model; frontstage
approach
market variables. *See* priorities, ranking
marriage, interracial, 12–14, 185
marriage markets, 23
Mauss, Marcel, 26
McRoy, Ruth, 164
medical conditions. *See* health profiles of
children
Melosh, Barbara, 118, 130
MEPA-IEP, 18–19, 163–165, 199
Mexico, 209n26
minority children, 5; demand for, 137, 139–
140, 143–144; in racial hierarchy, 14–15
(*see also* racial hierarchies). *See also*
Asian children; Black children; Hispanic
children
Mississippi, 102

mixed-race families, 168
Modell, Judith, 6
Montreal baby market, 59
Moynihan Report, 156
multicultural families, 174–176
multiculturalism, 174–175
Multiethnic Placement Act (MEPA), 18–19,
    163–165, 199
multiracial people: dating and, 211n41;
    racial hierarchy of, 146–151 (see also
    racial hierarchies)

National Association of Black Social
    Workers (NABSW), 130–132
National Public Radio Race Card Project,
    7, 138, 145
National Survey of Adoptive Parents,
    26–27, 100, 119, 152
National Survey of Family Growth (NSFG),
    24
Native American children, 130–132
"The Negro Family" (Moynihan), 156
Nepal, 50–51, 61, 207n29
Nicaragua, 51
Nigeria, 152
nontraditional parents, 99–100, 102–110

Obama, Barack, 129
Oh, Arissa, 95, 132
older adoptive parents, 82, 99, 102
older children, 103, 202. See also waiting
    child adoptions
online training, 187–189, 198
open adoption, 25, 68, 108, 118–122
organ donation, 9–10
orphans, 48, 85, 91–92, 95, 117
Ortiz, Anna, 156–157

Pande, Amrita, 25
parents, prospective: as adoption profes-
    sionals, 72–73; Black, 140–142, 144;
    Chinese American, 113; as clients, 2, 8–9,
    55–58, 63, 65, 77–79, 190; and declining
    of referrals, 80–90, 126; demographics
    of, 39, 56, 64, 142; eligibility of (see eli-
    gibility of prospective parents); Jewish
    American, 59; priorities of, 81–83, 96,
    111–127, 170–171; racial preferences of,
    133–162, 181–183 (see also racial hierar-
    chies); ranked by family structure, 2, 96,
    101–110; recommendation letters for, 199.

See also heterogamous couples; same-
    sex couples; single prospective parents;
    White prospective parents
Park Nelson, Kim, 41, 131–132, 191
Passel, Jeffrey, 14
Patton, Sandra, 190–191
pediatricians, evaluations by, 87. See also
    health profiles of children
Pertman, Adam, 29, 66, 129
Peruvian children, 182–183
phenotype. See skin color
pigmentation. See skin color
placement agencies, 48, 53
police brutality, 197
Posner, Richard, 23
postracial society, 129, 197
pregnancy discourse, 6, 203n13. See also as-
    if-begotten model
pregnant women. See birth mothers
priorities, ranking, 111–127, 170–171;
    age-race-health comparison, 122–127;
    gender, 117–118; open adoption, 118–122;
    time, 111–113; tolerance for uncertainty,
    113–117
private domestic adoption, 3, 38; costs of
    (see fees); description of, 71; duration of
    (see wait time); education and training
    requirements in, 195; increased interest
    in, 43, 202; predominance of White par-
    ents in, 142, 144; racialized pricing in, 7,
    8, 132, 136–148, 182; turning down situa-
    tions in, 80–86; uncertainty in, 114–115;
    of U.S.-born Asian and Hispanic chil-
    dren, 138–139
privilege, White, 10, 178–180, 188–189
prospective parents. See parents, prospec-
    tive
Putin, Vladimir, 208–209n40

Qian, Zhenchao, 14
Quiroz, Pamela Anne, 8, 15, 18, 64

race: adoption workers' discomfort talking
    about, 176–181; culture and, 170–176,
    189; minimization of, 33–34, 128–130,
    150, 155, 163–189; in terms of power and
    privilege, 163, 178–180, 188–189; as a
    variable, 96 (see also racial hierarchies).
    See also transracial adoption
Race Card Project, 7, 138, 145
race matching, 39–41, 163–164

racial boundaries. *See* color line

racial diversity, lack of, 155, 175, 179–180, 187–188, 198

racial hierarchies, 13–16, 18, 128–162, 192; Asian and Hispanic children, 133–136; biracial and multiracial children, 146–151; color-explicit depictions and, 182–183; dark-skinned children, adoption fees for, 132, 136–148, 182; foreign-born Black children, 151–162

racial identity, 95, 160–161, 171–172, 177–180

racial integration, 179–180

racialized pricing, 7, 18; dark-skinned discount, 132, 136–148, 182; opposition to, 140–144

racial socialization, 18, 164, 190–191

racism, 13, 17, 132, 148, 151–153, 179, 186, 196–197; of White adoptive parents, 168, 185, 192–193

Radin, Margaret, 7

recommendation letters, 199

regulations, 2, 4, 196; agencies opposing, 199–200; on birth parent visitation rights, 120–121; on education and training, 195, 197, 200; on fees, 138; on foster care adoptions, 19, 163–164; on international adoption, 19; on same-sex parent adoptions, 102. *See also* Hague Convention on Intercountry Adoption

rescue narrative, 159–160

risk: in foster care adoptions, 156–158; tolerance for, 113–117

*Roe v. Wade*, 111

Rothman, Barbara Katz, 10–11, 15, 101

rural areas, racially segregated, 175, 180, 187–188, 198

Russian adoption program: and ban on U.S. adoptions, 45, 123, 208–209n40, 210n39; and children with developmental delays, 89–90, 157; eligibility requirements of, 94, 103–104; popularity of, 47; wait times by gender in, 118

same-race role models, 199

same-sex couples: barriers to reproduction for, 65; domestic adoption and, 106–107; and eligibility and access to adoption, 102–110, 127, 191, 209n26; homogamous, use of term, 207n4; international adoption and, 104–106

Savage, Dan, 203n13

segregated areas, 155, 175, 179–180, 187–188, 198

Selman, Peter, 5

Simon, Scott, 129

single fathers, 99, 102, 109

single mothers, 25, 99, 102, 111

single prospective parents, 65, 99; and eligibility and access to adoption, 102–110, 127, 191; Ethiopian children and, 70; independent attorney-led adoption and, 107–108

skin color: of Black children, 34, 146–151, 158; color-explicit depictions, 163, 181–183; dark-skinned children, adoption fees for, 132, 136–148, 182

slave trade, 136

social service model, 33, 41, 63, 67, 74. *See also* child welfare

social workers: adoption providers as, 75; emotional labor of (*see* emotion work by adoption workers); and professionalization of adoption work, 39–41, 81, 101–102. *See also* adoption workers

socioeconomic inequalities, 10–11

Solinger, Rickie, 11

sound adoption practice, 39–41

South Korea. *See* Korean adoption program

Spar, Debora, 9

special-needs children, 78, 86–87, 103

stigma: around adoption, 6, 127; around birth mothers, 25; around single mothers, 111; around transracial adoption, 129, 161

Sunder, Madhavi, 7

supply and demand, language of, 29–32, 51. *See also* children, demand for; children, supply of

surrogacy, 24–25, 190

Sweden, domestic adoptions in, 10, 204n31

Sweeney, Kathryn, 16, 132, 147–148, 185–186

Taiwan, 103

Taylor, Paul, 14

time. *See* wait time

training. *See* education and training

transgender women, 99

transnational adoption. *See* international adoption

transracial adoptees, 20, 72, 169, 190–191

transracial adoption, 18–19; adoption worker attitudes toward, 33–34, 37; age-race-health comparisons, 33, 93, 122–127; Black and Native American opposition to, 130–132; and color-evasiveness by adoption workers, 163–189; compared to interracial marriage, 12; compared to transnational adoption, 130–133; market demands and, 96, 109–110; nontraditional parents and, 107–110; race and culture issues in, 17–18; racial hierarchies and, 130–162 (*see also* racialized pricing); stigma against, 129, 161; use of term, 132; White social worker support for, 19. *See also* Asian children; Black children; White prospective parents

Tuan, Mia, 132

two-tiered adoption system: and eligibility of adoptive parents, 101–110, 191; and foster care, 28 (*see also* foster care adoption). *See also* racialized pricing

Ukraine, 46

uncertainty, tolerance for, 113–117

UNICEF, 45

U.S. Department of Health and Human Services, 27

U.S. Department of State, 26, 45, 199–200

Vietnam, 15–16, 21, 51

waiting child adoptions, 54–55, 86–87

wait time, 98, 124–126; for Black children, 112–113, 125; by gender, 118; as market variable, 111–113; for nontraditional parents, 107; for White infants, 111–113, 124–125

Wang, Wendy, 14

Waters, Mary, 151–152

*We Are All Multiculturalists Now* (Glazer), 174

webinars, 69

websites, 65–66, 208n30

White children: adoption fees for, 7 (*see also* fees); demand for, 41, 96, 111–113, 127, 137; in racial hierarchy, 15, 137; shortage of adoptable infants, 41, 81–82, 96, 111–113, 138, 148; wait times for adopting, 111–113, 124–125

White ethnic immigrants, 12–13, 151, 158

Whiteness, 18, 134–135, 151; honorary White status, 133, 138–139, 161

*Whiteness of a Different Color* (Jacobson), 151

White–non-White divide, 13. *See also* color line

White privilege, 10, 178–180, 188–189

White prospective parents: Asian or Hispanic children and, 127, 133–136; Black children and, 34, 125–127, 136–147; choices of, 28 (*see also* priorities, ranking); and preparation for transracial adoption, 5, 17–18, 22, 35, 95, 129–131, 161–189, 193–202 (*see also* education and training); racist attitudes of, 168, 185, 192–193; transracial adoption as marketed to, 4–5, 29, 33–34, 109–110, 133–162, 202

Williams, Joan, 9–10

Wilson, William Julius, 23

win-win paradigm, 41–42, 62–63

Yakovlev, Dima, 210n39

Yancey, George, 13

Yngvesson, Barbara, 25, 156

Zelizer, Viviana, 6–7, 9–10, 23, 136

Zhang, Yuanting, 28

**Elizabeth Raleigh** is an Assistant Professor of Sociology at Carleton College in Northfield, Minnesota.